CREATION,
SCIENCE,
AND THEOLOGY

CREATION, SCIENCE, AND THEOLOGY

Essays in Response to Karl Barth

by

W. A. WHITEHOUSE

edited by
ANN LOADES

WILLIAM B. EERDMANS PUBLISHING COMPANY
GRAND RAPIDS, MICHIGAN

Library of Congress Cataloging in Publiction Data

Whitehouse, Walter Alexander.
Creation, science, and theology.

Bibliography: p. xxi
1. Barth, Karl, 1886-1968—Addresses, essays,
lectures.   2. Theology—Addresses, essays, lectures.
3. Barth, Karl, 1886-1968—Bibliography.   I. Title.
BX4827.B3W47   230'.044   80-29332
ISBN 0-8028-1870-6

CONTENTS

ACKNOWLEDGEMENTS

The editor acknowledges with gratitude the support of Professor T. F. Torrance in this publication project. Mrs. Margaret Gilley gave invaluable help in producing a perfect typescript, as did Mr. David Hewlett in proof-reading and in compiling the index. Professor C.E.B. Cranfield, Sir Derman Christopherson, Dr. Peter Brooks, and Dr. Colin Gunton provided information and assistance at various stages.

The editor and publishers also wish to thank the following for their kindness in granting permission to reprint material that has previously appeared: *Scottish Journal of Theology*, for "The Christian View of Man," "Providence," "God's Heavenly Kingdom," "The Command of God the Creator," "The Modern Discussion of Eschatology," "Towards a Theology of Nature"; Lutterworth Press for "The State and Divine Law" and "Christ and Creation"; the editor of *Durham University Journal* and Durham University for "R. B. Braithwaite As an Apologist for Religious Belief"; the Rev. D. T. Jenkins for "Theology and the Natural Sciences"; and Mowbrays for "The Christian in the University."

PREFACE

Walter Alexander Whitehouse was born on February 27, 1915, at Shelley, a village between Huddersfield and Penistone in the West Riding of Yorkshire, the eldest son of Walter Whitehouse, a foundry and then a textile labourer, and his wife Clara. He was educated at Shelley Council School and Penistone Grammar School (where he began to learn German) and was brought up to become a member of Shelley Congregational Chapel. In 1933 he entered St. John's College, Cambridge, to read Part II and then Part III of the Mathematical Tripos, graduating in 1936 as a Wrangler (taking his M.A. in 1941). In his last year at Cambridge he had decided to enter the Congregational ministry, and went to Mansfield College, Oxford (with membership of Balliol College), to study theology under Nathaniel Micklem, with whom he established a lasting friendship. The writings of Peter Taylor Forsyth and Austin M. Farrer were also to be of permanent significance for him. He took his B. Litt. in Oxford in 1940 with a thesis on "God and Creatures in the Philosophy of Thomas Aquinas and A. N. Whitehead." He was ordained as a Congregational minister at Elland, Yorkshire, in 1940.

While at Oxford, WAW found himself with an extraordinary opportunity to investigate the problems of the German Church in its trials under Hitler. Nathaniel Micklem had been invited to write a book on *National Socialism and the Roman Catholic Church*, and WAW went with him in 1938 on a short visit, between March 31 and April 16, to the land of "Ein Volk, Ein Reich, Ein Führer." The visit enabled WAW to make his first contacts with members of the Confessing Church, to hear at first hand of the suffering of many imprisoned pastors, and to meet their families. Martin Niemöller was one of the most distinguished of those who were suffering intensely from solitary confinement at that time. A diary of the visit makes disturbing reading, even now; WAW wrote, for example, at Koblenz: "Pastor Timm had had four four-hour interviews with the Gestapo one week for saying that the imprisoned pastors were suffering for Christ."

The presence in Mansfield of Hans Herbert Kramm (with whom WAW shared the Tower Room in the year before Naval Intelligence took over the main part of the College) provided sustained contact with the Church struggle through one who had been intimately involved as a young pastor and a possible future leader. WAW had met Kramm in 1938 in the Swedish Embassy Chaplaincy in Berlin, and Kramm served as best man at his wedding in 1946. WAW also translated a work by Heinrich Vogel (one of those to whom Barth had dedicated his *Credo* in 1935), and after the war translated one of Vogel's papers on the question of "German Guilt."

In the meantime, WAW became a member of a group convened by Alec Vidler at St. Deiniol's Library to study "natural law," a group whose members included R. P. McDermott, H. Cunliffe-Jones, Victor White, O.P.,[1] Richard Kehoe, O.P., Eugene Lampert, Hans Ehrenberg, and occasionally Eric Mascall. The fruits of the interest generated in these meetings appeared in the paper on "Theonomic Thinking," the Christian reconsideration of natural law; in his later work on the Biblical doctrine of justice and law; in the first of his contributions to volumes of essays in Barth's honour, "The State and Divine Law";*[2] and in a recent paper, "Theology and Human Rights."* This last was initially delivered as one of a series of public lectures on human rights organized by Professor F. C. Dowrick of the department of law in Durham University in the autumn of 1978.

WAW's concern to inform readers in Britain of the character of the German Church struggle led him to join the efforts of Mrs. Dorothy Buxton and the "Friends of Europe" organization to publicize the difference between the "intact" churches and those which had not been able to exclude "German Christian" administrators.[3] From his base as chaplain and tutor at Mansfield since 1943, he was the English Free Churches' representative in a delegation of British churchmen to the British zone of Germany in October 1946 (a fortnight after his marriage to Beatrice Mary Kent Smith). The delegation was led by George Bell, Bishop of Chichester, and was exceptional at that time for including representatives of the Roman Catholic Church, as well as of the Church of Scotland, and the British Council of Churches, with Pastor Dr. J. Rieger, Dean of the German congregations in England, as interpreter. The object of the delegation was "to study the ecclesiastical situation in Germany, and to take counsel with Church leaders in the British Zone and in Berlin on the needs and task of the Churches in Germany."

By this time, WAW was a superb preacher, with a number of notable sermons and addresses to his credit. Sermons were a remarkably effective

---

[1]See "The Concept of Justice in the *Summa* of St. Thomas Aquinas," *The Presbyter*, 5 (1947).

[2] * indicates material included in the present volume; complete bibliographical citations for all the essays are contained in the Bibliography.

[3]See K. Robbins, "Church and Politics: Dorothy Buxton and the German Church Struggle," in *Church, Society and Politics: Studies in Church History* (London: Blackwell, 1975), vol. 12.

way of getting across to his hearers his response as a Christian minister
to the devastation which he and his fellow-delegates saw for themselves,
as well as his respect for the dedication of members of the Confessional
movement to the care of the oppressed. The contacts he had forged on
his visit brought him back into living touch with the situation. From the
deputy bishop of Hamburg who visited Mansfield in the early part of
1947, he learned of the appalling conditions in which the Church was at
work:

> In Hamburg the homes of 500,000 people were destroyed by bombing,
> and the total population today is 60,000 more than before the war. Some
> of them live in the huge concrete air-raid shelters, great rabbit-warrens
> ten storeys high, divided into rooms where sixteen two-tier bunks can just
> be packed in with room to squeeze between them. In each room are 32
> people whose bunk is all they can call home. For two months there was no
> heat and no light. No light—there are no windows in an air-raid shelter.
> Church members said that to go into these Bunkers was like being in a
> cave full of wild animals.

But, as WAW reported,

> their obedience goes deeper. In the Civil Internment camps there are
> thousands of Nazis, many from the eastern territories who have not a
> penny or a stick of property. Their cases come up for trial and they cannot
> pay a lawyer. The Church in Hamburg has provided 20,000 RM to pay
> lawyers to defend the SS men from whom many of these Christians have
> suffered much. In 1935, they say, we took the Jews into our homes. In
> 1947 it is these Nazis who are the poor and oppressed, and however bad
> they are, it is for us to see that justice is done to them.

Such commitment led WAW to comment in one address, "Let's have no
more May Meetings at which the plight of Germany is ignored and we
spend our time boosting Congregationalism!"

However, the fate of Congregationalism mattered very much to WAW.
On one occasion he reported that he had been deeply moved by some
words spoken by a deacon of a Congregationalist church in the Yorkshire
Dales, a man who knew the shepherd's life at first hand, and was able to
remind a gathering of ministers that the shepherd's task is not a gentle
stroll with the flock through green pastures and beside still waters!

> The true shepherd is on the look-out for everything that hurts the sheep:
> from the germ or maggot in their constitution, to the mad dog or fox
> which brings terror to the whole flock. He must defend the rights of
> pasturage and build the protective fences. When the flock strays from its
> rightful heath, it is his job to find why they have wandered, whether from
> physical hunger, carnal desire for excitement, or fear of an enemy at the
> gate. He strives night and day to preserve their joy and peace. He goes
> before them in the dangerous places, to foretell and to forestall the pitfalls.

He reads the signs of the times to know what the morrow will bring, and prepares in good time for the coming storm. Do we recognize in Christ, one who cares for us at such a cost? Are we as utterly dependent on him in our own responsibility as the shepherd's dog is dependent on his master? The temptation to put beside his wisdom, love and power, some other influence of our own, which we suppose might contribute to his pastoral care, is enormous.[4]

(Put to a different, but related purpose, the imagery of what it is to be one of the "sheep," however talented and enterprising, is explored in the later sermon "The Christian in the University."*)

Apart from such comments as the one on Congregationalism and its relationship to the Church of England, published in the *Christian World Pulpit* (a supplement to a paper, *The Christian World*, purchased largely by Congregationalists and free churchmen), it was possible to explore the self-understanding and theology of Congregationalism in the pages of *The Presbyter: A Journal of Confessional and Catholic Churchmanship*. This periodical was primarily under the editorial leadership of Daniel T. Jenkins, assisted by an interdenominational team, with Reinhold Niebuhr having agreed to act as a collaborator from America. *The Presbyter*'s subtitle and statement of intentions signify a theology renewed in the current stress and strain:

> *The Presbyter* understands the Church to be created by God in Jesus Christ. It therefore seeks to show how the whole life of the Church in doctrine, worship, witness and structure derives therefrom, and how all its activity must continually be submitted to reformation according to the will of God. It will be clear, therefore, that its primary purpose is neither denominational nor sectional.

Further, the pages of *The Presbyter* provided WAW with an opportunity to publicize the theology of Barth, of whose importance he had received indisputable evidence in 1938 from pastors he met in Germany. The translation by G. T. Thomson of the first half-volume of the *Church Dogmatics* had appeared, but Vol. II was as yet untranslated when T. F. Torrance sent WAW Vol. III, 1 on the doctrine of creation. The *Scottish Journal of Theology* had not been brought into existence, so WAW's first exposition of Barth appeared in *The Presbyter* in 1946.* By coincidence, there was a reading in October 1946 on the B.B.C. of the English translation of Barth's "The Christian Churches and Living Reality." In October 1950 WAW himself introduced B.B.C. Third Programme listeners to Barth's *Dogmatics in Outline.* This broadcast followed the first of his contributions to the newly founded (1948) *Scottish Journal of Theology*, where with masterly clarity he introduced readers to Barth's understanding of the Christian doctrine of man,* providence,* heaven and the angels* (an

---

[4]*Congregationalism Today*, ed. John Marsh, pp. 14-15.

extraordinary and difficult subject, not commonly tackled in recent times), and ethics*[5]—all before the volumes of *Church Dogmatics* III were available in English.

WAW had been invited to Sydney as Principal of Camden College, but had been reluctant to leave post-war England, and so by this time was to be found teaching systematic theology (among other things) at Durham University where he was a Reader in Divinity from 1947 to 1965. The Durham theology department was at that time a small department in a small university on the verge of post-war reconstruction, but had some teachers who were to become distinguished in a variety of ways. A. M. Ramsey, S. L. Greenslade, C. K. Barrett, H. E. W. Turner, C. E. B. Cranfield and D. R. Jones all joined by 1950. An acquaintance from WAW's days at St. Deiniol's library, R. P. McDermott, was teaching religious thought in the department, and was also rector of St. Mary-le-Bow, which functioned as a "university church." The Honours syllabus at Durham was largely in the grip of the teachers of Biblical studies and patristics. However, A. M. Ramsey as Van Mildert Professor had followed up the initiative of O. C. Quick and established a course in systematic theology for postgraduate candidates for ordination in the Church of England who were reading for the Diploma in Theology. WAW and Ramsey shared the course between them. WAW also contributed an option on "Philosophy and the Christian Religion" to the Honours school. By the 1970's the Honours school had been radically transformed; the syllabus now included systematic theology and philosophy and the Christian religion, both taught by John Heywood Thomas, as compulsory components of the option in theology taken by the Honours majority of a very much larger department.

WAW's earlier interests in mathematics and natural sciences had not been abandoned, however. He had already worked out the fundamentals of his view of the achievements and possibilities of science from the standpoint of a Christian in his comments on C. S. Lewis's *That Hideous Strength* in 1946. He expanded his view in his first book in 1952, and in 1953 commended to a wider public the perspective of Karl Heim's *Transformation of the Scientific World View*, a translation which could only have been undertaken by someone familiar with the vocabulary and concepts both of theology and of modern physics. The Riddell Memorial Lectures delivered in Newcastle (then still part of Durham University) and published as *Order, Goodness, Glory*; the papers on a theology of nature* and theology and the natural sciences*; passages in *A Declaration of Faith* which clearly reflect his understanding of what it is to hold to Christian faith in relation to the modes of the appreciation of nature fostered by members of the scientific community—all these reflect his determination to make sense

---

[5]See his review article of R. E. Willis, *The ethics of Karl Barth*, *Scottish Journal of Theology*, 29 (1976), 177-82.

of the theology of creation which he was expounding as teacher and preacher in a variety of contexts. The last essay in the present volume, "Authority, Divine and Human,"* was developed from the Boutwood Lectures delivered at the invitation of the Master and Fellows of Corpus Christi College, Cambridge, in 1967, with the title "Divine Authority and Natural Science."

From his base in Durham, WAW became one of the founding members of the Society for the Study of Theology, whose first meeting took place in Cambridge in July 1952. The Society had made its aim "the scholarly study of Christian Theology in all branches of the Church with a view to fresh historical, dogmatic and constructive work in the field of Theology today." The theme of that first conference was "Eschatology," and four of the papers were published by the *Scottish Journal* in its series of occasional papers (No. 2; Edinburgh: Oliver and Boyd, 1953). (There were two other papers, delivered by Professors G. Florovsky and D. M. Mackinnon).[6] WAW's paper on eschatology* may be read as one of a pair (the other being "New Heavens and a New Earth"* given at a meeting of the Society in 1969) which together bracket in this volume the papers on a theology of nature* and theology and the natural sciences.* All these are obviously to be evaluated particularly in connection with the paper "Christ and Creation,"* another of the pieces produced in Barth's honour.

An honorary D.D. from the University of Edinburgh in 1959 was a splendid way of recognizing WAW's contribution to the renewal of theology in Britain, an effort he had made in concert with his development as a university administrator of the best kind. He is an academic who understands the purposes of the university, who believes that good administration exists to further those purposes, and who does not let inappropriate industrial or bureaucratic management styles determine results incompatible with the university's academic interests. From 1955 to 1960 he added a further commitment to his Readership in Divinity, that of being Principal of the St. Cuthbert's Society in Durham University, a non-residential Society in a collegiate university, which helps to provide an alternative form of student association. Sir James Duff was coming to the end of his career, and was due to retire as Warden at a time when the Durham colleges were about to separate from King's College, Newcastle, and to exist as separate universities, quite different in character. WAW served as Sub-Warden from 1961 to 1963, and Pro-Vice Chancellor when Derman Christopherson was appointed Warden of the Durham colleges (Christopherson was Vice-Chancellor after the separation of Durham from Newcastle). The alterations to the 1963 University Statutes included a number of significant changes which seem to reflect preferences of which

---

[6]For a recent appreciation of the latter, see WAW's review article of D. M. Mackinnon, *The Problem of Metaphysics, Scottish Journal of Theology*, 28 (1975), 573-6.

WAW would approve. For example, there were to be no more permanent heads of department, Boards of Studies were to become part of the constitutional machine, Canon Professors were no longer to be ex-officio members of Council, not all professors were to be members of Senate, and there was to be a higher proportion of elected members. The experience of Congregationalism seems to have been put to good purpose in university government! (see "The Christian in the University"*).

Apart from the offices he held, the invitation to deliver the Riddell lectures already mentioned was a tribute to the high repute in which he was held by his colleagues in Newcastle as well as in Durham. One paper which reflects collaboration with the Newcastle philosophy department has been included here. Karl Britton, professor of philosophy in Newcastle, and WAW produced a joint critique of R. B. Braithwaite's empiricist's account of the nature of religious belief, and WAW's appreciation of it seems to be the only instance of a theologian explicitly interested in Barth bringing himself to write a constructive assessment of Braithwaite's paper.* Remarkably few theologians have been able to equip themselves to learn anything other than scepticism from post-World War II critics of religious belief, but one of WAW's advantages was that he continued to teach philosophy and the Christian religion as well as grapple with the work of the great theologians, of whom Austin Farrer and Barth were splendid modern examples.

WAW had long been alert to the importance of treating ethics in relation to dogmatics, though many syllabi in theology neglect the connection shamefully. His essay "Christological Understanding,"* the third of his contributions to volumes in Barth's honour, is central here. His sermons especially reflect the connection, and it is appropriate at this point to quote from his 1962 Whitsuntide broadcast with his comments on Braithwaite in mind. For instance, he remarks on the significance to be attached to evidence

> afforded in persons who show unusual ability to adjust their interests and behaviour to the complex demands and opportunities of life. This, indeed, has come to be regarded as the product which religion has to sell and by which it may be judged. It is easy to be contemptuous of the salesmanship, but it may be a mistake to lose all taste and admiration for what is often put quite simply as the power to be good. This ought to cover an expression of vitality which is both rich and appropriate in all aspects of being, and no doubt it is a pity that the moral core of it, on which I am Puritan enough to insist, is often taken to be the whole substance of goodness. Human behaviour does sometimes suggest that the energies and insights necessary for doing things reliably and effectively, and with human graces, have been enhanced; and this is particularly impressive with behaviour which strikes one as a new revelation of authentic human dignity. Such behaviour does not come by way of cleverness or by way of conditioning.

It springs, fresh and glowing, from unusual insight and unusual purity of
will. This . . . may be no more than a suggestive parable. . . .

To go beyond suggestive parable, however, WAW went on to refer to St.
Paul's attachment, at one stage of his career, to the word translated as
"simplicity":

> As he used it, it drew attention to the fact that some people give themselves
> to life, and in the course of it to other people, with direct confident gen-
> erosity, not, as one might suppose, because they are fools, but because they
> are free and this is how they express their freedom. This is something
> which may appear only fitfully. When it appears, it seems to rest on one
> of the few things worth calling a miracle. Such people have not been freed
> merely from this cramping obsession or that one. They have been freed,
> if only for the moment perhaps, from self-preoccupation altogether. They
> have managed to abdicate the throne of self-possession from which a man
> maintains whatever grip he has on life. But their life has not fallen to
> pieces. They seem to be accepting as their own manhood one which is
> being given to them in the course of a grateful and generous response to
> what is all about them—to everything which God is providing by the way
> of nature and by the way of saving grace. That anyone should come to see
> life, and live it, in these terms, is not, to my mind, a natural possibility;
> though it is one to which religiously disposed human animals have aspired.
> It is however before us as an actuality in the manhood of Jesus Christ.
> Where the God who expressed himself in that manhood comes to dwell
> in the rest of us, something of the same result is likely to appear. Where
> it does appear, the question which I put about religion has been answered
> in practice, and I can account for it in no other terms than that God is
> here.

WAW's contacts with theologians in Europe led to some fruitful expe-
ditions for him at a time when English-speaking theologians read the
work of their European colleagues more frequently than they met them
or came to know them as friends. He took part in preparations for the
World Council of Churches Assembly at Evanston and attended meetings
at the oecumenical centre at Bossey in Switzerland. One of WAW's pieces
of systematic Biblical exegesis for a meeting there in August 1956, "Sanctity and worldliness in the Bible,"* is an example of the exploration of
connections between dogmatics and ethics which continued to preoccupy
him in the thick of his administrative responsibilities. And the paper
"Towards a Theology of Nature"* was originally produced for a conference of scientists, theologians, and philosophers at Bossey in April 1963.
Professor E. Schlink (an Honorary D.D. of Durham) became a friend as
a result of these meetings, and the contact enabled WAW to go to Heidelberg University in 1959 as a British Council-sponsored visiting lecturer.
From there he was drawn into the meetings of the Göttingen circle of
theologians, philosophers, and physicists associated with Professor C. F.

von Weizsäcker. WAW contributed one of the papers to the 1961 conference on "Act and Being," which focused on a reassessment of Bonhoeffer.
For many years, WAW was the sole British representative at the meetings
of the European Societas Ethica, founded originally in Basel by Professor
Van Oyen, who had been a pupil of Barth's.

WAW's career at home was about to take a new turn with the expansion
of British universities in the 1960s. The University Teachers' Group had
been formed to take up the concerns voiced by Walter Moberley in *Crisis
in the University*, and WAW produced his paper "Theology As a Discipline?"
for a meeting convened by Alec Vidler at Highlea, Hoddesden. It was
widely assumed that new British universities would not include departments of theology (though they might tolerate departments of religious
studies). A department of theology could so easily be regarded by university opinion as "an enclave of the Church, to be tolerated because of
the charm and culture of those who inhabit it—or not, as the case may
be—but to be contained as an academic phenomenon by techniques of
polite indifference." WAW's view was that

> the time is ripe for theology as a discipline to be re-orientated so as to
> become more open towards science, morals, law, letters, art and religions.
> . . . This openness will be for the sake of directing attention to the ways
> in which men ask and answer fundamental human questions, and there-
> fore for the sake of uncovering what it is that makes human life the
> rewarding, rich, tragic, enigmatic adventure which it is known to be in any
> culture worth the name. Here there is new and exacting work to be done.
> It is arguable that it would be done most vigorously in new environments
> and not as a by-product of a department which exists primarily to serve
> other interests.

He was well aware that in theology the advancement of learning can so
easily be a matter of antiquarianism, or the tidying up and re-classifying
of existing learning, and that hope of genuine illumination from new
learning was required. WAW was quite clear that genuine illumination
from new learning had been released at Basel during Barth's tenure of
the chair of dogmatics there, and his proposal was that in the new British
context new learning was likely to be generated by provision for theological studies as strands in joint honours degrees. The object initially would
be "to find out whether theological insights and judgements can be given
currency and validity in wider fields, beginning from further clarification—suggested in part by what comes from attending to the wider fields—
of the currency and validity of such judgements and insights in the discourse of the Christian churches and in matters of 'religion.' " This would
be done by way of commitment to undergraduate teaching and to postgraduate research (not commonly characteristic of departments interested
in the production of ordinands).

When he wrote the paper, WAW thought it "highly improbable that any university where theology is not yet established would be prepared to risk acting on a precarious and unconventional proposal" such as the one he had outlined. However, WAW's extraordinary capacity to combine teaching, writing, and administration in a way rarely emulated by other members of theology departments, and the existence of his paper in print, made him more than acceptable to the founding members of the new university of Kent at Canterbury—or at any rate to some of them. For some senior members who had experienced Oxbridge, theology was academic poison, though as a non-conformist he was free at any rate of one criticism that might be made of him. The invitation to become the founding Master of Eliot College (1965–1969) put him in a strong position to introduce theology into the various degree patterns, though initially he was content simply to contribute to courses on "science and religion" proposed in the first instance by the philosophy teachers. As circumstances evolved, however, Kent's Professor of Theology (1965–1977) was able to add members to his team and establish a lively and successful department. From a joint honours subject with two students and two-and-a-half teachers a single honours course was established, and when WAW chose to retire a year or two before retirement might have been expected, the success of the department was such that he was replaced at professorial level, and the department continues to flourish. Not the least of his achievements was to have enabled the Roman Catholic Franciscans to locate their "house of studies" but half a mile from Eliot, with their novices coming to read a humanities course before beginning specialist work with the Order. In the meantime, between 1962 and 1967 he chaired the commission appointed by the Congregational Church in England and Wales to compose *A Declaration of Faith*. The 1970 *Declaration* represents the final phase of his contributions toward an outline of a Congregationalist systematic theology.

WAW's work as Master of Eliot required all his resources; he fostered a wide range of academic talent, chaired the college governing body, and presided at high table—all this at a time of student unrest, since Kent was easy of access to agitators from London. It was a period of great grief for him too, since his wife Mary was ill with the cancer from which she died in 1971. The task of Master of a college at Kent was meant to be short-term, and WAW had done more than his stint, but a deadlock over a later appointment led to his return to the responsibilities of Master for two further years (1973–1975). It was in 1974 that he married Mrs. Audrey Ethel Lemmon, with whom, in semi-retirement, he returned to parish ministry, this time as a member of the United Reformed Church. The High Chapel at Ravenstonedale, near Kirkby Stephen in Cumbria, has had many distinguished ministers, including now Kent's Professor Emeritus of Theology, a great man of extraordinary modesty who continues to produce fine sermons, translate German theology, and sally forth, when invited, to deliver lectures and addresses. His revision of the Boutwood lectures for this present volume pull into focus his understanding of divine authority after reflection on a lifetime's experience as minister, university teacher, and administrator. Those who come to know him only through his writings might find it helpful to bear in mind the circumstances with which they are connected. These essays, and the books and articles to which the bibliography directs readers, offer many reflections of interest for other theologians, whether they regard themselves as aspiring or accomplished. The point of Christian theology is, after all, a simple one:

> The world goes on putting its questions to those who go with the shepherds and are finding out what happens. Can our fears be cut at the root? Can men hope to stop pumping into society the poisons bred from these fears? Can we hope for even more—that the effects of the poison can be neutralized by goodness and by suffering springing from fearless love? Yes! We dare to reply. Life as you and I face it and live it, self-centred and fear haunted, can be broken and then picked up and re-made in communion with a divine life which is free from fear. And here is this divine life, traced out on earth in our midst with no resources but our own, linking itself to ours for our salvation.

> St. Luke's Christmas story takes us from politics and politicians to God, to the fear of God and to a lively hope grounded upon His love. We have to come back to politics, and to all the rest of mankind's interim concerns; and we come back realizing that the fear of God and hope in God hardly seem to touch public life or even private life in these days. God is still content to hide his strength in weakness, as he did in the manger and on the Cross. . . . But for my part, I find the angel's word convincing and will go with the shepherds to see this thing which the Lord has made known to us.[7]

---

[7]From the 1959 Christmas Day broadcast sermon.

FOREWORD

I count it a great privilege to be asked to commend this volume of the collected papers of W. A. Whitehouse. It is owing to his considerable modesty that we do not have more of them, although he is certainly one of the ablest theological minds of our day, and many others have stood upon his shoulder. Alec Whitehouse has been a very good theological friend of mine ever since we used to meet regularly in Oxford in connection with the "SCM Theological Club" in the years immediately after the Second World War. About a dozen of us met to read papers to one another and think through basic theological questions in an ecumenical perspective, in the hope also of finding ways to stimulate a genuine rehabilitation of serious theology in British churches and universities. Those were the years prior to the launching of the *Scottish Journal of Theology*, the Society for the Study of Theology, and the English edition of Karl Barth's *Church Dogmatics*, to which Alec Whitehouse made signal contributions.

I was greatly impressed from the start of our friendship with the remarkably fertile way in which the precision and realism of his Cambridge mathematics and his Oxford theological studies came to be combined under the impact of the profoundly realist theology of Karl Barth, and not least those volumes of the *Church Dogmatics* concerned with the doctrines of providence and creation. Far from retreating from the formidable intellectual challenge of Barth, like many of his contemporaries, Alec Whitehouse set himself to think through the far-reaching implications of Barth's thought for our understanding of the physical world and also to put them severely to the test in coming to grips with the seismic change in the ontological foundations of knowledge. As he fed the results of his own inquiries into his lifelong concern for the bearing of our knowledge of God upon the consistent structure and integrity of the created order, he found that he had also to engage in critical dialogue with the reactionary empiricist philosophy, including the philosophies of science and of law, that prevailed in postwar Oxford and Cambridge under the influence of Viennese positivism. Karl Barth's christological and eschatological critique of the immanentist naturalism that had corrupted German moral and socio-political thought, as well as German theology, had provided Whitehouse a perspective. Using that perspective, Whitehouse devoted much of his energy to examining the material relations between scientific and theological subject matter, to developing a theology of nature, and toward the clarification of the vexed problem of natural law in the fields of ethics and jurisprudence, both of which, like natural science, needed to be set back again on proper ontological foundations. How all this affected his church theology is very evident in the justly praised document *A Declaration of Faith* of 1967, in which he clearly had a masterly hand.

Thus the profound realist orientation of Alec Whitehouse's thought in science, ethics, and law, as well as in theology, together with his commitment to interdisciplinary relations at a deep level, ruled out of the question for him any trimming of his ideas to meet the fluctuating fashions of current opinion. It also put from him any thought of substituting a phenomenology and sociology of religion for the serious enterprise of systematic theology and a rigorous philosophy of theology, and made quite impossible any lapsing back into the loose and damaging dualist thinking of the nineteenth century, which now seems to be a strangely anachronistic feature of some current theological writing. On the contrary, these papers alone, apart from his major works, reveal a determined wrestling with fundamental issues, giving them an integrity and a distinction which will long be admired. Readers will find in them evidence of a shrewd perception and a reliable judgement to guide them in their own understanding of Christian theology in its bearing upon the real world of space and time, that world in which God has set us and through which he has revealed himself to us in the grace of our Lord Jesus Christ.

THOMAS F. TORRANCE

BIBLIOGRAPHY

of the
Works of W. A. Whitehouse
(excluding reviews and review articles)

* indicates that the essay or address is included in the present volume.

1940
Christendom on Trial. Anonymous pamphlet published by the Friends of Europe.

1941
Translation of Heinrich Vogel, *The Iron Ration of a Christian* (Preface by Hans Herbert Kramm). London: SCM, 1941.

1943
The Man in the Street. London: Independent Press (Forward Books No. 5), 1943.

A sermon, in *Congregationalism Today*, ed. John Marsh. London: Independent Press, 1943.

1945
"On Prayer" (sermon). *The Christian World*, Feb. 15, 1945.

"Theonomic Thinking." *The Presbyter*, 3 (1945).

1946
"Dona Nobis Pacem" (sermon). *The Christian World Pulpit*, Nov. 21, 1946. (Originally preached at the Control Commission Chapel in Berlin, October 1946.)

*"Karl Barth and the Doctrine of Creation." *The Presbyter*, 4 (1946).

Natural Law: A Christian Reconsideration, ed. WAW and A. R. Vidler. London: SCM, 1946.

"That Hideous Strength." *The Presbyter*, 4 (1946).

1947
"The Evangelical Church Between East and West." *The Presbyter*, 5 (1947).

Translation of Heinrich Vogel, *The Grace of God and German Guilt*. London: SCM, 1947.

"The Situation of the Evangelical Churches in Germany." *The Presbyter*, 5 (1947).

*"The State and Divine Law," in *Reformation Old and New* (*A Tribute to Karl Barth*, ed. F. W. Camfield. London: Lutterworth, 1947.

Signatory to *The Task of the Churches in Germany* (a report from a delegation of British churchmen after a visit to the British zone, Oct. 16–30, 1946). London: SPCK, 1947.

"The Wrath and Mercy of God" (sermon). *The Congregational Quarterly*, 25 (1947). (Originally preached in Mansfield College chapel in Nov. 1946 on returning from the visit to the British zone.)

1949

*"The Christian View of Man: An Examination of Karl Barth's Doctrine." *Scottish Journal of Theology*, 2 (1949), 57–74.

1950

"The Bread of Life" (sermon). *The Christian World Pulpit*, Oct. 12, 1950.

*"Dogmatics in Outline." BBC Third Programme broadcast, Oct. 1950.

1951

*"God's Heavenly Kingdom and His Servants the Angels." *Scottish Journal of Theology*, 4 (1951), 376–82.

*"Providence: An Account of Karl Barth's Doctrine." *Scottish Journal of Theology*. 4 (1951), 241–56.

1952

Christian Faith and the Scientific Attitude. Edinburgh: Oliver and Boyd, 1952.

*"The Command of God the Creator: An Account of Karl Barth's Volume on Ethics." *Scottish Journal of Theology*. 5 (1952), 337–54.

"Creation" (sermon). BBC broadcast, and published in *The Christian World Pulpit*, March 13, 1952.

1953

*"The Modern Discussion of Eschatology," in *Eschatology*, ed. W. Manson, G. W. H. Lampe, T. F. Torrance and W. A. Whitehouse. Scottish Journal of Theology Occasional Papers No. 2. Edinburgh: Oliver and Boyd, 1953.

Translation of Karl Heim, *The Transformation of the Scientific World View*. London: SCM, 1953.

1955

The Biblical Doctrine of Justice and Law, with Heinz-Horst Schrey and Hans Hermann Walz. London: SCM, 1955.

"The Christian Doctrine of God." *The Student Movement*, 57 (1955).

1956

*"Christ and Creation," in *Essays in Christology for Karl Barth*, ed. T. H. L. Parker. London: Lutterworth, 1956.

"A Reformed National Church: Could Congregationalists Cease to be Dissenters?" *The Christian World*, Sept. 13, 1956.

"Shall the Dead Praise Thee?" (sermon). BBC broadcast.

1957

"Behold Him Come . . ." Two Advent addresses, BBC overseas service, Dec. 1957.

1958

"A New Year" (sermon). BBC broadcast, Jan. 1958.

*"R. B. Braithwaite As an Apologist for Religious Belief." *Durham University Journal*, New Series 19 (1958).

"Teaching Genesis 1–2: The Primeval Story." *Religion in Education*, 25 (1958).

1959

"Christmas Day" (sermon). BBC overseas service, Dec. 1959.

1960

Order, Goodness, Glory. (Riddell Memorial Lectures, Durham University.) London: Oxford University Press, 1960.

1961

The Six Days of Creation. (BBC broadcast talks.) London: Independent Press, 1961.

1962

"Is God Here?" (Whitsun meditation). BBC Third Programme broadcast, June 1962.

"Theology as a Discipline?" *The Universities Quarterly*, 16 (1962).

1964

*"The Christian in the University" (sermon), in *The Christian Way Explained: Durham Sermons by the Archbishop of York and Others*, selected by R. J. W. Bevan. Oxford: Mowbray, 1964.

"The Ordinance of the Lord's Supper" (sermon). BBC broadcast, June 1964.

*"Towards a Theology of Nature." *Scottish Journal of Theology*, 17 (1964), 129–45.

1965

*"Theology and the Natural Sciences," in *The Scope of Theology*, ed. Daniel T. Jenkins. Cleveland: World, 1965.

1966

*"Christological Understanding," in *Service in Christ: Essays Presented to Karl Barth on His 80th Birthday*, ed. James I. McCord and T. H. L. Parker. London: Epworth, 1966.

1967

Chairman of the Commission of the Congregational Church in England and Wales, and contributor to *A Declaration of Faith*. London: Independent Press, 1967.

1970

"Making the Declaration of Faith," in *Christian Confidence*. Theological Collections No. 14. London: SPCK, 1970.

*"New Heavens and a New Earth," in *The Christian Hope*. Theological Collections No. 13. London: SPCK, 1970.

1979

*"A Theological Perspective," in *Human Rights: Problems, Perspectives and Texts*, ed. F. E. Dowrick. New York: Saxon House, 1979. (Originally delivered as a lecture in the Durham University department of law, autumn 1978, as "Theology and 'Human Rights,' " the title it has in this volume.)

1981

*"Authority, Divine and Human." First publication in this volume. (A revision of the Boutwood lecture delivered at Corpus Christi College, Cambridge, in 1967 with the title "Divine Authority and Natural Science.")

*"Sanctity and Worldliness in the Bible." First publication in this volume. (A revision of an address delivered at the Bossey Ecumenical Centre, Switzerland, in 1956.)

PART ONE:

Essays in Response to Karl Barth

DOGMATICS IN OUTLINE:
KARL BARTH

THE PUBLISHER SAYS THAT THIS SMALL BOOK CONTAINS THE QUINTESSENCE of Barth's systematic theology.[1] The full statement is not available in English, though we have, from the same translator, G. T. Thomson, the first half-volume which was written in 1932. Then Hitler was rising to power, and Barth was settling down to a colossal task. If he lives to complete it, one will find, in 1962, twelve or thirteen volumes of *Church Dogmatics*, each of them five to eight hundred pages long, in every good theological library. In scale and quality the work is that of an intellectual giant. The term "Barthian" has been used in this country as a mild term of abuse for those who followed this so-called "prophet of Protestant irrationalism": those who retailed his Biblical insights, his stimulating paradoxes, and the rhetoric of his dialectical theology. Rumour has it that one British university is still unwilling to grant to Barth the status of doctor of divinity because he is a Barthian and therefore not intellectually respectable. But Barth can no longer be dismissed as an *enfant terrible* masquerading among the theologians. He is a figure of European, perhaps of world-wide, importance, destined for good or ill to exert a great influence on human thought. Why? Because he is writing a vast technical work of theology! By what right nowadays does a *theologian* exert such influence or make such heavy demands on his readers? Thoughtful people who themselves are not theologians at all and have no obligation to read the massive tomes, may nonetheless have an interest in what is being done. And therefore I shall discuss this small book in relation to the great *Dogmatik*. If, as I suppose, Barth is producing systematic theology, matched in scope and quality to the revolutionary state of the world, that is an event of far-reaching importance—provided of course, that theology still matters, as it did in the days of Augustine, Aquinas, Luther, or Calvin.

During the summer of 1946 Barth lectured, at seven in the morning,

---

[1]Karl Barth, *Dogmatics in Outline*, trans. G. T. Thomson (SCM, 1949); trans. from *Dogmatik im Grundriss* (Christian Kaiser Verlag and Evangelischer Verlag, 1947).

to students of Bonn university. It is these lectures which we now have in English. They offer an exposition of Christian faith not unlike those which have been fashionable in England during the last fifteen years; for instance, Dr. Whale's lectures given in Cambridge at a more respectable hour. The articles of the Apostles' Creed are discussed freely, for Barth had to dispense with a manuscript and we owe the book to a shorthand transcript. So it is possible for us to see what kind of Christian Karl Barth fundamentally is. It may surprise many people that his understanding of Christian existence is not at all outlandish; his thought is not wildly paradoxical; his insights are not inherently foreign to the British mind. But this simple exposition reflects the profound and coherent clarifications for which Barth has worked so strenuously in the big *Dogmatik*, so it is a very distinguished exposition.

Before I talk about those clarifications, let me lay to rest a couple of ghosts: the ghost of Barth's irrationality, and the ghost of his indifference to culture and humanity. From his early days, as a pastor of the Swiss Reformed Church, he has had a desperate concern for the languages used and the things done in the Christian Church. He believed they ought to be based on reasoned and responsible conviction, guided by ascertained and clearly conceived truth, and not upon something obscure to reason such as habit or impulse. Faith includes clear and ordered human thinking. It is knowledge, or better, it is *wisdom*—knowledge by which to live. And Barth is intensely aware of the rich complexity in human life. He is by no means indifferent to culture and humanity. His theology illuminates that rich complexity, yet it does not pretend to usurp the functions of other disciplines which add to human wisdom. I am sometimes asked what value Barth does set on philosophy, the arts, and the sciences. The answer is not clear to me. His negative verdict is well-known. There is no sign in these activities of any natural disposition among men towards the Word of God. To some, that verdict is a pathological reaction to "liberalism" in theology, and to the growth of modern paganism. To my mind it is clearly entailed by an authentic Christian doctrine of God. But this is not all that he has to say about it. In the chapter on the Second Coming, where he discusses the goal of time, Barth refers to men who, in their pursuit of secular hopes, often put Christians to shame. These hopes, and the thought and effort which accompany them, are not irrelevant to the Alpha and Omega believed by Christians. I suspect, therefore, that Barth's evaluation of philosophy, science, culture, and history, is an eschatological evaluation. I mean that it will finally appear only when he offers a full statement of the doctrine of the world's consummation in the fifth part of the *Dogmatik* which is to deal with redemption.

But now I have referred to "the Word of God," and you feel a trifle sceptical about the clear and ordered human thinking stored in this theological cupboard. I have mentioned eschatology and Christ's Second Coming, and, quite appropriately, the skeleton in the cupboard tumbles out. What trustworthy knowledge can there be of such matters? What value does Barth set on *theology*? How does he propose that it be practised? And what kind of result is he achieving? These questions will occupy the rest of our time.

Systematic theology is an orderly criticism of what is thought and said in the Christian Church. It is an attempt to clarify, by an appropriate method, the facts of Christian existence. Here are men and women thinking and living in some kind of relation to Jesus Christ. Here are churches which for 1900 years have publicly professed a theory and practice of communion with God which is distinctive and authoritative. They profess this communion to be one which God Himself has initiated through events which are described as the utterance of His Word. These events appear to be random historical facts upon which an absolute value has been set by some people. What is thought and said in the Church is evoked by the man Jesus Christ; it is controlled by the writings of certain prophets and apostles, which are our only documentation of His person and work. In offering his critical service to the Church, the theologian must take the measure of these difficult facts. He has to work in a world which is now almost persuaded that Christian existence is built on a delusion. Like the rest of us, he finds it hard to suppose that men are being summoned, along channels like these, to decisions of absolute significance and absolute validity. Has Barth closed his ears to the major questions which are being raised about the Church's integrity? It has seemed to many people that theology as he understands it is an anachronism, and that the method he has prescribed for it is irresponsible. The facts of Christian existence are the subject matter of history, philosophy, anthropology, psychology, and literary criticism. How do they become the subject matter for another science, theology? The answer is that this common subject matter has an avowed *raison d'être* to which these other sciences cannot give proper attention. That *raison d'être* is divine "dogma," with which mankind has been confronted in quite unpredictable fashion. Dogma, in the first instance, does not mean doctrinal propositions. It means an imperial summons, a behest or decree. It is the decree of God, His claim upon His creatures, and His promise to them. Barth has decided, with good reason, that no natural disposition towards Christian existence can be discovered among men. The dogma which summons them to Christian existence therefore demands special investigation. Christian existence must be submitted to *theological* examination and reformation in relation to this avowed *raison d'être*.

Is this divine decree a fact or not? Is there any such dogma, properly called the Word of God? Is it found where Christian faith says it is? Barth has refused to discuss these questions in the abstract. He begins by acknowledging such a Word of God. He has worked out a method by which to measure Christian existence in relation to it. And he is working to clarify what should be thought and said in a Church which is true to its *raison d'être*. The result is that he is probing the questions raised about the Church's integrity more thoroughly than any theologian since the Reformation. And he has shown, I think, that in the nature of the case, the ground of Christian communion with God must *disclose itself*, with divine self-evidence, in the course of true Church life and in the theology which serves it. It cannot be established or refuted *a priori*.

To discuss his method fully I should have to wander off into a maze of technicalities. It is decisively different from that of Roman Catholic theology. And though it is very near to that of the Reformers, it is designed to deal with the matters on hand with greater range and precision than was required of them four hundred years ago. His task is to conform the thought and speech of the Church to the Word of God. His data are the world of public fact and the divine dogma which impinges upon that world. How does he become aware of the dogma? First, he tries to see in the testimony of Holy Scripture the reality of Jesus Christ. Then this same Scripture directs his attention to the world of public fact, and under its direction he tries to state the significance of Jesus Christ for that world. As he does so, the divine dogma comes into view, and he finds that he has to expound it in orderly fashion. You can only see what this means, and the discipline which it entails, if you see him actually at work in the big *Dogmatik*. He has emphasized that theological exposition is always provisional, and there is no room for claims to infallibility. Though the dogma does not change, the doctrine in which it is expressed is in constant need of renewal. Barth has seen to it that there will never be a sect committed to his doctrine in the way that Lutherans or Methodists were committed to that of their founders. But that does not mean that Church history will be unaffected by what he is doing. Nor, I think, will the effect be confined to the Reformed or Calvinist churches to which he is principally responsible. He is summoning all the churches to new decisions in the realm of doctrine, and in these decisions they will be committed to new modes of thought and action which cannot easily be predicted at this stage.

Dogmatics in Outline shows clearly enough the kind of reformation which Barth has already achieved in Christian doctrine. Let me mention three points where his doctrine has a bearing far beyond the field of academic theology.

First, I know of no other theologian who speaks to me with such clarity and persuasiveness about *God*, and His method of working in history, with persons, and with material things. If one studies the controversies of the eighteenth century, between the Deists and their orthodox opponents, one finds a common framework of reference within which both sides understand the being of God and human religion. Barth has eradicated the last traces of that framework. Biblical scholars have been recovering for us the framework used in the Bible, and Barth has proved in practice how well it meets the intellectual needs of modern men. The result is a doctrine of the life of an active God; a life lived in sovereign freedom and love; a life which He has chosen to express in a covenant-transaction with mankind, grounded in everlasting wisdom, and perfected, despite appearances, in the person of Jesus Christ. With this background he has been able to re-coin the simple terms of Christian discourse; heaven and earth, for instance, as the two parts of creation; soul and body as the two poles of manhood. When you find him using such terms, do not dismiss him as a naive pious reactionary. He is putting them back into circulation with an acuteness worthy of the Logical Positivists. The result is to dispel the cloud of unreality which haunts so much talk about God, both the hollow platitudes of hymns, prayers, and sermons, and the pale philosophizing which has so often passed for theology. The consequences, for religion and for upright human living, may be very great.

Secondly, Barth speaks with incomparable power about the cosmic significance of Jesus Christ. Something happens in the life of God, and we have evidence of it in the history of the man Jesus, which explains both the creation of all things and the destiny which is assured to them by grace. The action by which God is moulding the world for His own glory, is the action which He has performed publicly before men in the flesh of Jesus Christ. The theologian has to expound this decisive divine control of the cosmos, and Barth does it very effectively without ever talking nonsense about the cosmos itself. He shows a scrupulous respect for the truths of science and humanism. He regards their non-theological wisdom as a parable of theological truth. A good parable must be true in itself, as well as being true to that of which it is a parable. Further, the cosmic Lordship of Jesus Christ lies at the heart of political realities. And there is ample evidence in Barth's occasional writings that his theological clarifications have led to clarifications in the broad field of political decision and political responsibility. Here he shows marked divergence from the Church of Rome, and from the bourgeois sentimentality of much Anglo-American and Swiss religion.

Thirdly, he has of late been actively drawn into the Ecumenical Movement. He is suggesting how to consider the Church from new perspectives. What place does the Church hold in the covenant-transaction of God? And how is she commissioned to serve the world between the times of Christ's withdrawal from it and the unveiling of God's completed purpose? This may prove an invaluable stimulus to reunion by the road of common reformation.

Barth's best admirers are not slow to criticise him, sometimes on matters of great importance. But even his detractors are coming to agree that we must learn from him how to pursue, with a deep sense of vocation and with no apologies, the distinctive task of the theologian.

(1950)

KARL BARTH AND THE
DOCTRINE OF CREATION

THIS FIRST PART OF BARTH'S TREATISE ON THE DOCTRINE OF CREATION HAS not been in my possession for a sufficiently long time to warrant any serious discussion of it.[1] In this article I aim only at an outline of its contents. Those who are familiar with the one translated volume of the *Dogmatik* will know how Barth provides, in the course of his own exposition, long sections printed in smaller type which exhibit the Scriptural basis of his teaching in the light of previous theological discussion. To work through these sections is particularly important and rewarding in the case of this present volume, but it is a task which I have hardly had time to begin.

Two other volumes are promised on the doctrine of creation, the first on the doctrine of man, and the second on the doctrine of providence, creaturely freedom, and the command of God the Creator. In the chapter on "Science and Society" in *The Era of Atomic Power*, the Commission appointed by the British Council of Churches says: "The Church has been so pre-occupied with its message of sin and redemption that it has given far too little thought to the place of man's creative activity in God's purpose for the world. We need a wholly fresh interpretation of the doctrine of creation, and of man's co-operation in God's creative work." Whether or not Barth's exposition will meet this need remains to be seen; the later volumes will prove it.

Meanwhile, the outstanding thing to remark about this first part is that the doctrine of creation is here to be closely integrated with the doctrine of redemption. As one would expect, it is from the Person and Work of the Redeemer that the Christian believer attains to faith in the Creator. Further, the Christian understands the work of creation only in virtue of its essential relation to the covenant fulfilled in Jesus Christ. After an

---

[1]Karl Barth, *Die Lehre von der Schöpfung*, III, 1 of *Die Kirchliche Dogmatik* (Zollikon-Zurich: Evangelischer Verlag, 1945). [Since the English translation was not published until 1958, all the translations in this essay are WAW's own.]

opening section on "Belief in God the Creator," Barth devotes the major part of his book to a section on "Creation and Covenant." It is a sustained examination of the first two chapters of Genesis. First he wrestles with the *form* in which the witness to God's creative work is given in these two chapters: "Creation, History, and the Story of Creation" (*Schöpfung, Geschichte, Schöpfungsgeschichte*). Then he expounds Genesis 1 under the heading: "Creation as the External Ground of the Covenant," his thesis being that in the P account the world which is built, and the order of its building, is a world designed for the dealings of God with His people through which the Covenant is established. The earlier account, in Genesis 2, he expounds under the heading: "The Covenant as the Inner Ground of Creation," and here he takes every narrated event, every turn of phrase, and shows how its inner significance lies in the relation ultimately to be established between God in Christ and the Church. The third main section, "The Yea of God the Creator," draws out the significance of this Christian understanding of the work of creation in three directions, where, apart from such a secure and objective basis, the human mind is left vacillating between optimism and pessimism, vague assurance and despair: (a) that creation is a beneficent work; (b) that the created world is real; (c) that creation is a work of justification. Lest it be thought that he is tilting against windmills in this third main section, he devotes many pages of small type to the careful assessment of the important philosophical points of view to which his theological doctrine is most clearly related whether by affinity or by contrast; to Marcion and Schopenhauer in the first matter, to Descartes in the second, and to Leibnitz and the general movement of eighteenth-century optimism in the third.

Barth provides, at the head of each section (numbered consecutively throughout the entire *Dogmatik*), a carefully worded statement of his theses, and these perhaps should be quoted.

40. *Belief in God the Creator*

The judgement (*Einsicht*) that man, together with all reality other than God, owes existence (*Dasein*) and actuality (*Sosein*) to God's creation, is made only in receiving and responding to the divine self-evidencing, i.e., only in faith in Jesus Christ; in acknowledging the unity of Creator and creature actualized in Him, and in the life which is mediated through Him in the presence of the Creator, under His law, and in the experience of His favour (*Güte*) to His creation.

41. *Creation and Covenant*

Creation is first in the series of works of the triune God, and thereby the beginning of all things other than God Himself. Since it includes within itself the beginning of time, its historical reality is removed from all his-

torical observation and report, and testimony to it, in the Biblical creation-
stories as anywhere else, can only be given in the form of pure saga (*Sage*—
legend?). According to this testimony, the purpose and also the meaning
of creation is to make possible the covenant of God with man, the origin,
centre, and end of which is in Jesus Christ. The history of this covenant
is thus the goal of creation just as creation itself is the beginning of this
history.

42. *The Yea of God the Creator*

The work of God the Creator subsists especially in the beneficence that
what He has made can, within the limits of its creatureliness, *exist* as actualized by Him and can *be good* as justified by Him.

Such a treatment of the doctrine of creation deserves all our attention
for it has many qualities calculated to shatter the shameful silence which
too often prevails in Christian theology to-day on the subject. First, it is
really theological, with a secure foundation in the Biblical testimony, not
a pale philosophizing built up laboriously and inconclusively from scientific or metaphysical reflection. Second, it takes seriously the *activity* of
God in creating the world. Something has been done, and done by a
personal agent. There have been events of which account can be given
only in story form, not in the form of "eternal truths." Third, it embodies
a robust affirmation of the goodness of what exists. And fourth, it is not
peripheral or preliminary to the main Christian theme, but rather does
the Lordship and saving work of Jesus Christ sparkle within it from every
point. Profound questions are raised as to whether Barth has theologized
faithfully in this volume, some of which may be mentioned later. But there
can be little doubt that this is the way to treat the doctrine of creation,
and that he is right and illuminating in finding the relation of creation
and covenant to be the key to the whole mystery of what God the Creator
has done.

It has become customary to indicate the Christian teaching about creation by discussions conducted from a speculative physical or metaphysical
point of view; to transfer this subject, together with the subject of God's
Being and attributes, to the frontiers or even into the domain of Natural
Theology. Those who are familiar mainly with contemporary theological
scholarship, particularly of English origin, are likely to receive a salutary
shock when they read genuine theological treatments of the subject. To
go back only so far as Dorner's *Dogmatics* is to discover a range of questions
and discussions with which we have grown sadly unfamiliar. The theological question at stake here is the relationship between creation and redemption, and it could easily be demonstrated that this question lies at
the heart of the great theological controversies from the days when the
first article of the creed was formulated and the battles raged over Trin-

itarianism and Christology, to the Reformation disputes about Nature and Grace and a double ethic, and down to the German Church struggle of our own day and its counterpart in other lands including our own.

Barth maintains the crucial importance and relative integrity of a pure theological approach on the ground that it is only in faith that the otherwise unattainable knowledge is given that God does not exist alone and that the world is real. This cannot be proved against the possibility that only God exists and the world is somehow unreal; nor against the thought that the world may well exist of itself and by itself. Even if it could be proved (cf. *Finite and Infinite* by Dr. Austin Farrer) that the power and meaning of the world's existence are not from itself, rational theology cannot answer the question whence they are. Christian theology, wrestling with this question in the context of an Old and a New Covenant, declares that they are from God the Father. And the article of faith indicates an act, related in the perfect tense, denoting the *establishment* of a relation between God and the world, which act has been done in the good pleasure and free omnipotence of God's love. The result of this act of God is a non-divine reality, heaven and earth, the establishing of which is an expression of the inner life of the Trinity.

But what is the epistemological status of this "insight" or "judgement"? Barth takes pains to make this clear. (Maybe he has heard that there are theologians in England who think his theology lacks an epistemological foundation and therefore feel free to dismiss him virtually unread!) His answer to the question is basic to the whole volume, and is open to grave criticism—some of which has been forcibly made already from a Lutheran standpoint by Dr. Regin Prenter.[2] The Biblical testimony, focused on the Person of Jesus Christ, is that God is not alone. Neither the *Lebensraum* of God, nor that of man, is all-embracing. Now the Bible is the organ of the Spirit of knowledge of the Father through the Son; and in the personal relationship with Jesus Christ, in the integrity of Christian faith, established by the Spirit, the believer apprehends the unity of God and the non-divine creature, and comes to know how real is the non-divine creature, and how entirely dependent it is on God the Father Almighty. This "insight" like all others, comes supremely through the Cross, where the end of creatures is revealed in the *death* of the God-man. In the resurrection a *new* creation is revealed, and therewith the act of creation itself. This noetic relationship of Jesus Christ to the act of creation subsists in virtue of a prior ontological relationship—a truth to which the believer attains as his faith develops into understanding. The Christian understanding of God's creating work has its origin in the contemplation of Jesus Christ, and of course we see Him in the (now perfected) act of accomplishing His redemptive Lordship over men. An understanding

---

[2] *Theologische Zeitschrift* [Basel], May/June 1946.

of creation derived from this particular contemplation will bear distinctive marks of its origin. The resultant doctrine is of a perfected act of God the Father through His Son (the Word which makes this known is the Word by which it was done); an act whose purpose and effect is integrally related to the historical establishment of the covenant of grace.

When we scrutinize the Biblical testimony to this first of God's works, we discover that true exegesis of it is possible only on these lines. The three prepositional phrases of Romans 11:36 affirm the act of creation as such, that it consists in the foundation, perpetuation and working out of the covenant, and that it issues in the redemption and perfecting of what is made. On pp. 52ff. there is an important, but not unfamiliar, discussion of the appropriation of this divine act to the Person of the Father. There is a proportion between the relation of Father to Son within the Godhead, and the relation of the Creator to the world. But this appropriation is characterized and qualified by the truth that what finds analogical expression in the act of creation is the eternal Being of the Father *with the Son*; and that the Son is not *causa instrumentalis* but *causa efficiens—socia Patris in creando*. Further it must be emphasized, with the Fourth Gospel, the Epistle to the Hebrews, and Irenaeus, that it is *Jesus* Who pre-exists in the eternal counsel of God, and Whom the Father sees, and so loves the world as to create it. (The whole question of a Logos-doctrine is investigated here.) The will of the Father and the Son is made explicit by the Holy Spirit, and He is thus the intra-divine guarantee of the creature's existence. The communion of Father and Son is not disturbed but rather glorified by the existence of creatures. Herein is the significance of the assertion that creation is the overflowing of divine love.

In distinction from the eternal generation of the Son, creation is an act which is of the nature of history. It is an event which "fills time"; a *Zeiterfullende Erfahrung*, not a timeless truth. This involves Barth in a discussion of time and history.[3] The bearing of this discussion is barely indicated by saying that Barth's exposition of the creation stories is governed by the principle that every detail in creation-history has its analogue in salvation-history. Creation-time is thus the "image" of salvation-time. Original and fundamental time ("time" being a form of experience) is the life of Jesus Christ, the pattern of events which embodied His finished work, together with the pre-history and post-history of these events in the history of Israel and the existence of the Christian Church. All other time is an image of this basic time. All other experience is conformed to this pattern of events, and may be seen as such by the believer.

The initiating event, creation, is of the nature of history, but cannot be recorded under historical forms, for the writing of history is dependent

---

[3]What he has to say here is extremely important, but liable, because of its novelty, to be obscure in a brief summary. Oscar Cullmann's book *Christus und die Zeit* (Zollikon-Zurich: Evangelischer Verlag, 1946) deals with the subject *in extenso*.

on the presence of human observers and participants. The form of the creation-stories is no accident or crudity therefore. This is the form, the inevitable form, through which we may come to comprehend this act of God. The stories are not "myth" as Barth understands the word; that is to say, they are pure stories, free from veiled philosophizing. And their interpretation must take account of their nature, and of the earthly human media through which they are given to us.

Barth therefore passes to his two long sections of exposition, and this, as has been remarked by others, is theology in the grand manner; an excellent example of the *pulchritudo theologiae* mentioned by Anselm. His Lutheran critic goes on to say that for Luther *"intellectus est breviter nihil aliud nisi sapientis crucis Christi,"* and where the Cross is, there is not merely beauty, but there are insoluble riddles, there is a *crux interpretationis*, there are irresolvable perplexities and ample occasion for humble waiting upon God. But Barth has an answer to everything. One feels the same uneasy doubt which is aroused by the slick assurance of much Fundamentalism. Dr. Prenter in the article already cited exhibits the root of this glittering success as lying in a robust supralapsarian *knowledge* of the unity of creation and redemption; a knowledge which leads Barth to utter dependence on the *words* of Scripture, and to a method of analogical and typological exegesis which is not, *prima facie*, the product of the *fides* which Luther described once as *"Arduissima res."* The heart of the Lutheran objection to Reformed theology comes out in his comment that Barth takes the significance of creation for redemption to be the *essence* of the work of creation. This is all of a piece with his Anselmic assumption that belief in God the Creator is a *judgement (Einsicht)*. To make the noetical transfer from *credere* to *intelligere* is to imply an ontological transfer from *Est* to *Significat*. This famous controversy from the days of the Reformation and of Protestant scholasticism is perhaps one in which we must again engage before a true oecumenical theology is achieved.

To indicate the content of 300 pages of exegesis is an impossible task. It is impossible even to select "important" topics and themes, for it is all important. As a stimulus to German readers to study the book, I will only ask what you would say in a sermon on Genesis 1:20-22. Have you realized the significance of birds and fishes, living an ordered and productive life in those terrifying frontier regions between the formed earth and chaos? It is to a spectacle awakening trust and confidence that man's attention is here directed, and this gracious provision of God is integrally related to His focal dealings with men in Jesus Christ. Likewise in chapter 2, how many of us have thought of relating the deep sleep which fell upon Adam before the creation of Eve, to the burial of Christ which preceded the creation of the Church?

Nowhere, to the best of my belief, have the eyes of modern men been opened to the meaning of God's work in creation, as in these pages. The question which lurks in an English mind is similar to, but less profound than, the Lutheran question. Must we not set a value on the created world in and for itself, recognizing that even so in God's mind its significance is inseparable from the chief of His works, but confessing that our minds are incapable of attaining to the divine comprehension. If, aided by Barth, we penetrate to the secret of why things are, and find that secret in the fact of Christ and His Church, dare we suppose that the whole existence and worth of flowers, beasts, sunsets, and storms, has been exhausted by such understanding? Barth rightly claims that there is a *theology* of creation, which is independent of the results of scientific observation, but has the spirit and method of scientific observation no place in the understanding which is of faith? The results of such observation, during our earthly existence, seem necessarily to retain an irreducible autonomy vis-à-vis theology, but is a genuine theological and exegetical method only possible by ignoring them? Is there not something to learn about life from created things, seen as for the most part we are bound to see them, out of relation to the Gospel? If so, then Barth has overstated his case. But this is not to deny that the task he has performed is an essential and neglected one, and that he has done it magnificently to the enrichment of all Christian thinking. The question remains, however, whether the unity of creation and covenant is a unity which can be laid bare to human knowledge by analogical exegesis of the words of Scripture conducted on a basis of certain understanding; or whether this certainty is *seen* only in the light of glory, and in the light of grace may only be *believed*. (Incidentally, Barth's position depends on, and perhaps necessarily follows from, a robust decision in favour of supralapsarianism; a decision which most of us have hardly come within sight of in recent years.)

I have left myself no space in which to comment on the third section of the book, that in which Barth shows that Christian faith implies that creation is an act of divine benevolence, an expression of God's goodness. . . . The created world is real. We should accept it, and our part in it, as something given by the act of God, Who has deliberately abolished Chaos and the Void that this may exist. All things exist to participate in the overflowing of God's own fullness, that is to say, for the sake of His gracious covenant. To be a creature means to be destined to this, to be affirmed by God, chosen and accepted. To be a creature means to be in the manner of Israel, of the kind that God in His Son has not been ashamed to make His own. The creation, whose ultimate reality and justification is always dubious by human valuation, issues in the covenant choice of man for eternal life with God, and the believer comes to share God's affirmation of it by seeing how it is ordered towards this covenant. It has its dark side as well as its immanent goodness, and it is the duty of the Christian to affirm both sides, to participate in life to the full, and above all to recognize the succession of divine acts in which the end and goal of the process are being fulfilled. Such a summary sounds trite, but many pages would be needed to show the force of Barth's contention that an estimate of the goodness of the world cannot be dependent on the opinion of the individual believer or unbeliever, but is firmly and objectively rooted in the unity of creation and covenant.

His book compels us to face the full implications of Christian faith, and exposes the confusion and uncertainty in which human thinking is involved where that faith is denied.

(1946)

THE CHRISTIAN VIEW OF MAN:
An Examination of Karl Barth's Doctrine

VOLUME III OF THE *Dogmatik* IS CONCERNED WITH CREATION, AND THE FIRST part dealt with the act of creation, elucidating from a specifically Christian point of view the relation of creation and covenant. In this second part, it is the creature which is studied.[1] For a theology bound to the Word of God, the questions at issue concern the nature of man, and the enquiry is controlled by the fact of God having become man. The material which is handled in this vast volume is a selection from man's varied attempts to speak about himself. The aim is to illuminate and to correct the speech of the contemporary Christian Church on this subject, and to do so by proper theological method and criteria. The resultant doctrine may not be very different from what is said in section I (A) of the Lambeth Report Part II, but one cannot help asking whether the statements made there have been reached by the searching discipline of dogmatic theology, practised with the seriousness found in Barth's work. His declared purpose is to seek "comprehensive clarifications in theology, and about theology itself," which will give the Church strength to offer "clarifications in the broad field of politics," a strength which is not strikingly obvious in the Lambeth conclusions about "The Church and the Modern World" and "The Christian Way of Life." Barth is aware that in the present situation, every problem turns on a fundamental decision about the nature of man, and on p. 273 he asks where, outside Christian anthropology and ethics, is there ground for branding as inhuman anything which entails a hostile or an indifferent attitude to one's fellow man. His task here is to probe the foundations of Christian speech about man, mindful of the fact that in Christian anthropology all is not gold that glitters. (His careful criticism of Brunner's *Man in Revolt*, on pp. 153–157, is salutary reading for British theologians.) The desperate concern for truth, which underlies this book and justifies its length, was brought home to me afresh by the important

---

[1] Karl Barth, *Die Lehre von der Schöpfung*, III, 2 of *Die Kirchliche Dogmatik* (Zollikon-Zurich: Evangelischer Verlag, 1945). [The translation is WAW's own.]

little book by Schrödinger, *What is Life?*, where in an epilogue he invites us to ponder the two premises: (1) My body functions as a pure mechanism according to the laws of nature, yet (2) I know that I am directing its motions, of which I foresee the effects, which may be fateful and all-important, in which case I feel and take full responsibility for them. Can one set, alongside and prior to these premises, the fact that I am confronted by Jesus Christ, and draw out correct and non-contradictory teaching about God and eternal life, which is radically different from that to which Schrödinger points the way? The task is not so easy, nor has it been as securely done in the past, as the Anglican bishops seem to assume when they invoke "the Christian understanding of man."

In regard to method, Barth first lays down that:

> **43.**[2] Because man, beneath heaven and on earth, is the creature whose relation to God is disclosed to us in the Word of God, he is the particular object of the theological doctrine of creatures. In that the man Jesus Christ is the revealing Word of God, he is the source from which we come to know human nature made by God.

That the theme of the Bible is God's relationship with *man*, carries consequences for the theology of creation which were drawn out most notably by Luther. Scholastic theology is open to criticism in so far as it works with an *a priori* world-view, and claims knowledge of a relationship of God and creatures to which the God-man relationship must conform. Knowledge of this general relationship, and the relationship itself, appear to be established in some independence of Jesus Christ. The anthropocentric procedure characteristic of Reformed theology is not to be confused with that Idealism which makes man the measure of all things. Idealism sees man as the all-important reality, in whom all things in heaven and earth combine to form a microcosmos. The theologian must not proceed as though the significance of non-human creatures were exhausted by their contribution to the being of man. He must rather recognize that man's existence is *limited* by the reality of heaven and earth, angels and animals. But his starting point is the fact that in the Word of God the God-man relationship is made explicit, whereas in respect of all other being, the Creator-creature relationship is concealed (for which reason, theology, when bound to the Word of God, cannot work out an ontology of heaven and earth to which it is irrevocably committed). All that can be said of God's purpose with the rest of the cosmos is based on what is disclosed in the explicated God-man relationship. The being of man is knowable; an ontology of this special creature is possible; and this carries with it a theological knowledge of heaven and earth as the cosmos of man. Theology cannot ignore the question of how the cosmos subsists in itself, but

---

[2]The principal articles of doctrine are numbered consecutively throughout the *Dogmatik*, and the five included in this volume, 43–47, will be quoted in full.

its relationship with cosmological speculation can at best be an external, opportune one. It takes into provisional service the best available cosmology (and Barth assigns to non-theological thinking a positive significance which should disarm some of his cruder critics), but it is free to withold its confidence, say, from a self-contained ontology of angels such as St. Thomas took over from Dionysius. Its theme is God, and His making of the world. This theme includes the fact that He has made what He has, and the theologian is bound to pay attentive and discriminating regard to the science of his day, but there is no cosmology to which he is committed.

There is no substitute for theological knowledge of man. The exact sciences, taking for granted *that* man is and *what* he is, describe his possibilities. This may be a starting point for speculative anthropology, where, however, the subject is still phenomenal man, and the subject who truly exists never makes a complete appearance. He does so only in the history which he shares with God, to which the theologian is granted access in the Word of God.

A difficulty at once appears, and the attitude adopted in face of it is of far-reaching importance. In the Word of God man is displayed as a traitor to his essential being. It may be said that existence in original sin is an accidental determination of human being; or, if this is rejected (rightly in Barth's judgement), it may be said that there has been virtually a new creation. This is equally false. Sin does not produce a new creature. The sinner is God's good creature, of whom we are trying to speak. Yet it must be admitted that we cannot penetrate past sin (as past a mere accidental determination) to reach undisturbed human nature. Man's nature cannot be traced from "surviving lineaments," nor can it be inferred dialectically from knowledge of sinners. Real man is known because we can see *the sinner existing by God's grace.* When we see God's revealed grace concretely in the man Jesus, we discern a Being unaltered and unalterable because of sin, and it is at this point alone that an answer is offered to the question "What is the created being of man?" (In summary this sounds highly arbitrary. The importance of the whole book lies in the necessity and the profound implications of it.) In the Gospel we see the freedom of God to mean that He is ever and anew the gracious Creator of man. Theological anthropology is rooted in Christology, and it is well to observe that any reversal of this process leads inevitably to Docetism or to Ebionism at the focal point of Christian faith.

It is therefore the relation of God to *the man Jesus* which clarifies for us both the faithfulness of God the Creator and the unalterable character of that human nature which He has made. There is a valuable discussion on pp. 51–54 of the Biblical foundation for Christology which contains explicit safeguards against the natural tendency to reach the mystery of Christ's human nature via preconceived general anthropology. In Him, manhood is so realized as to be the ground of our manhood, by God's grace. In Him, manhood is original, preserved and revealed. The epistemological difficulty caused through the contradiction of manhood in sin can therefore be overcome, by treating sin neither too lightly nor too seriously: by treating it as man's choice of an ontological *impossibility*.

44. The being of man is the history wherein one of God's creatures, chosen and summoned by God, is apprehended by Him in its own act of response, and wherein its capacity for such an act is demonstrated.

This article (pp. 64–241) is introduced by a discussion of Jesus under the heading "Man for God." There follows a discussion of the phenomena of humanity, and a clarification of "real man." The first step is to see Jesus and to find His manhood in the work He does and the office He holds. Here first we must break with the Aristotelian habit of preconceiving manhood as one among many fixed species which can be known in general, and which will be found exemplified in the "personality" behind this work and office. Jesus *is* Kyrios and Christ. It is precisely as Son of God, one with the Father, that He is man. The so-called "human touches" all safeguard this truth. There is no content to His manhood apart from this. (The evidence of the Prologue and the "I am . . ." sayings in the Fourth Gospel become decisive here.) Hence we must affirm of one who lives with us the same human life in the same world:

(a) that of this man alone can it be said that he is identically God;

(b) that this presence of God in man is an *act*, a saving act;

(c) that this act takes place in a *history* with which God's glory is bound up;

(d) that this man *exists* in the glory of God, in the act of His Lordship;

(e) that he has no neutral existence behind the history;

(f) that he *is* essentially *for* God, in order that God's work may happen, His Kingdom come, His Word be expressed.

We learn also from the Gospel to regard all human life as a partaking of what Jesus is; so, though there is unlikeness in this partaking (not only from the fact of sin but because of the unique identity of Jesus with God), these affirmations carry consequences for human nature in general:

(a) man as such must be conceived as belonging to God;

(b) his existence is determined in a history which stands in recognizable relation to the divine redemption established in Jesus;

(c) he is not an end in himself, but is for the glory of God;

(d) whatever freedom means, he can never escape the Lordship of God;

(e) his being is a participating in what God does for him; his freedom is freedom to decide *for* this in the course of a history initiated and sustained by God (whence the "ontological impossibility" of sin);

(f) his being is existence in the service of God.

By these criteria the theologian can come to terms with anthropological thinking which seeks truth by abstraction, and does not acknowledge that man belongs to God, exists only in relation to God's act, exists for the glory of God, under His Lordship, and in His service. Such thinking is governed by the question of what it is that marks man off from other creatures, and what it yields is predicated without a subject. "Rational animal," for instance, points to a subject only when it is made into a theological definition by exploitation of the *Imago Dei* concept. Barth therefore surveys recent work in this field to discover the dogmas which have served to counter scientific modes of thought. Zöckler, in conflict with Darwinism, claimed that humanity is a natural realm, like those called animal, vegetable, and mineral, which is characterized by "spirit," of which ethics and civilization are the expression. Otto played with the significance of "personality." Titius maintained that the "ideals of Jesus" are the culmination of a plan which can be traced in the scientific account of natural human origins. Barth, obviously enjoying himself here, regrets that these "ideals" of love to God, love of men, and life in God's kingdom, are not more convincing phenomena of humanity, and wonders why no Apologist has yet used the facts that men alone trouble to laugh or to smoke! A survey of the British scene would be useful. Philosophers too have made their suggestions. Idealism, particularly in the form which derives from Fichte, has affected the current conception of man, and its limitations easily give rise to work such as that of Jaspers. Naturalist, ethical-idealist, and existentialist anthropologies are, in Barth's judgment, the most important contributions of late to the search for self-knowledge. And there is much to be learned by the theologian who makes his way critically through the best work. But it is not by "Apologetics" that he will fulfil his task. Brunner, no less than Zöckler, Otto, and Titius, fails to reach the true subject, man, when he speaks of human freedom, intelligence, responsibility, personality, historicity, and capacity for decision, in a fashion which suggests that man has a certain neutrality in respect of God's covenant-history.

Real man is disclosed by an *actual* response, an *actual* decision. And if there were no Christological foundation for anthropology, the fact of sin would preclude all knowledge of the real subject—a point which Brunner has not seen clearly enough. It is necessary to make a complete break with the notion of fixed permanent "natures" in settled timeless relations and to think in terms of "behaving" (*Verhalten*) not of "proportion" (*Verhältnis*). What does it mean for the ontological determination of man that Jesus Christ is our neighbour on the plane of history? To be human is a history, a "being together with God" which derives from God, rests on His choice, and is constituted by hearing His Word. Its content and its meaning is the interaction of grace and gratitude. (The soteriological reference of χάρις and εὐχαριστία depends on a prior reference in the context of creation.) From the human side, this is the being, directed towards God, of a subject whose active response is at the same time pure spontaneity. The human creature can be identified without remainder with a history whose marks are: knowledge of God, obedience to God, invocation of God, and God-given freedom. The basis for this teaching was laid in Volume II, 2, and may be studied in Dr. Camfield's summary in *Reformation Old and New*, particularly ch. IV, "God's Election of Grace."

Man is the creature with whom God binds Himself in covenant in the pre-existent Jesus Christ; the creature created *ex nihilo* by the Word of God. He is who he is by having a real history, given within the primary history (or happening) which is God's Word. In this primary history, God's creatures are protected from annihilation, actively redeemed, and enlightened; and in the history given to them, they participate in the happening of the primary history. Man's existence as a subject is existence by the grace of God, in a relation never to be dissolved and ever to be renewed; it is existence in gratitude. And however free and spontaneous it may yet be seen to be, it is wholly encompassed by God's grace. Here, however bald and unconvincing this sounds in summary, there is to my mind a "Christological correction" of the Church's doctrine of man whose implications can hardly be envisaged at this day.

We note that once the true subject has been disclosed, there is room for a science of the condition (nature in that sense) of human life; though real man will always transcend what it says. It is a science built on insights obtained from sources other than the confrontation of man by his fellow-man Jesus. It will exhibit man's *capacity* to be what theological anthropology says he *is*. Natural science, displaying man's capacity to exist in his cosmic environment; ethical idealism, displaying his capacity to be the subject of his own life; existentialism, which shows him related to what is wholly other, and displays his capacity to exist in a history where he questions, decides, and is called into question; theistic anthropology (philosophical theology rather than apologetics), displaying his capacity to exist as partner with God; all must be developed. But they will not yield an autonomous ontology of man.

Now follows a detailed discussion of human existence, which is manifestly determined as that of a person with persons, as an existence of soul and body, and as temporally ordered life. This, it is well to remember, is an exploration of faith, and a criticism of its expression from within faith. In his engaging *Vorwort* Barth points out that he has followed a road to theological knowledge of man which no previous theologian has chosen to follow, and that his work carries the blemishes of all such pioneering. In respect of one article, "Der Mensch und die Menschheit," dealing with the individual, societies, and society, he has not seen his way through, and so has suppressed what he wrote. He does not claim to have included all the matters which fall within an orderly theological doctrine of man. And he has had to devote much space to Biblical exegesis where his professional colleagues have not yet fulfilled their dogmatic responsibilities as exegetes. He has found, however, liberation from the distorting fetters of traditional thought on the matter, and is acutely sensitive to the challenge of modern thinking, and the result is that familiar ideas are set in new and illuminating contexts, with effects that one may hope to see in more "popular" writing. These three sections, 45–47, are books in themselves— the last one a substantial volume of 250 large pages—and cannot be adequately reviewed.

45. That real man is appointed by God for life with God finds ineradicable expression in the fact that his creaturely being is being in encounter—between I and Thou, between Man and Woman. In this encounter he is human, and his humanity is the likeness of his Creator's being. It is being which is related to God in hope.

46. Through the Spirit of God, man is the subject, the form, and the life, of a material organism; he is the soul of his body—both, completely and simultaneously: in irremovable distinction, in inseparable unity, in indestructible order.

47. Man exists in the time of his present, past, and future life, which is appointed for him. The boundary of his being, behind and before, is the eternal God, his Creator and Covenant-partner. He is the hope wherein man is permitted to live in his appointed time.

The problem in these sections is to see how the form of human life is related to that theological determination of human creatures which is discerned Christologically. The thought in the sections is governed respectively by studies of "Jesus, man for the rest of men," "Jesus, complete man," "Jesus, Lord of time." It is important not to ease the problem by treating sin as an ontological possibility. Man's present existence is a token of what he really is in God's knowledge. We must not speak as though sin had replaced God's creature by another creature and so annulled the Covenant. It is necessary to understand human existence from these three aspects by a method which truly discovers in sinful man a continuum of God's creature.

MAN DETERMINED AS GOD'S
COVENANT-PARTNER

The solidarity of Jesus with His fellow-men is integral to His human reality. Its depth is exposed by consideration of the verb σπλαγχνίζεσθαι, which points to an act of compassion which is not, so to speak, cultivated in an individual in order to bring himself into solidarity with his fellows. Rather does it imply that He takes His being, *qua* man, from those (fallen) men to whom He gives Himself completely. And thus the "kindness and love for man of God our Saviour appeared" (Titus 3:4). In Jesus, man for the rest of man, is the *Imago Dei*; for in this being of Jesus we see also the Being of God.

Allowing for the speciality of the life Jesus lived, we must approach the matter of the general life of humanity by seeing it as that *for* which Jesus is all that He is. But we cannot escape the implication that there is a common form of existence in which it is possible for Jesus to be thus, i.e., to be for the rest of men. It is existence as God's covenant-partner. But man is God's covenant-partner, not in virtue of an inherent potentiality for entering into covenant, nor in virtue of any claim he can make, but solely because *Jesus is for him*. The being of man is thereby determined as co-being with his fellow-man. (Note that this being is constituted by the relatedness of singular subjects, and only under that condition is it found in pluralities.) The notion of egocentric man must therefore be eradicated from Christian anthropology, and no one saw this more clearly than Nietzsche. His clear-sighted attack, analysed on pp. 266–290, is a summons to more responsible theological thinking at this point.

This analysis of "being-in-encounter" cannot easily be summarized. Much that has been written of man's nature, which purports to speak of it from the possibilities which are peculiarly open to man, fails of its purpose, because, in all that pertains to man-in-himself (i.e. not in concrete encounter with a neighbour), he can be either human or inhuman. That which is definitive of humanity appears through the achievement of encounter. The moments of human existence which demand attention are, therefore:

(a) seeing one another with the eyes—a moment which bureaucracy rules out;

(b) speaking and hearing—a moment corrupted by propaganda, the inflation of verbal currency, and loss of confidence in speech;

(c) lending a helping hand—an activity which can, unfortunately, be simulated without any breach in the autarchy of one's life;

(d) enjoying these congenial activities—a moment which is denied where encounter is marked by indifference or resentment.

Barth draws out the truth of personal relationship with a power of which few in Britain might think him capable. And then he insists that he has not been talking about Agape. In a most interesting discourse on Christian love (pp. 329–344), he corrects the fashion of the last ten years to write off Greek life and thought as hostile to the Gospel, and to force the contrast of Eros and Agape. There is a *tertium quid*, humanity, and of that we must speak from this foundation, to enable all men positively to appreciate what they are by creation.

In the man-woman relationship, the one point where there is structural differentiation between human beings, the continuum of God's creature in sinful humanity is manifest. Barth said a great deal about this in his previous volume, and it has received a certain amount of exposition and comment (cf. H. Hirschwald, "The Teaching of Karl Barth on the *Imago Dei*," *The Presbyter*, 5 [1947]). The section on this demands a review to itself, more especially because of the interesting account given of the exegetical basis in Genesis 2:18–25 and the Song of Songs.

Thus man's existence is determined as the being of God's covenant-partner. By nature we are covenant-partners, but this is only true and only knowable because, in the history of His free grace, God has made us His covenant-partners. There is no point of departure here for Natural Theology. But in this, our permanent and continuing humanity, man is in the Image of God, an existence not destroyed by sin but maintained inalienably by reason of our *hope*, i.e., the objective grounding of human existence in the Gospel grace. In developing this *Imago Dei* concept, it is of course fundamental to think of analogy of *relations*, and not in terms of the Thomist *analogia entis*. We exist in the Image of the Living God who Himself confronts Himself to become one God in the *koinonia* of the Holy Spirit. And, as we at once go on to see, it is through this same Spirit that human existence is rendered possible.

MAN AS SOUL AND BODY

Human existence is being in encounter with God and with fellow-man. The term "soul" refers to its *Dasein*, as "body" refers to its *Sosein*. There is in the Bible only an incidental basis for the use of these terms, and in this matter the theses of non-theological science are intensely relevant. We begin, therefore, from contemplation of "Jesus the complete man," noting that language which (in Fourth Gospel terminology) would seem appropriate only to the Logos is used of this *man*. Two things stand out. First, the soul-body distinction, which carries with it in our thought the distinctions of internal from external, and of intelligible from sensible, is manifestly a provisional one. Jesus is in no sense a compound of two kinds of being. Secondly, the life which Jesus lives in the flesh is one from which all trace of disorder has vanished because it is under His control. The novelty of this manhood is interpreted through what is said of His relation to the Holy Spirit—a relation with the *abiding* Holy Spirit, in distinction from the manhood which is possible in virtue of partial gifts of the Spirit. Human nature has been degraded to "flesh"—soul and body lacking Logos—but the triumph of His incarnation is the rectifying of sinful flesh, so that human existence is established in peace and order. The soul of man is the soul of a body, and his body is the body of his soul. This ordered distinction in unity has analogies (and no more than analogies) in the co-existence of God and man in Christ, in the co-existence of Jesus and His Church, and, in less accessible form, in the duality of heaven and earth, justification and sanctification, Gospel and Law, faith and works, preaching and sacrament (the Word is never *signum audibile*, though the sign is *verbum visibile*), creed and orthodoxy, Church and State. Those who are tempted to systematize doctrine from this point of view should be careful not to extend the analogy to Creator and creature, nor to grace and sin.

The existence of man as soul of his body is established, constituted, and preserved by God, and this truth is expressed by saying that he has spirit. Jesus is man as Messiah and as Son of God. *Because* He is Messiah and Son of God, the Holy Spirit indwells His manhood completely. (To invert this statement would be to admit Adoptionism.) Upon this ground, all men are granted to have Spirit and to participate in the manhood which He is. But, remembering that the Covenant is "the inner ground of creation," the statement that "man is in that he has Spirit" means that he is established in a covenant-role. His existence is by God's free grace. As living man, whose body is not a corpse and whose soul is not a shade, his existence is preserved before death and saved beyond death through this free grace whereby God is for him. It is to be understood in the same perspective as the existence of a prophet or judge, of a member of Christ's body or of the Messiah Himself. And this grace of God in creation extends over body as completely as over soul. The term "Spirit" therefore, which points to these truths, has as its peculiar meaning God's being and action for men, whereby the soul is awakened as the life of the body which man is. This action is, however, related immediately to soul, and to the body through the soul. The term "Spirit" can therefore, in certain contexts, be used of "soul." But it may never be taken to mean something identified with man in himself, a third element in his constitution. It is identical with God and shares His immortality. A text such as Ecclesiastes 12:7 brings no "comfort of immortality" to men. If the term be construed with reference to the breath which makes life possible, the breather with whom alone it can be identified is God. As breathed by man, it is not part of his identity as are soul and body.

Barth turns then to consider man's existence as soul and body from three points of view: soul and body in mutual involution, in distinction, and in order.

Soul and body must be *conceived* together. The dichotomy must be transcended (as, for instance, that of God and man can never be).[3] The inner structure of human creatureliness discloses two poles, one creative and spiritual, the other created and natural, but together (a togetherness of nature, not of grace) within a creaturely whole. This wholeness is the ground of man's being a Subject, and so a being in covenant-relation with God. To make clear the fact that soul is not a continuation within man of the divine Being and Action denoted by Spirit, one may note that soul must be soul of a body, whereas Spirit needs no such complement. The existence of soul is the existence of a creature with its own being and action; it is the self-maintaining life of a corporeal being; the life of a genuine subject, and therefore the life of a body which is spatial and material. This unity in conception of soul and body is developed to serve as a corrective to three major misconceptions: the abstract dualist approach of Greek anthropology (followed frequently in the Fathers); abstract monism of the materialist kind; abstract monism of the spiritualist kind. The last is an erroneous attitude more widespread than one had perhaps realized. It is to be regretted that Barth does not give a more extended examination of the first.

But if soul and body are to be conceived without separation, it is equally important that they be conceived without confusion. The subjectivity of man involves a centre at which his life happens, and a periphery where it is articulated. Soul and body are to be understood together as the potentiality of his being in the Word of God, which Spirit makes actual. Their differentiation becomes important when we recognize that the being of man as man is to be self-conscious and accountable to oneself. And here we reach something of which we are sure in the case of man, but of which we are by no means sure in the case of animals. We do not know how they have Spirit, nor that they have soul unified with body. The right differentiation of soul and body in man discloses the seat of his power to recognize God as other than himself, and the seat of his capacity for action in that situation.

The being of man is *Vernehmendes Wesen* (being which comes to an understanding by hearing, questioning, perceiving, etc.). The Bible has no interest in epistemology for its own sake. Its concern is that men should in fact know God. But it is important to discuss man's capacity for knowledge in general terms, since God regularly treats with men indirectly by signs. In fact, human knowledge and understanding is alienated from its proper content, God, and by talking of an abstract capacity for

---

[3]The God-man dichotomy can never be transcended *in conception*, but *is* transcended in the Person of Jesus Christ, and there alone. The "togetherness" of God and man is of grace, never of nature.

knowledge as such, there is danger lest we give to this sinful understanding a relative justification. The Bible does provide directives for an analysis of human nature from this point of view, however; God acts so that man *encounters* Him and *acknowledges* Him, the latter being an act of acceptance in which man becomes himself. There is warrant therefore for our distinguishing the act of *perceiving* (*wahrnehmen*) and the act of *thinking* (*denken*). The empirical moment in knowledge and the moment of acknowledgment are distinct, but (as we are warned in the case of the prophets and apostles) they are inseparable. The Biblical terminology does not permit an analysis into an act of purely external contemplation and one of purely internal reflection. Even the Greek terms of the New Testament are coloured from the Hebrew, so that νοῦς, for instance, is not purely theoretical reasoning, but "what you do in your heart." Perceiving, however, has a special connexion with body, and thinking with soul. Body is the capacity in man to expose himself to what is other; soul the capacity to make what is other his own. Neither pole of activity is conceivable without the other. Man therefore "perceives in that he is soul of his *body*: he thinks in that he is the *soul* of his body. In such differentiation, the act of knowing is the act of the whole man who is seen in the Bible to be confronted by God." The priority of soul must be expressed by saying that soul is the agent of knowledge, the pole at which the real man comes to himself; knowledge being an act in which body only participates. Barth invites us to ponder what kind of creature it is who can be charged with "seeing yet not perceiving."

To know God, in the Biblical sense, is also to act. It is the being of man to *desire* and to *will*. The act of willing has a special connexion with soul. It is a deliberate decision in favour of some defined relation with my object. There is a special reference of desiring to the bodily nature of man. And the situation here is precisely parallel to the previous one. Desiring and willing are both *seelisch* (of the soul) and *leiblich* (of the body); and both are to be understood as primarily *seelisch* and secondarily *leiblich*.

The primacy of man as soul, soul of his body, has already appeared. But body is no accidental appendage of real man, nor inferior to soul. It may be thought of as the "openness" of soul. But the order established between these two poles of man's nature is important. God deals with man as with one who can *control* himself and can *serve* himself. This control by the soul and service of the body is a fact of human existence which is denoted by the terms λόγος, *ratio*, rationality. It is clear therefore that man must not think of himself merely as soul—as a thinking, willing being; he is the controlling soul of his body. Nor must he think of himself merely as body—a perceiving, desiring being; he is the body which serves his soul. In this total act, which throughout is an act of soul *and* body, he exists, a created person, for the Person who has made him. He is appointed to be God's creature and God's partner. Conceived thus, he is a being "whom God can encounter, to whom He can give His Promise and Command, whom God can make like unto Himself, in order to have intercourse with him, to bind him to Himself, and to have with him a common history" (p. 512).

MAN IN HIS TIME

To give even the bare bones of this last section in this context is an impossible task. British theologians are not familiar with the material involved, and unless, as is devoutly to be hoped, a translation speedily appears, a series of expository articles is called for. The time-form is characteristic of life, including the life of God. In the original uncreated time which is a perfection of His Being, past, present and future are *in* one another, not after one another as in created time. Time of this latter character is granted to man in his creation, as the form of his life. By this the world is established as a realm for free divine activity where creatures can live the life willed for them by God. The time which man has, by gift of the Creator, is such that every act of living has its moment, these acts cohere in durations, and measured limits are appointed for the creature's life. Existence in time is characterized by a beginning, a duration, and an ending. The existence of man is then to be examined under the four headings: Time which is given; Time which is appointed; Time which begins; Time which ends. The point of departure for this examination is our knowledge of the man Jesus in *His* time. The New Testament shows Him to us as "the Lord which is, and which was, and which is to come" (Revelation 1:8), the Lord of Time.[4]

To understand how the time of Jesus is the time of God, and how the time of man is related to it, we note (p. 556f.):

(1) That every other time begins, and so from the standpoint of earlier times it *does not yet exist*.

(2) Every other time continues (*dauert*), and so from a contemporary standpoint its reality is *limited to that duration*.

(3) Every other time ends, and so from the point of view of later time it *no longer exists*.

But the time of the man Jesus is not limited thus. The man Jesus *will be*, in that He is and was; He *is*, in that He will be and was; He *was* in that He is and will be. Thus (pp. 527f.) He lives in the lifetime which He

---

[4]Barth refers to the following books: Bultmann, *Offenbarung und Heilsgeschehen* (1941); Kümmel, *Verheissung und Erfüllung* (1945); Cullmann, *Christus und die Zeit* (1946); Markus Barth, *Der Augenzeuge* (1946); and Buri, *Die Bedeutung der neutestamentlichen Eschatologie für die neuere protestantische Theologie* (1935). But he provides material of his own, both exegetical and theological, which British scholars cannot afford to neglect.

needs, as do all men, to live as man. But He lives the life of One who represents God to man and man to God, the life of the Judge who establishes God's right before men and among them, and man's right before God and among his fellows. This life that He lives is thus not exclusive to Himself. The time in which He lives this life becomes not only His time, but the time of God's life and of man's. This time becomes the time which always was where men have lived, which always is where men live, and always will be where men shall live. He makes all men His contemporaries, though in different fashion for those who respectively live with Him from 7 B.C. to A.D. 30, live before 7 B.C., and live after A.D. 30. Thus He is the Lord of time.

The riddle of man's existence (and apparent non-existence) in the past, the present, and the future, can now be tackled from Christian faith. But it is in Jesus, and in Him alone, that we find ground for affirming the reality of its time-form. It is real because it is given to men by God, as the form of existence which He wills and creates. To be in time is to be in relation to God's eternity. This is the inner aspect of the riddle.

Its outward aspect is that man's lifetime has the character of a fixed term (*die befristete Zeit*), and discussion of this leads to further discussion of its two aspects, that it begins and ends. The second of these is the most pressing problem, but Barth does well to raise the problems involved by the former limit, beyond which "we as yet were not," the problem of *Woher?* What is said here serves to clarify what is involved by the Christian practise of baptism. In regard to the other limit, towards which we are moving, the burning question arises whether it is the edge of the abyss— the abyss of not-being. One would expect from Barth a powerful exposition of what it means to live in the shadow of death. It is provided, with a restraint appropriate to this high matter, substantially through the medium of Biblical exegesis. But his object is to distinguish that *limiting of life's span which is natural to the human creature* from the unnatural rejection and condemnation by God towards which we are moving. That God's annihilating curse falls in the end upon sin gives to death a sting which it is impossible to alleviate by soothing words. But what is condemned and annihilated is the ontological impossibility which man is ever choosing and which is ever denied him by the gracious God. Once this is made plain— as it is in contemplation of the man Jesus—we are free to speak *positively* of the term set to man's life. For man's limited existence is not "unto himself" but unto God whose good creature he is.

In this last section I have done no more than scratch the surface of a rich vein of theology, and may even have failed to indicate properly how the vein runs. I would plead once more for the speedy appearance of a translation.

Barth's work is important not least because of the decision he has made as to the nature and method of theology. It has been a fruitful decision, and we cannot afford in Britain to neglect its fruits. But what matters more is that the challenge involved in that decision has hardly been heard yet, and the translation of this masterly book on such a live contemporary issue could not fail to make plain what is involved. Those who have followed him in the decision about theology will have questions to ask about the work done here. They may have suggestions to make, and they cannot but be stimulated to produce in English dress books which deal with the subject on a more popular level. And for them too, the existence of the book in translation would greatly ease the task of coming to terms with it. That task I have not attempted in this review. I hope that the book, displayed even in this skeleton form, will speak for itself.

(1950)

PROVIDENCE:
An Account of Karl Barth's Doctrine

HERE IS THE ELEVENTH *Kapitel* OF BARTH'S *Dogmatik*, AND HE ENTITLES IT *The Creator and His Creation*.[1] Its three great themes are: God's Fatherly Providence, the "Negation" (Chaos or Void) of which He rules and against whose opposition He safeguards His creatures, and the ministry of angels. Before he passes on from the first to the second article of the creed, Barth promises a further *Kapitel* dealing with the ethical doctrine which rests on our understanding of God as Creator. The doctrine which he has to expound and establish in this sector of the theological field is at once the most familiar and the least secure element in the Christian outlook of modern men. We all know the kind of thing we are expected to say about God's Fatherly care. Professor Farmer's book *The World and God* gave substantial help towards saying it in the modern climate of thought. But there are plenty of signs that Christians tremble in face of the obligation to relate the vast and complex range of experience to the action of God. It becomes increasingly difficult to speak as though the wealth and variety of cosmic reality can be intelligibly related to the God who reveals Himself in Jesus Christ and to the action which He takes at that focal point. And what one expected from Barth was a rethinking of the doctrine of Providence on a Christological basis. What he has to say is not excitingly novel. He is happy to work with the analysis of the subject found in older works of theology, notably in the *Summa Theologica* of Aquinas and in the Reformed (rather than the Lutheran) divines. Those who now have Heppe's *Reformed Dogmatics* on their shelves may even be able to reconstruct for themselves the process by which, in study and lecture room, this book took shape. And such as find Barth's "sources" a matter of interest will be duly intrigued by the ascendancy of Cocceius over Quenstedt. In my judgement he has re-told the story of God's government of the world so that it becomes a convincing and well-established story, and the secret of his

---

[1]Karl Barth, *Die Lehre von der Schöpfung*, III, 3 of *Die Kirchliche Dogmatik* (Zollikon-Zurich: Evangelischer Verlag, 1950). [The translation is WAW's own.]

success is precisely his fidelity to Christocentric theological thinking. It is not a new story, but an old one, drawn out in its full depth, so that the main theses, about whose status we have become steadily less sure, are reaffirmed, and notorious difficulties (such as that of reconciling any significant divine government with a real spontaneity of events) are properly faced. A busy reader will be moved by this volume more than by its predecessors to join in the fashionable chorus of protest against Barth's literary technique. If he had time to write books elegantly and economically instead of printing material hot from the lecture-room, how grateful we should be! But though one may thus occasionally cry for the moon, one may be profoundly grateful for what one gets instead. And indeed, the aid to easier comprehension which one longs for may be the false aid which is afforded when the treatment of a wide range of subjects is co-ordinated by a distorting "system." By the present technique, the truth of every thesis is brought to light in a manner appropriate to that thesis, and one is rebuked time after time for one's churlish complaint against repetitive and seemingly rhetorical thinking.

And now, as far as may be, granted the present reviewer's limits, we will let the content of the volume speak for itself. A translation of the fundamental theses may serve to introduce it:

48. *The Doctrine of Providence, its basis and structure*

The doctrine of Providence is concerned with the history of created being as such, more especially in that it pursues its course in every detailed respect and in its totality under the Fatherly Lordship of God the Creator, whose will takes effect and is recognizable in His Election of Grace, and therefore in the history of the covenant between Himself and man, and therefore in Jesus Christ.

49. *God the Father as Lord of His creation*

God exercises His fatherly Lordship over His creation in that He preserves the course of its particular existence, accompanies it, and governs it. He does this in that His mercy in Jesus Christ has appeared and is powerful in the created world, so that the glory of this His Son may be made manifest in it.

50. *God and the Negation*[2]

By the counsel of God, a threat to, and actual corruption of the world have also appeared, by reason of the Negation which is hostile to the Creator's will and therefore hostile also to the good nature of His crea-

---

[2]The term *Das Nichtige* is not readily translated into English. I imagine that "the Void" would convey its sense to those familiar with existentialist thinking. My wife, who neither knows German nor is a theologian, suddenly came to my rescue with "chaotic insubstantiality," which deserves, I think, to be placed on record. After all, she knows more about it than I do (cf. Gen. 3:1).

tures. In having passed judgement upon it through His mercy which appeared and is powerful in Jesus Christ, God decides where and how, to what extent and in what ministerial relationship to His Word and Work, it may still retain a place until its refutation and destruction (which are already accomplished) are generally revealed.

51. *The Kingdom of Heaven, God's Ambassadors, and their opponents*

God's action in Jesus Christ, and therefore His dominion over His creation, are therefore called "The Kingdom of Heaven," because its claim is primarily and peculiarly upon the upper world. From this upper world, God elects and sends His ambassadors, the angels, who come as forerunners (in the sense of objective and authentic witnesses) of the revelation and actualization of His will on earth, who accompany it as true and powerful servants of God and of men, and who stand as an excelling guard against the opposing forms and powers of Chaos.

Section 51 is the one best calculated to hit the headlines, were there any to hit, but section 49, though more pedestrian, is more important.

I

In section 48 Barth examines our belief in Providence; he takes critical account of how it has been handled in older systematic theology; and he proves that we are committed to a distinctively *Christian* belief which is not to be regarded as a modification of insights within the reach of all good men—insights derived from a "general revelation."

First he maintains, with an eye on Thomas Aquinas (*Summa Theologica* I, qq. 22–23 and, after a long interlude, 103ff.), that the theology of this matter is in no respect part of the doctrine of God. In so far as it must, of course, rest on the doctrine of God, it does so, not because *providentia Deo conveniat* as do *scientia, vita, voluntas, amor, justitia, misericordia*, but because *praedestinatio* (understood as God's Election of Grace) pertains to the Being of God, and that Election carries with it both Creation and Providence. Further, the Calvinist assimilation of Providence to the doctrine of Creation, and the interpretation of it in terms of *continuous* world-creation, is wrong (cf. Heppe, p. 251: "There is a single divine act by which God creates the world and determines its government"). The dangers thus entailed are that one either abandons the precise significance of *creatio ex nihilo*, or that one interprets Providence in a falsely deterministic fashion. The action referred to here as the **Fatherly Lordship of God the Creator** has its ground not only within the **Godhead** but also outside Himself in the already established being of creatures. It is, if you like, a *continuing* of creation, but it is an act with a different "time" from that which the act of creation has. Its content is to guarantee, rather than to found.

But that is not to say that there is anything arbitrary in this further action of the Creator. We are in a position to resist any suspicion of Epicureanism that the world is at the mercy of Chance; and we must leave no room for an Aristotelian suggestion that creation is moved by a God who is in any sense indifferent to its being. But a doctrine of Providence which is not Christocentric (governed, that is, by texts such as John 5:17; Col. 1:16f.; and Heb. 1:3), must inevitably seem speculative and insecurely grounded, and in no better case than similar doctrines which arise in pantheist and polytheist religions, as also in Judaism and Mohammedanism where the lack of a completed *Heilsgeschichte* means an attenuated belief in Providence. Therefore we must examine with care this act of faith, and no better indication of it can be found than in Questions 26–28 of the Heidelberg Catechism. Paul Gerhardt's hymns are a classical expression of the way in which the doctrine came to its own in the climate of thought created by the Reformation.

The question at issue is about the Lordship under which history develops. There is no answer to the question from world-history itself. It cannot yield the revelation which Natural Theology is concerned to find here. If, by faith, we are able to affirm that it does carry within itself the glory of God, this faith is not a response to the creatures, their life, their goodness, their beauty, etc. (and queer things begin to happen when you try to identify the glory of God with the bright side of creaturely reality). It is faith in *God*, the history of whose glory (i.e., His Lordship) is concealed in, with, and under the history of the creatures which are His veils (*larvae Dei*). This glory is not felt nor seen, nor affirmed in dialectical judgements, but strictly *believed*. But this act of believing is sustained by perceptions which Ritschl in particular banished from Protestant thinking under the opprobrious label of *Metaphysik*, leaving nothing stronger than value-judgements. These perceptions (the subject matter of Section 49) do not afford a secure conception of how God's Providence works and the doctrine of Providence is not an essay in the Philosophy of History. But in so far as our belief in God is *Christian* belief, in so far, that is, as we have found in "God with us" and "God for us" the eternal God who is therefore "God above us," we can pass beyond any abstract speculative theory to a securely based belief. Calvin pointed the way in isolated passages, but abandoned it in the *Institutes*, where he perpetuated the abstract handling of this matter which received its death-blow from the Lisbon earthquake.

We may begin to work out the doctrine by recognizing that though the covenant-history witnessed by the Bible is only a tiny strand in the whole of world-history, yet if we have seen it aright it is the strand towards which everything else converges. And again, this strand is all of a piece with general history, so the faith which is evoked by the *Heilsgeschichte* must be faith in the God who is Lord of all events. There seem to be two histories, the history of creatures as such, and the history of God's action with His covenant-partner, and there is a positive, essential, inner connexion between them. How the history of creatures is annexed to the covenant-history is known to God alone; but *that* it is so annexed is revealed in the covenant-history itself—in the very fact, if you like, that man as God's partner is man *in the cosmos*. And the faith to which we are brought by the Gospel is that in the very act of creaturely existence we are in the Kingdom of Christ and in no other. Therefore we cannot regard universal history as something hypothetically governed by God with a hidden left hand, and therefore beyond our power to correlate with the history in which His right hand is laid bare in Jesus Christ. The strand of *Heilsgeschichte* teaches us to regard all history as the field where the Providence so clear in that strand holds universal sway. Pursuing its own course, cosmic history furnishes time, space, and opportunity for the fruition of God's covenant, and it is preserved by the right hand of God to serve that covenant purpose. Not by passivity nor by an imposed conformation to the life of Israel and the Church, but precisely by *its own* activity, does it "work together" with the coming of the Kingdom of God. It is the seemingly larger strand of a double history where, instead of the open presence of Jesus Christ, there are only images or reflections (heaven and earth reflecting the relation of God and man; man and woman reflecting the relation of Christ and the Church; light and darkness reflecting the relation of grace and sin, or life and death), and because these are only reflections or echoes, they give no ground for absolute affirmations of any *analogia entis*. By creation it has been *prepared* for this "co-working," though it has no competence in this respect in itself. It was not, however, made for anything else, nor made in vain. It has no status as *creatura corredemptrix*. But in so far as it proceeds under God's Providence, it is given a constitutive significance for the covenant-history. It is too ambiguous in its working to support any *Weltanschauung* which abstracts from the Kingship of Christ, not even so innocuous a version as that it is constructed for the growth of personality! When, therefore, we affirm its regularities, and assess their meaning, what we can say is that God will give to His creation its function, its purpose or goal, and its character, tomorrow as He has done to-day. But the man of faith will not prescribe to God nor to himself *how* this will take place. To affirm *this* constancy is to affirm Providence.

II

The action of God the Father, conserving, accompanying, and governing His creatures as Lord, is the theme of Section 49, for, as might have been mentioned earlier, the Providence of God is an ever-present active Lordship, not a mere envisaging of possibilities. *Non minus ad manus quam ad oculos pertinet*, as Calvin put it.

The term *conservatio* suggests an action of making safe or keeping unharmed, and the prefix has been queried in the past because it might suggest that God's action is an auxiliary aid to the creature's effort to be its own *servator*. Barth, of course, is inclined to retain it with the very different suggestion that the grace by which the creature is maintained in being is something which expresses in another way the true grace of its redemption in Jesus Christ. We have to ask whether it is proper to attribute to God an irrevocable decision to maintain, moment after moment in their limited being, creatures such as the world contains; and when we see how they are capable *in their very limitation* of participating in the history which is made by Jesus Christ, we find this to be securely grounded in God's eternal love. They are conserved in the mutual order which the notion of "second causes" expresses. The mode of God's conserving action is incomprehensible to us because in His grace there is none of that "necessity" which we find to be a necessary means for comprehension. They are conserved in face of "evil"—the possibility which God has rejected in His decisive act of creation; for "evil" is a standing threat to the being of creatures. God has power over it, but they have not. Called into play by the rejecting decision of God, it stands like a minus sign outside a bracket, affecting every creaturely plus within the bracket. It is only because God's affirmation of His creatures remains an affirmation, that the creature continues in its creaturely goodness. *Creatio*, in other words, is preceded by a *servatio*, and guaranteed by a *conservatio*. This trustworthy action of God, from which our existence hangs as by a thread from moment to moment, is disclosed (both in regard to its necessity and in regard to its trustworthiness) by the Gospel events, and the "preserving" or "establishing" words used in the New Testament repay careful lexicographical study. They bring to light the ground upon which the New Testament Christians based their expectation of continuity in Christian life, which carries within itself a firmly secured continuity in human creaturely life, and warrants the freedom from care and worry which marks New Testament humanity. Within their appointed limits, therefore, we can take for granted the lasting reality of God's creatures.

This conserving action of God is the divine factor which faith tries to apprehend in all natural and human history. We go on to understand it as the *concursus divinus*, God's accompanying of His creatures through their history with Fatherly Lordship over them. The Deist story about God in His relation to creatures will not do. God does not leave them to work out the genius of their inherent nature. He accompanies them as Lord, so that His will is done on earth as it is in heaven; and yet He acts throughout with respect for their relative autonomy and spontaneity. Familiar questions come under discussion in this section—the relation of the First Cause to second causes (the proper analogical use of "cause" in this context being carefully elucidated), and all that falls under the topic *De Potentia Dei*. Barth insists that these questions can be tackled properly only if we work with fully Christian concepts:

> By "God" we understand: the one, who as the Father, the Son, and the Holy Ghost, is eternal love, has life in Himself—and *as such* is also *per se* Being, the Almighty in the Height above His creation, and *causa causarum*. By "the will of God" we understand: His fatherly good will, His decision of grace in Jesus Christ, the mercy in which He has set Himself from eternity to rescue His creation and to give it eternal life in community with Himself—His will which, *as such*, is also His kingly lordly will, disposing the existence and operation of His creation unconditionally and irresistibly. And by "the operation of God" we understand His action in the history of the covenant founded on His decision of grace, with its fulfilment in His giving of His Son, and its establishment in the work of the Holy Ghost to awaken faith and obedience—His operation which, *as such*, is also His mighty operation in the whole created realm, over and in, before, with, and after all creaturely operation, in virtue of which the whole of this pertains to *His* operation and is completely subordinated to Him (pp. 132f.).

The *concursus divinus* can be further elucidated by distinguishing three moments within it: *praecurrit, concurrit, succurrit*. The observable processes whereby creatures are determined in their being are held within a predetermination by God, which is an unconditioned and irresistible expression of His Fatherly Lordship. Readers will remember what Barth has already done (in II, 2; cf. Camfield's summary in *Reformation Old and New*, ch. IV) with the doctrine of predestination. Here he has to take careful account of the status of the semi-hypostasized laws and norms under which the course of nature proceeds, and to indicate a significant act of God preceding their operation in every given case; an act which does not abrogate, but which does relativize them. To make this act of God significant in the mind of modern men is one of the great difficulties in this field, and I do not think that Barth has wholly succeeded. His exposition needs to borrow from that of *succurrit* before it strikes home to my mind at any rate. In regard to *concurrit*, the difficulty is to see in creaturely being an act of God simultaneous with, but not to be confused with, the act of the creature. *Sic intelligendum est Deum operari in rebus, quod tamen ipsae res propriam habent operationem* (*Summa Theologica* I, 105, 5c). The act of God is intimate and particular to each creaturely event. Formally its relation to the creature's own act is not mere parallelism. In an unconditioned act of Fatherly Lordship, God established the act of the creature precisely as the act of the creature. If we try to say something about *how* this happens, and work with the analogy of inter-creaturely acts, we fall away into a "mechanistic" picture, or else we begin to talk of "emanations" or "infusions" of the divine being. This particular Christian doctrine of the divine *concursus*, which matters so much, yet is so hard to state, makes sense only with the belief that in every creaturely event there is an *encounter* of two radically different realities, an encounter such as we know about in our own meeting with God by means of His Word and Spirit. Can we understand the general working of God, with and over His creatures, from that focus? It is the obligation to do so which faith recognizes (though theology tries to find other grounds), which has produced the elements of this doctrine—that all creaturely being is good, and to the glory of God, and directly produced by His action out of the richness of His grace, and yet is produced as the proper act of the creature, achieved in genuine freedom and spontaneity. We say something significant about God's action in these terms, without needing to pretend that we have probed the secret of its mode (for the secret of our incorporation into the covenant of Grace by God's word and Spirit remains a secret until the *Parousia*), and without needing to detract from the sole glory of God the Lord by postulating some kind of synergism in this *concursus*. And what we say does not detract from the worth and the freedom of the creature in its own right. Barth offers three pages of theological argument (cf. 166–170), drawn from the Reformed tradition as opposed to all others, which may be of service to those who have an "anxiety-complex" about human freedom vis-à-vis the sovereignty of God; but he points out that because this is an instance of demon-possession and not a mere intellectual difficulty, his arguments can only avail to speed the departing demon on its way. Its actual casting out comes only by prayer and fasting. So much for *concurrit*. In regard to *succurrit* we are in the realm of the consequences or effects of creaturely action, over which the creature has manifestly little if any control. Do we lapse into resignation in respect of all this? Or is there ground for trust, confidence, and hope? It depends ultimately on what you can say about the action of God, and the freedom and Lordship with which He acts, subsequent to the creature's own act. The Christian story, taken seriously, requires you to say of God: *succurrit*.

It is the exposition of the third aspect, *gubernatio*, of God's Fatherly Lordship over His creation, which brings most clearly into view the truth acknowledged in the doctrine of Providence. What we see when we look at the world is not God's government of creaturely life, but rather a nexus of necessities and freedoms or contingencies which defies our imperialist will to comprehend. God rules creaturely life, in and through what we see, and He rules effectively as Lord, with His own self and His own glory as the goal for creatures. We cannot see this, but we may and must believe it because we believe the Biblical witness to the "Kingdom of God." What we say about the government of the cosmic scene is securely based only if we are able to relate it to the action of the King of Israel and to the

Kingdom of God taken in its full New Testament sense. The older Protestant theology shows a cleavage at this point between Lutheran tradition, which is so anxious to rule out the Stoical thesis of government by Fate that it lies open to the charge of Occasionalism, and Calvinist tradition, which is more anxious about the Epicurean thesis of Chance and therefore lays itself open to the charge of rigid determinism. Neither charge can be fully sustained. But one must take due account both of the triumphs of *common-sense* (referred to in the German text by the English phrase) in which the bourgeois finds the most congenial manifestations of the Kingdom, and of the eccentricities of waywardness or miracle which make the gypsy as well as the bourgeois a servant of the Kingdom.

The action which faith attributes to God is one of *ruling* something other than Himself, which takes place by an *ordering* of all things through His presence with them both as planner and plan. It is a direct action of God in each separate event, where He gives to the creature a prescribed opportunity of freedom, decrees the effect of its act, and gives it its own validity and worth. But this means in practice its *co-ordination* with its environment, so that out of individual specialities a significant *unity* is secured. It is the glory, not the shame, of creatures to be utterly dependent upon God the King, though this glory is misconstrued where the notion of absolute dependence is taken abstractly as the key to creaturely existence, and grossly misrepresented where the creature is regarded as utterly dependent on the Whole within which it is ordered.

In fact we cannot pretend to maintain a thesis like this as though it were a self-authenticating idea, or a formal notion to be established prior to any content it may receive from faith in God as the King of Israel. The history of Israel is the place where the government of God is concretely revealed, and it is a history which happens, not for the sake of Israel in itself, but as the "inner ground" of all world-history. It is a history (from Abraham to Christ) which serves as a stock on to which all other nations are grafted, and once we read its true meaning we find that all world-history begins to look like a river, not like "the endless wave-beats of an unbounded, colourless, formless sea, each part of it like the rest, flowing out of itself, and being sucked back into itself." We begin to picture it on the analogy of a life-history of plant, or animal, or man, or as a work of art; not as a meaningless sphere whose points are interchangeable. The covenant-history of Israel, seen from its centre where the king appears in His beauty, is the place where the true "economy" or "disposition" of creatures under the rule of God appears openly, and though the same economy is hidden outside this place, we are constrained to believe that it is real. *This* economy is the case wherever creatures live. The King of Israel, Jesus Christ, is Lord over all. We know *that* this is so. We do not know *how* it is so, and therefore we must acknowledge that His rule continues beyond the focal events, still in the form of a hidden *Heilsges-*

chichte which comes into the open only in the once-for-all history of Israel which culminated in the Ascension of the King, and the appointment of the Apostles (from the seed of Israel).

But what about the Church, and the Bible? What about the continued history of *the Jews*, which is of the same significance? These are constant elements in the panorama of world-history which serve as reminders of how the whole world is under the Providential government of God the King of Israel. To draw the proper outlines of God's universal Providential government, we must attend to these signs, and read them aright. For we learn, precisely from the history of Israel, that the wise government of God is no crude affair of open power yielding unmistakable evidence of its reality in the persons of subservient puppets. The "constants" in world-history, each a sign in its own right and with its own purpose, are signs which *can be* but *need not be* read in their true significance. And this very ambiguity is part of what we may read in them. The history of the Bible, its formation, its translation, its exposition, and its effect on history; the history of the Church, with its peculiar claim that our time is now *Endzeit* where everything is ordered to the proclamation and believing of the Gospel with its peculiar power of resistance drawn from its own experience of Yahweh's faithfulness conquering human rebellion and its strange capacity for renewal (not *perpetuo mansura* save as *perpetuo reformanda*); the history of the Jews since A.D. 70 which testifies to the action of Israel's King by continuing in so disturbing a fashion to display the negative side of His saving act, the history of those who are "not a people" now that they are no longer Yahweh's people, who are not marked off by any clear racial distinction, nor by language, culture, religion, or common history, and who nevertheless are held in being in this form of "not a people" by Yahweh who still holds to His word that "he that toucheth you toucheth the apple of mine eye": these are signs which disclose the true character of God's Providential government. The exposition of them in these pages should have far-reaching effects on other parts of theology.

Barth has added to these three well-known "constants" a fourth which is of much greater significance to the modern mind: the evidence in the structure of human life which is "given" and "taken away" either by Chance or by Fate or by God the Father who is the King of Israel. He notes how every such life is profoundly affected (or "disposed") by the time of its birth and of its death, and how it thus becomes a *unique* participation in common experience. What happens between the two limits is a *history*, which can be brought under judgement *as a whole*; and in its finite particularity, the whole of world-history is somehow focused. These facts can be read without serving in the least to remind us of the Fatherly Lordship under which we exist, but when the King of Israel confronts us in a life which moves "from His poor manger to His bitter cross," our own condition of life shines with a new light.

Another "constant," of quite a different order, namely the angels, is referred to in this context, and the matter deferred for fuller discussion in Section 51. For Barth knows well enough that this "sign" has been overlooked deliberately in many discussions of Providence within serious Christian theology. "But one wonders whether such discussions are not also remarkable in paying little or no attention to the other constants as well!"

I am aware that I have communicated little or nothing of the real content of this all-important Section 49. But perhaps a better purpose will be served by indicating its structure rather than attempting to characterize its doctrine by neat labels drawn from the history of thought. Readers will note the absence of one familiar bit of apparatus, the distinction between general and special providence. Unless these terms can be used to point more clearly than they have done to the relation of the history of Israel and general history, Barth considers they are better dropped.

The doctrine is further clarified in a long treatment of the Christian life under the universal Lordship of God the Father, a life expressed in faith, obedience, and prayer. These matters have been sufficiently expounded by English writers, influenced by Barth, for me to pass over this section without comment.

III

And so we come to Section 50 on "the Negation," the third element which confuses the relation of God and His creatures, the "foreign body" with its queer negative reality, powerful within yet alien to the sphere of God's Fatherly government. The problem is to affirm God's Lordship over it without impairing His holiness and omnipotence. There is danger in denying its status as a "third element"; the danger to which Calvinism has not been immune, of finding causality of evil in God, and the danger which makes Pelagianism what it is, wherever it appears, of finding this causality in creatures.

There is a profound danger also of failing to recognize the real thing, and of arguing instead in terms of the "shadow side of creation," its precarious status, its tragedy and darkness, which are not in opposition or contradiction to God, though until they are "turned to His praise" they are eloquent of the deeper hostility to His will by which creation is imperilled. To treat this shadow-side as the Negation is to defend God's cause at the wrong point and thus to leave the real Negation in power so far as we are concerned. (*The Screwtape Letters* went a long way towards making this point clear in Britain.) If you want to know what to do with the darkness which God created by dividing from it the light, you can learn from Mozart who alone in the eighteenth century seemed capable of dealing with the Lisbon earthquake. For he *heard*, though of course he did not see, the whole creation with its joy and tragedy, and heard it bathed in the *lux perpetua* of divine glory. I learn that his grave, like that of Calvin and that of Moses, is unknown; but what does a grave matter in the case of such great witnesses to God!

But how can we talk about the real thing which God's action is directed against? Barth refers us to the work of Julius Müller, *Die christliche Lehre von der Sünde*, written 1838–44 to expose the limits beyond which the Christian Monism of Schleiermacher and Hegel breaks down. And he offers his own extended examination of Leibnitz, Schleiermacher, Sartre, and Heidegger, as the most important guides for those who want to recognize the Negation for what it is.

They are all fallible guides, because the Negation is known to God alone, and He knows it in the action where the Word was made *flesh*, that is to say, a creature open to attack by the enemy, estranged from Himself and from God by coming into the context where the Negation makes human sin its point of attack against both God and His creatures. He knows it by this victorious action against it. My recognition of it comes by being conformed to this Word of God made flesh. I recognize that I am responsible for the queer reality of the Negation, by being its bearer and its agent; but no self-analysis can disclose in my experience of sin the real Evil which brings real Death in virtue of a real Devil and a real Hell. God alone knows where and what to attack, and I cannot do battle with it save under His election of Grace. His command, in Jesus Christ, makes plain to me that disobedience is not mere imperfection judged by a Law, but rather guilt vis-à-vis the grace and kindness of God; and this is knowledge of the Negation, acting through sin, primarily against God. Knowledge of it as active in evil and death is also granted when I see how its powerlessness has been exposed by an event of physical suffering and historical degradation. I recognize that this happened because man is fallen prey to a real Death (not merely subject to an act of dying), and to a real "physical" corruption with its own dynamism. In this "physical" mode of attack, which is just as important as the "moral" mode suggested by sin, the Negation acts primarily against the creature of God, and thus against God in a less direct way.

What account of the reality of the Negation may be offered from this foundation? I will summarize Barth's points as best I can.

(a) We cannot say that it "is," as we use that term of God or Creatures; but because we recognize that God is confronted by it and in conflict with it, we cannot treat it as "nothing."

(b) Nor can we identify it with that which God and creatures "are not," for that *privatio* belongs as such to their perfection, establishing in creatures the "shadow-side" which does ultimately redound to the praise of God.

(c) It has no "nature" discernible *by creatures* and no existence which they can discover. They know it only by knowing God in His action against it.

(d) Its ontological context is the *electing action* wherein God is who He is. It is "the impossible possibility" which is given real power to threaten this action precisely by His Lordly and Sovereign rejection of it. But this is not to be understood as though its reality could be caught up by synthesis into what He wills for the ultimate purpose He pursues. Barth's doctrine is not an extreme form of dialectical system. At this point, *all* synthesis is impossible. But we must not follow the obvious alternative of treating it therefore as mere illusion or appearance.

(e) Privation of *grace*, rather than privation of being, indicates its character, its power to threaten, and its status as the object of God's *opus alienum*.

(f) God attacks it, and gives His creatures their part in the attack, by carrying through His *opus proprium*, the gracious covenant-action with man. Man's "good" is thus to cleave to the covenant-action of God; and if, Faust-like, he tries to master the Negation himself, claiming to "know good and evil," he is himself mastered by it.

(g) God's zeal, wrath, and judgement, give no proper substance or content to this queer reality, but they do give it the perverse "truth" of lies, the "sense" of nonsense, the grotesque "possibility" of the impossible. But it has no stability, and, so far from being a permanently "necessary" element in God's design (which we are always tempted to say by some kind of synthesis), it is in fact finished, a truth still to be revealed, but which our joy and freedom can already proclaim.

Those who see it clearly see it fearlessly, and they alone see its true fearfulness. They see only the echo or shadow of a ruined reality, but they recognize it to be effective even as such. And if you use the concept of "God's permissive will" to theologize about it, the content of this permissive will is simply that we do not yet see the Kingdom of God in open glory, and until we do, this echo of a ruined reality is made to serve His purpose by an act of royal Providence which no synthetic thinking can comprehend.

(1951)

GOD'S HEAVENLY KINGDOM
AND HIS
SERVANTS THE ANGELS

MODERN EXPONENTS OF THE DOCTRINE OF CREATION SKATE AS LIGHTLY AS possible over the thesis that God is Maker of *heaven* as well as of earth. And St. Matthew's habit of referring to the Kingdom of Heaven does not commend itself as important to most scholars in their elucidation of the Kingdom of God. For Barth, whose doctrine of Providence was outlined in the last issue of this *Journal*, "God's Kingdom which comes to us on earth is the Kingdom of Heaven; and when God's will is done on earth as it is in heaven, that is not only a *divine* event, i.e., one established, governed, and consummated by God, but also a *heavenly* event, i.e., one worked out in the presence, power, co-operation, and co-revelation of heaven on earth" (p. 558).[1] Though this is a secondary aspect of the event, a theology which ignores it is gravely impoverished. And a proper recognition of this aspect entails a further recognition that man's encounter with God in His saving act is also an encounter with the angels of God, the creatures who inhabit heaven. Schleiermacher wrote a notable appendix *Of the Angels* (§§ 42–43 in the second edition of *The Christian Faith*) which dismissed the topic from Protestant theology for 150 years, but now it has come back in a treatise which will surely rank with the other two great monuments of angelology, the *Celestial Hierarchy* of Pseudo-Dionysius, and the *Summa Theologica* of Aquinas (I. 50–64, 106–114), both of which are sympathetically evaluated.

Is this a field of knowledge of which Christian theology must take serious account, and if so, with what methods and safeguards? It is clear that the notions of heaven and of angels form part of the framework within which the Christian Gospel is proclaimed and believed, and that the Biblical writers have something to say about the heavenly angelic function which has for them a necessary connexion with their primary theme.

---

[1]Karl Barth, *Die Lehre von der Schöpfung*, III, 3 of *Die Kirchliche Dogmatik* (Zollikon-Zurich: Evangelischer Verlag, 1950), § 51. [The translation is WAW's own.]

It is equally clear that this has for a long time been regarded as a case for *Entmythologisierung* by those parts of the Church which are not committed to the theology either of John of Damascus or of Thomas Aquinas. Once Dionysius could be branded Pseudo, his theme was relegated to the hands of poets and children. Biblical angelology became a minor theme of study for those concerned to elucidate the mental climate of some Biblical writers. And occasionally a philosophical theologian has proposed an explanation of the patristic or medieval interest in angels to show that some "equivalent concept" would still be of use to us to-day. For my own part, I have been uneasy about treating this theme as dispensable or superficial to the essential Christian Gospel, but at the same time utterly unconvinced by the various kinds of treatment it has received. I now think that Barth is right when he says that a theology which has no account of angels, or a non-Christian account, is an impoverished theology; for the problem of angelology is "the problem of the *mystery* of the presence, the speech and action of God, in our neighbourhood, i.e., in the lower cosmos—the problem of heaven and earth, which is the problem of the significant nearness *and* distance, distance *and* nearness, without which God would not meet the earthly creature as majestic and trustworthy, holy and gracious, and therefore not as God" (p. 605). The story of God's action, incorporating us into His Kingdom by the Holy Spirit, is not fully told until the secondary emphasis is brought out that this Kingdom is the Kingdom of Heaven; and that creatures belonging intrinsically to the Kingdom of Heaven exist in the service of that Kingdom, and their service is precisely to accompany the extension of that Kingdom to earth and effect its purposes, not by any power of their own (it is the mark of demons to claim such power), but because the effective glory of God is reflected in them as the glory of a king is reflected in the ideal ambassador. Such a doctrine of angels, which is significantly different from anything formulated before and wholly Biblical, fills a gap in our account of God's dealings with men which, in default of it, may be filled by exaggerated accounts of Scripture or of Bishops to the undoing of the Church's integrity.

Barth realizes that this is a field where extreme care is needed if our assent to the Biblical testimony is to develop into understanding, and he works out the "limits of angelology" in a long section which includes a review of all that has happened in the past. Biblical history, he points out, is always on the verge of "saga," and the theme of angels is always introduced on the very edge where what is proclaimed passes over into the mysterious or non-verifiable region of events. Therefore we have only "poetic indications," savouring of divination or fantasy. But in the Bible they come under the control of that real event, God's grace in Jesus Christ, which also governs the empirical history. This makes them orderly, meaningful, and disciplined, and therefore one can and must think through them, albeit incidentally and with a light touch. But this theological task was distorted almost from the outset, by the desire to answer a question which from the Bible alone is unanswerable. What are angels by "nature"? *Ex eo quod est, spiritus est. Ex eo quod agit, angelus est.* By this remark Augustine confirmed the tendency to build up a background for the Biblical angels, which in time became so interesting as to obscure the sole Biblical interest which is their office. To call them "spirits," as in Heb. 1:14, was originally to confess ignorance about their nature, but it came to suggest that they should be taken generically with the souls of men, and a story was built up on this assumption about the independent mode of existence which may properly be attributed to "intelligent spirits." Rev. 4–5 added force to the adjectives in Heb. 1:14, and the Biblical evidence was sometimes used to suggest that the essential function of angels is to participate in the heavenly cultus which established the whole rhythm of creation. But this must not be pressed too hard against the Fathers, for Dionysius, whose great merit was to reduce patristic angelology to some order, felt himself under no obligation to turn an *angelus* into a being whose characteristic function is to sing hymns. To his neo-Platonic mind the angels appear as hypostasized moments in the heavenly motion, the cascade of light which brings knowledge and redemption to men. But at least his account of them was fundamentally "functional," dynamic, and soteriological, whereas in Thomas the counter-tendency comes to full expression, and they become elements in a stable heavenly system, whose "mission" brings them out of their proper sphere. Barth's question is whether this ontology of angels, which has taken the Church so very far away from the Biblical witness, is necessary to systematic thought. He finds that Protestant theologians who have recognized its alien character have still complained that the Biblical symbols are so obscure that even though they must still control the final story they require to be interpreted in the light of non-Biblical principles. Against all this he insists that there is positive illumination for us in the Biblical silence about the "nature" of angels, and that if we concentrate on the Biblical presentation, and keep our thinking true to its suggestion that they are relative to the God-man relationship and properly knowable *in their office*, we can do full justice to the claim that they are so bound up with the Word of God that any response of faith which ignores them is inadequate. The fundamental weakness of "the Intellectualism of St. Thomas" comes to light very clearly (p. 464f.) in the theology which earned for him the title of the Angelic Doctor. That theology is the grandest expression of the attempt to produce an ontology of heaven and of angels. Such theology is ill-conceived, but nevertheless Thomas and Dionysius are masters who press upon us the truth of a heavenly part in the created cosmos, whose participation in the history of God's covenant with mankind is an indispensable theme of theology.

Can one, however, work out the theology of the matter if ontological

questions cannot be raised in this field? Barth reminds us that the question
of heaven is raised by the Biblical witness to God's action, for the sake of
which action He has created the cosmos. Though He is apart from His
creation and "the heaven of heavens cannot contain Him" (nor yet His
Son—Eph. 4:10), He has His throne within the cosmos, in the region of
heaven which is the *terminus a quo* for His action here. The action itself
is one to which we have become subject. Its central moment is the *coming
to earth* of the Word of God in the fashion of *a heavenly man*. We acknowledge it as the coming of the Kingdom of God from heaven to earth, and
we cannot evade the intellectual consequences of conceiving the focus of
all God's action to be the history of man on this planet. The exegesis of
the Biblical witness to this history in which God and man participate must
clarify first of all the meaning of "heaven," and no *raison d'être* is ever
suggested for heaven or for its inherent created life apart from this action
of God the covenanting King. His will is done in heaven *in order that* it
may be done on earth. In the witness to His action, we note a concomitant
witness to the action of a heavenly host. The army of Israel, as well as the
stars in their courses, are often taken to be tokens on earth of properly
heavenly creatures, to whose action their own is related. It becomes clear
that within the fundamental theme of God's action, the heavenly host
must have within itself ordered variety, multiplicity, and diversity of office,
for only so can we acknowledge the detailed particularity with which the
Kingdom of Heaven bears down upon earth.

At this point one needs to examine at length the Biblical material in
order to deal with the suggestions of a hierarchy of angels, and of named
angels with identifiable functions. Barth finds no basis whatever for the
suggestion of hierarchical ordering. He interprets Paul's terminology
against the background of Daniel where the heavenly creatures are called
sarim to express their function of imposing upon earth the peace of God;
and this activity of the heavenly *sarim* is brokenly reflected, to Paul's mind,
in the action of various political ordinances on the human scene. In a long
and powerful exposition of Rev. 4–5, Barth makes the point that in every
angel God is "represented" in His relation to a particular realm of earthly
reality. And it is significant that the immediate guardians of the throne
are precisely the "four beasts" which on any showing are the angels most
intimately associated with God's movement towards earth, and it is they
who initiate the praise of heaven. This in turn helps to clarify the truth
in the notion of a "heavenly cultus." To the angels must be attributed
perfect knowledge of the whole "mystery of God." Their entire existence
is an "exemplary service" to that mystery, not only in their office of accompanying its fulfilment, but also in the antecedent praise which they
give because what God has determined in heaven must happen on earth.
Thus the angels are the creatures made to inhabit heaven, the region of
God's throne in the cosmos, from which His Kingdom is being extended

to earth. They exist in the service of this extended Kingdom, which is the service of God and His earthly creatures. That is the definition which we should work with, and it is an exclusive definition for the purposes of Christian theology.

What then can be said of angels on the basis of this definition? I have space only for a bare list of observations. God's action is mediated to His creatures by His creatures. But, unlike the humblest earthly thing, an angel cannot belong to itself as well as to God. It has no "substance" of the kind sought by ontology, and it is lost to human view in God. (This explains why "to be as the angels in heaven" solves the problems of marriage without annulling marriage.) They are plenipotentiaries because their testimony to God's action is unadulterated testimony. Ambassadors, remember, are not members of the government they represent, but their presence demands the respect appropriate to the government. It is the ministry of angels which alone makes manifest the "Otherness" from which God comes to us. Omit the angels, and you create havoc by ascribing their office either to the Holy Spirit or to Bishops. Their service is to give to God's relation with men its cosmic contours and concreteness.

We must remember, however, that though their authority is something which neither prophet nor apostle can have (though it is precisely the authority claimed by the Pope), theirs is not the most privileged role in creation. As Barth points out, in using the illustration of an ambassador, a businessman has greater freedom than an ambassador ever enjoys. And here it is instructive to examine the places where they are introduced into the Gospel story. They come only at the beginning and the end, to mark off the history within which lies all history, but which is itself wrought out by the man Jesus. Before and after that history, it is for human witnesses to take up the tale.

I do not claim to have understood all that Barth has written in this chapter. Nor do I think that the issues he is pressing will come home to us simply by our having available a translation of his work. We must have a book from a British theologian on the subject. But I am persuaded that the God of whom the Bible speaks must be represented to us, when He confronts us, by creatures whose office is clearly indicated in Scripture along the lines which Barth has worked out so magnificently. It is clear to me, though not, perhaps, to the reader of this bald sketch, that here is a clarification in the field of theology which is much nearer to the heart of the Church's *malaise* than one would ever imagine. What has been misrepresented in the "Catholic" tradition, and *entmythologisiert* in the "Protestant" tradition is something vital to our apprehension of the Gospel.

I follow Barth's example in respect of demons. He dismisses them in 15 pages, for "a short sharp glance at the waste places is all they should have." They are not bad angels, but opponents of the angels. You don't believe in them for they are the Lie basic to all lies; *der in alle Mythen spukende Mythus*. They represent the dynamism of Chaos, whose reality consists in God's conflict with it. Not created, they are there by the divine No! But they triumph over the angelic ministrations wherever men are persuaded to deny their reality. To deviate from this paradoxical line, and to work out in the name of Biblical realism a demonology alongside angelology, eschatology, soteriology, and Christology, is to commit the fundamental mistake which led to the witch-hunts whose major effect was to provoke the Enlightenment. I think that awkward questions remain which cannot be silenced by this line of argument, but fundamentally I believe it is right.

(1951)

THE COMMAND OF GOD
THE CREATOR:
An Account of Karl Barth's
Volume on Ethics

THIS TWELFTH CHAPTER OF THE *Dogmatik* IS AN EXPOSITION OF THE
ethical teaching which follows upon an understanding of the doctrine of
creation.[1] Further chapters on ethics will come at the end of the volumes
on reconciliation and redemption and Barth notes that the whole complex
of state, community, and law must wait for more thorough treatment until
the next volume is completed. Here we have a generous and moving
exposition of man's freedom in relation to God; his freedom in the community of male and female, parent and child, near and distant neighbours; his freedom for life with due evaluation of reverence for life, its
protection and its industriousness; and his freedom within appointed limits where opportunities do not recur, where each person has his "station"
and must live with the honour appropriate to his limitations. The exposition follows the formal lines worked out in the volume on man. It is
studded with careful reviews of the more important recent books dealing
with the themes under discussion. In this field Barth shows the greatest
respect for Schleiermacher who of course worked out his theology with
a profound sense of the richness and complexity of human life, though
here, as well as in his grasp on the Gospel, Barth's understanding seems
to be both richer and more sensitive. The distinctive feature of the work
is its firm adherence to the conviction that ethics, as the doctrine of God's
command, exhibits the law as a form of the Gospel, grounded everywhere
in the knowledge of Jesus Christ and of God's gracious election of man
to covenant fellowship with Himself in Christ. Grace and freedom are
therefore the fundamental categories, even in respect of those moments
in the divine command which are appropriately examined in the light of

---

[1]Karl Barth, *Die Lehre von der Schöpfung*, III, 4 of *Dir Kirchliche Dogmatik* (Zollikon-
Zurich: Evangelischer Verlag, 1951). [The translation is WAW's own.]

the Creator's "ordinances." Brunner's *Divine Imperative* receives sustained criticism throughout the volume on the ground that its approach is ultimately "legalist" and therefore fails to exhibit the true character and full range of God's command.

Barth's general discussion of God's command and the problem of ethics may be found in *Dogmatik* II, 2, a summary of which was made by the late Dr. Camfield in *Reformation Old and New*, ch. V. The question raised by general ethics concerns the ground and possibility of the fact that "in the multiplicity of human actions and modes of action, there arise certain constancies, laws, rules, customs and continuities." Their rightfulness, suitability and worth are brought under question. Theological ethics tries to grasp the fact that human conduct is good insofar as it is *hallowed* by God's word, which is the content, measure and origin of such hallowing. It shows how God's command comes to men as a permission, a sovereign, concrete, and gracious decision, and as God's judgement by which they are at once condemned and forgiven. It indicates whence and how *rightness* is bestowed on actions and courses of action wherein men find themselves engaged in the rough and tumble of life. In this volume Barth passes from general ethics to special ethics and asks what it means, in the context of Creator and creature, that man is under God's command, that here he is hallowed by that command and has freedom *vis-à-vis* the will of God and thereby freedom for eternal life. In substance, his answer is to indicate with precision the regions of life which call for special attention in this context and to work out the criteria of obedience to God's command.

It will be impossible to give a proper summary of this tremendous account of human conduct, or even to mention half the points where, if Barth is right, the Church needs to re-think its ethical pronouncements. I must be content to translate the five main theses, to discuss the method by which Barth conducts this inquiry, and to indicate the broad outlines of his exposition, providing first by way of sample the content of one small section.

52. *Ethics as a task within the doctrine of creation*

The task of special ethics, within the doctrine of creation, is to inform men both of the fact, and of the extent to which, the one command of the one God who is gracious to man in Jesus Christ is also the command of man's Creator, and is therefore the present hallowing of man's creaturely action and of his refraining from action.

53. *Freedom before God*

God the Creator wills that man, as His creature, should account for himself in His presence. His command says in particular that he shall[2]

---

[2]The verb is *dürfen*, not *sollen*. It indicates a summons to man to take advantage of a freedom to which he is given access by the grace of God.

keep His day holy, as a day of celebration, freedom and joy; that with heart and mouth he shall acknowledge (*bekennen*) Him; and that he shall come to Him as a suppliant.

54. *Freedom in association*

In that the Creator calls man to Himself, He also turns him towards his fellow-man. God's command says in particular that in the encounter of man and woman, in the relation between parents and children, and on the path from those who are near to those who are distant, man shall affirm the other person in affirming himself and affirm himself in affirming the other person, that he shall hold him in respect and gladden him.

55. *Freedom to live*

In that God the Creator calls man to Himself and turns him towards his fellow-man, He tells him to honour his own life and that of each other man and to defend it against all caprice in order to make it effective in His service and in preparation for His service.

56. *Freedom within circumscribed limits*

God the Creator wills for man and lays claim to man (who belongs to Him, is bound up with his fellow-man, and is summoned to affirm his own life and the life of others) within the special purpose which is indicated by the time-limits, the vocation and the dignity which, as his Creator and Lord, He has marked out for him.

Only 50 pages out of 800 are devoted to considerations of method. The rest of the book is positive exposition. In view of the prevailing confusion about method in theological ethics, however, and in view of the widespread opinion that Barth (despite what was said in II, 2) can only deal with ethics in terms of a point-to-point inspiration theory, it may be helpful to consider this first section with some care.

The task of "special ethics" is often discharged by casuistry, the exposition of an amalgam of Biblical texts, "natural law," and western tradition with reference to "cases of conscience." This is deemed to bring to light God's "law" as a formal command which is applied to cases in an appropriate way by interpretation. It rests upon a misreading of man's existence under the command of God. In place of the concrete divine command which is revealed in the ethical experience, it sets up the opinion of the moralist; it violates human freedom by subjecting man to law rather than to grace; and it leaves men bereft of the full and certain knowledge of the concrete divine command which comes from the living God and requires no interpretation. How, then, should we raise the question about God's command in respect of concrete acts of human will, decision, conduct, and forbearance?

All ethical occasions are moments in the encounter of God with men, where His command, which comes "vertically from above," is addressed to men living also within "horizontal" relationships. There is unity and constancy in the divine command, for all ethical occasions are moments in the *Heilsgeschichte*, and there is a corresponding stability and continuity in the horizontal realm. The problem is to work out an account of this "horizontal" which will afford an indication of the character of ethical experiences and serve as instructive preparation for them, which is what Brunner has done with his "ordinances" and Bonhoeffer with his "mandates." These impositions of authority are relationships to be fulfilled wherever God commands. The analysis of them offered by Brunner and by Bonhoeffer (in his posthumous *Ethik*) is precarious and, in Brunner's case, inadequate to the Gospel of God's grace and man's freedom. He claims to find, by scrutiny of "reality," certain ordinances of creation. But this "reality," our "field of action" which has to be expounded in special ethics, is known only as we participate by faith in the meeting of God with man in the person of Jesus Christ. It is God the Holy Trinity, encountering man the creature made to be His covenant-partner, man the sinner to whom in grace God remains true, man the child of God who already enjoys the certainty of expected sonship in an eternal future, who enter together into every ethical experience. The field of action disclosed in each such experience, in its integrity, complexity and differentiation, is not known *a priori*, nor is it known by postulating a self-contained economy of the first article of the Creed and finding laws peculiar to a Creator according to which God's command is given, which is how the "ordinances of creation" are usually conceived.

Special ethics is therefore a commentary on the meeting of God with man in the concreteness of *Heilsgeschichte* and its orderly differentiations will post-scribe what is pre-scribed in the Word of God. And here we can say that the command of the God who is gracious to us in Jesus Christ is also the command of man's *Creator* and is the hallowing of *creaturely* action and forbearance. Here Barth's method rests on the conviction that the election of Jesus Christ and of man in Him is the inner ground of creation. Creation's meaning is to be found in the grace which forgives sin and awakens man to life from death. Jesus Christ is the *Realgrund*, not merely the *Erkenntnisgrund* of creation. Thus the Creator's command is given, not in and through an obscure "world-reality," but in a reality of grace, which establishes a province where God is man's friend and benefactor in quite precise ways, and man may be God's friend and the recipient of His benefit. Instead of "orders" or "ordinances" it is better to speak of "provinces" (*Bereich*) in the being and action of God and in the being and conduct of man where God knows man with a Creator's knowledge, and where man's liberation and hallowing by God's command can be grasped only by commentary clearly based on the doctrine of creation.

In this volume, therefore, Barth is concerned to open up for us the horizontal field of action where men live under the command of God; to prepare us to hear that command insofar as it conveys to us the will of our Creator; to help us to understand it as a command which aims always at human freedom and exaltation; and to suggest the right questions which we must be prepared to face in particular moments of ethical experience. He follows the lines laid down in II, 2, where he worked out the theology of man as the creature of God, and asks first about the freedom proposed by the will of the commanding God in the relationship of man to God Himself; then about the freedom which God desires for man in his relationship to his fellow-men; then about the freedom which man is to achieve in the act of living as soul of his body; finally about the freedom which man is to achieve precisely as a limited and circumscribed entity. These are the features of man, the responsible creature of God. The command of God is always the command to fulfil this responsibility and thus to live before God as one free for Him.

Barth's method is thus the same in regard to the exposition of ethics as he adopts for all other areas of dogmatic theology. It rests on the same epistemology and the same submission to the Word of God in its Scriptural attestation. It is best exhibited in practice, but in this volume, with its wealth of concrete particularity, a brief exhibition is peculiarly difficult and unsatisfying and we must be content to catalogue a few of the results.

II

The section of freedom before God lends itself to rather fuller exposition than do the others. It is interesting that Barth repudiates the notion that there are no acts of love to God which are not in the form of love for one's neighbour, and that he sets such store by a non-profane area of conduct. In its detail, his inquiry goes concretely to the heart of our inadequacies with tremendous stimulus. When it is translated I foresee that its theological power will be hailed in this country as robust generous Christian common sense, but it will bear rich fruit in transformed sermons and conduct. But the outline I propose to offer seems dreadfully bald and abstract. Three matters come under consideration: observance of the Lord's Day, confession of faith, and prayer.

The Lord's Day is marked by celebration, freedom, and joy. It is a time specially claimed by God because He claims the whole of our time, and He requires in response to this claim not merely an attitude to all our time, but deliberate concrete deeds arising from a resolution of mind and conduct. Unless we obey His command in its speciality, our whole obedience falls short of that *actualized* hallowing which Sabbath observance promised in Exodus 31:12–17 or Ezekiel 20:12 and 20. Its two notes, freedom from work and freedom for God, make it a radical demonstration that human life is ultimately a "resting in God." But either note, taken by itself, produces the imposition of new burdens which turn each Sunday into a *wasted* day of rest. The mandatory permission of God is that on His day man shall express joyful faith in Him and turn his back on all self-propagated willing or achieving. The theology of its celebration does not depend on religious or humanitarian grounds which appear in contexts other than this creaturely "resting in God," and Barth suggests its outline by raising four groups of questions, all of which bring the Sabbatarianisms of the one-time ruling classes under searching criticism. To approach Sunday with a programme is a dubious way of treating it as a day when our life is peculiarly acknowledged to be in God's hands. Should it not be open for the programme He suggests when we meet Him in His house? To celebrate it as a joyous feast presupposes the effective driving away of our cares, which only God can do. Does the Church, in its ordering of worship expect this from God? Does its worship leave us free to spend a good Sunday once we have left its portals? It is the Lord's Day of rest for His *people*, a social occasion which means more than spending it *en famille* or with old friends. Is the Church able to initiate a wider sociality, beginning from its own congregational life? Finally, it is the first day of a new week of work and domestic life. Do we learn more about its celebration next time when each Monday morning tests whether or not we have spent it well?

Confession of faith must also be considered under the aspect of a particular action with its appointed time, as witness the moments when men in the OT "worshipped God." It is active participation by a human spokesman in the *Heilsgeschichte*, whereby the name of the Lord is invoked and hallowed with precise historical consequences. Barth points out first that it is free invocation of God, a dancing before the ark of the covenant done purely for His honour, and it is spoilt by any calculation of effect. Second, however, the given opportunity for it is one for entering a protest against unbelief, doubt, or heresy. To regard its normal context as a festal or liturgical one is to insulate the act against the suffering and conflict which it properly entails. But God, when He requires this action, is seeking pacification for His world, not the guilt-laden martyrdom of His witnesses, and therefore they should not resort to confession as a kind of polite reaction to unbelief. Nor should they forget that it is meant to provide a light in darkness, a purpose seldom achieved by pious musing or lyrical gushing. Third, though privately held convictions may give to an act of confession the incisive relevance which is proper to it, the act should never be that of a soloist nor even of a chamber-music player. It is the community's witness to its Lord (required of Peter and thrice withheld by him) which has to be echoed; the witness to which the congregation is brought where the whole Bible is newly opened to them. And it should be echoed in the form of concrete truth from Scripture, not in the vague form of "Biblical truths." Fourth, the freedom within which the act is permitted includes freedom in the choice of language, and freedom from anxiety about its performance. To invoke God and to confess faith with an air of pedantry, or with an air of heroism, is to fall away from these freedoms, as Barth fears Melanchthon did by not really taking to heart the verse (Psalm 119:46) which stands at the head of the Augsburg Confession!

Prayer, the perennial undertone of all action, is related to confession as breathing in is related to breathing out. But it is required as a deliberate act; a motion of formal speech where the lips as well as the heart are engaged. It is the chief concrete act by which the festivity of the Lord's Day is carried into every day. Barth offers some criteria of proper prayer. First, it is man's freedom before God (the fact that he *may* pray) which is the ground of obligation. The arguments and impediments in the way of obedience only disappear where the act is seen to be grounded in the covenant relationship where it is strictly a matter of command, dealing with the constant threat to which our solidarity with Christ is exposed. "I can't pray" turns out in fact to mean "I won't pray; I won't submit to the judgement of God and live by His grace." Second, to safeguard the facts that man comes before God solely as a receptive vessel and that in His presence all masks must be dropped, the primary and decisive form of prayer is petition. Other moments come to expression, not in and for themselves, but in and with petition, to safeguard its holiness and purity. Third, the petition is offered by one whose cause God has made His own in the manhood of Jesus Christ. Petition is made representatively on behalf of the universal subject of God's grace (mankind) by the particular subject (the Church). It is a prayer that since God has made our interest His, then His interest may become ours. Fourth, prayer is made with the certainty of being heard; i.e., "in faith, not doubting." To pray, not with an eye on our ability to do it nicely, but with a conviction that what we ask will affect the detail of God's providential rule, makes a world of difference. Finally, since our engagement in prayer is an obedience which is also freedom, the form of that engagement calls for scrutiny and resolution. Here private and corporate prayer may be taken together. Prayer begins and ends with *asking*. The asking must have a disciplined courtesy. It is done by silent or open speech, and the offering of silent prayer *by a congregation* raises questions for a mind as clear, though generous, as that of Barth. It is a matter of formulated speech, because we ought to pray even when we don't "feel like it." The formulations will in principle be short, since requests are soon made. Whatever habits and set times be resolved upon, we hope always to get beyond the mechanism into glad and free and willing prayer. To achieve this in public worship, however, raises questions about the preparation for public prayer, by minister and congregation, which Barth discusses with realistic concern.

From these pages there emerges a vivid picture of modern man, and of the commanding grace which is summoning him to live as God's good creature in this first realm of deliberate relationship with his Maker. Those who would challenge its veracity, from Scripture, from historical theology, or from the sensitive appraisal of human experience, must reckon with a wealth of material which Barth has explicitly taken into account. I think it will hold its ground, not, let me repeat, as a codification of God's command, but as the proper form of theological preparation for experience of that command.

III

The remaining three sections are books in themselves, the first on human relationships with the man-woman relationship at their head, the second on the texture of psycho-somatic life, and the third on the ethical ramifications of each man's mysterious "placing" in the scheme of things— a region of inquiry which is not pre-ordained as a private preserve for existentialists. The pattern of discussion, in broad outline, is as follows.

First among human relationships is that of man and woman, with marriage as its centre and goal. Over against the supernaturalizing of marriage in the notion of it as a "sacrament," or the metaphysical speculations which follow upon Schleiermacher's affirmation of romantic love, Barth pleads for a measure of disenchantment. Further, by refusing to isolate in any way the discussion of physical sexuality from the total encounter of spirit-activated souls of bodies, he claims that the matter may be de-demonized as well as de-divinized. He pleads also for a de-centralized treatment which begins by looking at moments in the relationship other than the central one of marriage, for this estate is only one possibility which Christians undertake when called thereto, knowing that the relation of Christ and His Church can be presented through it. There is also a proper humanity of the unmarried, as, incidentally, there is no impairing of marriage by childlessness. Barth examines these matters with the utmost care and sympathy and incidentally produces the best exposition of St. Paul's mind which is known to me. There are three general directions in which to look for the issue between good and evil in respect of being a man or being a woman. The first of these bids each person be true to his sex, for in the diversity of man and woman (the analysis of which is necessarily precarious) there is a parable of the covenant of grace. By all means let the women dispense with veils and speak in Church provided they are not really hankering after feeling and behaving like men. And beware of the Androgyne myth, whether in the form of Berdyaev's "sexual polarization" or Simone de Beauvoir's existentialist de-mythologizing of woman. Second, any attempt to evade the mystery represented by the humanity of the opposite sex is the beginning of evil. Men and women carry a mutual responsibility to sustain the challenge arising from their diversity.

Third, their co-ordination is cast within an irreversible "ordering," which is dangerous to mention because the fundamental equality is so easily denied. Yet there is a precedence proper to the male, to be undertaken not by natural superiority but in subordination to God, and it calls for strength in the man and maturity in the woman. Disobedience here has for its symptoms the tyrannical man and the subservient woman, who then becomes the rebellious woman seeking to rectify the situation but at the cost of producing a weak man. Here is a *circulus vitiosus*. But against it there is a *circulus veritatis* where the mature woman educates the man's strength by winning his respect and turns him into the kind man. It is at the points of intersection of these circles that we find the questions about good and evil raised acutely.

Marriage is discussed under seven headings, but at every point Barth takes seriously its foundation in a decision of love. The choice of marriage, as of celibacy, is by call of God. It is a life association which constitutes a task in its own right which should not be subordinated to sexual satisfaction, the comfort of the wage-earner, the woman's home instinct, or the bringing up of a family. It means an obligation to realize complete community, with each partner brought to his freedom by the other. (This is peculiarly the man's concern.) It means an exclusive life-community, the safeguarding and effectuating of love's choice being inconceivable in any other terms to Christians who have experienced the community of man and God. It means partnership for *all* the common future of the two parties, but here it is important to take the radicalism of the New Testament as a summons to freedom, and it is wrong to neglect the limiting case where the painful but proper decision may have to be taken that N and N have not in fact been joined by God. To prohibit re-marriage in such circumstances is a scandalous mis-reading of commanding grace, particularly if it takes the form of refusing Christian hallowing. The hallowing of Eros, in order that the decision to marry may be reached in free and mutual love, is next discussed with rare insight. And finally the civic aspect of "matrimony" falls into proper perspective against the clarification of the reality of marriage.

The second relationship which men enjoy by creation is that of parents and children. From the standpoint of the child, which is common to all, the "honour" due to parents is what matters. He must respect their "weight" as teachers and counsellors. Their bearing on his life is from the same quarter as is the bearing of God. They represent, but do not exhaustively embody, the *a priori* out of which the child has come. Their nurture represents that of God, but under the new covenant the one authentic Fatherhood, that of God, establishes a nurture for human children in Christ alongside that nurture in its parental representation. Thus, while there is a real obeying of parents, it takes place "in the Lord" as a free and differentiated decision of obedience whose form Barth examines in the three stages of early childhood, adolescence, and maturity. The bearing of this divine command on the child's re-action to palpable weaknesses in his parents calls into play all the tremendous humility and sympathy of which Barth is capable, and again he looks with care at the limiting case (much illuminated in Scripture) where the decision may have to be made to live as one without father or mother. From the standpoint of parents two matters call for preliminary clarification: the state of childlessness and the question of birth control. Here as elsewhere the generous things said by Barth are less significant than the care with which he says them and the theology from which he gets them. He goes on then to sort out the wheat from the tares in respect of such statements as that parents must always be *for* their children, that they must exercise authority over them, and that they must equip them for life, and he ends with a reminder of the limits set to parental care.

The third topic of this section deals with man's existence as a member of some *Volk* (those who are "near") and within humanity (those who are distant). Here we have to do, not with the stringency of a Creator's command, but with the disposition of a providential Governor. Nevertheless, though there is a relativizing of the sanctity of race, language and culture, it is a fruitful relativizing which leaves room for the hallowing of man's historical responsibility as one of his own folk. This hallowing comes to effect in the presence amid the peoples of the covenant-history fulfilled in the one Lord Jesus Christ, which sets every form of life-with-those-who-are-near into relationship with a *centre* and with a *goal*. Life under the command of God is therefore always life "on the way out" from the national corner to the unity of the people of God and therefore to the broad acres of "humanity." Here, however, as in the next section, the whole story cannot be told in the context of the doctrine of creation. Barth leaves the topic with twenty packed pages of exegesis focused on the stories of Babel and Pentecost, which indicates what happened within Israel's own history to make room for the Church as the new people whose existence does not end that of the nations but brings to light their true significance.

IV

It is no longer possible to take for granted the "urge to live" and Barth grounds all that he has to say about "freedom for life" in God's command being a command to live. Barth takes very seriously the *Lebensangst* of modern men. He begins with a section of "reverence for life," but for life as the loan of existence *qua* soul of my body. "Reverence" is a practical exercise of my freedom based on recognition of the limits which give shape to what is loaned. It is not "theoretical-aesthetic admiration" of life, as of something divine. The command enjoining reverence for life has its explicit Biblical form in "Thou shalt not kill," but before he deals with the primary defensive aspect of this, Barth works out an account of its positive bearing. He deals in turn with issues raised by the instinctive levels of life, the relation of human life to that of plants and animals (showing the same delicate respect for the concern of vegetarians as he shows in so many other places for similar cases of conscience), the category of health, the achievement of *joie de vivre*, the naturalness of self-affirmation and the will to power.

When he turns to the significant negative aspect of the explicit command, in the section on the defense of life, the bearing of the command becomes more searching though not necessarily more important. Here there is an urgent unconditional protection of life, in contrast with the positive aspect where the respect which is enjoined is in every case conditioned. But when it comes down to cases, we have to face the fact that what is protected is not an unconditioned magnitude—Life, just like that! We have to reckon, therefore, with limiting cases where the relativity of the life which is unconditionally protected may permit, or even require, a proper act of killing. The New Testament identification of the coming Kingdom with the Son of Man means that these limiting cases are not to be found quite so readily as is assumed in the Old Testament which after all must now be read in the light of the Crucifixion of Jesus Christ, and Christians do well to believe that the protection of human life against arbitrary extermination is almost limitless. Barth looks at eight possible cases of inflicting death; suicide, common murder, abortion, extermination of the "worthless," euthanasia, emergency killing in self-defense, the death penalty, and, finally, war. Suicide is the extreme assertion of sovereignty over one's life and contrasts most sharply with obedience to the Lord of life which may indeed mean giving up one's life to death but in a quite different form. That it is not beyond forgiveness affords no excuse whatever. Barth maintains that here is the point where it is supremely clear that the offence in taking life is offence against the Gospel and faith, not offence against some law. And in view of known circumstances where men have been driven to suicide (one thinks of the Gestapo knocking on the door) it is most important to look at this whole field from the standpoint of God's gracious permission to men that they *shall* live and to look honestly at the possible limiting case. Again in the case of abortion, the divine No! has its root in the Gospel. Human life is upheld in freedom in grace; otherwise we miss the point of respecting it. But this enhances rather than alleviates the gravity of critical decision. If life must be weighed against life, the decision *can* fall in favour of the mother and against the child, but no legislation should ever take the responsibility for decision away from those most directly concerned. Extermination of the "worthless," like euthanasia, comes into the class of murder and there is no question of a limiting case. But these three possibilities are serious enough to call for serious theological exhibition of the grounds of prohibition. Self-defense and the death penalty go together for the latter is a communal instance of the former. The hallowing of the instinct for self-preservation is a question in itself and passages in the Sermon on the Mount stand in the way of any easy story at this point. Here again the limiting case is liable to be ruled out by treating the command as a law. The case for the death penalty is often thought to rest on grounds other than the Gospel, and it raises issues wider than those involved in a direct threat to the life of an individual or his immediate neighbour. Barth finds that there is little ground for practising execution as a punishment. The limiting case is that of the traitor and of the tyrant, where what is at stake is not the well-being but the actual being of the State. In regard to war, Barth does everything possible by way of sharpening conscience, but he sees a possible limiting case where a nation has to defend *within its own frontiers* an independence which on serious grounds it is not prepared to surrender—which is all very well for a Swiss, but not wholly relevant even to Czechoslovakia in 1938. Within its limits however (and these 23 pages are not a Christian Ethic of War) Barth's handling of the problem of bellicose killing, and of military service in preparation for it, is strictly to the point.

The third section of the paragraph about life deals with its industrious employment. The point about man's industry is that it co-operates with and corresponds to the activity of God. To see it as service commanded by God we begin from the work which is most clearly hallowed service, the work of the Church. This calls for clarification of what is involved in *belonging* to the Church, and incidentally of the status of the Church as a Church *for* the *Volk*, not *of* the *Volk*. Then of the responsibility which is laid upon every member by reason of the internal history in which the Church lives; each has to co-operate responsibly in maintaining the unity of the congregation, its quality of life, its theology and its practice of love. Then we turn to the Church's service in the world where the first requisite is love, the second is missionary activity, the third is clear proclamation of the Gospel, and the fourth is a prophetic declaration for right against wrong. Round this centre of the Kingdom and the community which proclaims it, God's fatherly Providence rules the entire creation, and in this periphery man has the peripheral privilege of work. The Christian understands something of the great context in which all men's work is set, and he finds the gracious necessity of it primarily in the fact that it gives to each man his point of attachment in the creation, the place where his life can be "spent." Here, as in the section on prayer, Barth throws what he has to say in to the form of "criteria" for right work. To work is to limit yourself to a particular job and *to identify yourself* with that self-limitation. The other criteria derive their urgency from this one, e.g., the worth and honour of what is done, the humanity with which it is done, the significance found in the doing of it, and the limitation imposed on its demands. The sociological significance of Sabbath observance receives proper consideration once these criteria have been probed.

V

The last section of this volume plays a role similar to that of *De meditatione futurae vitae* and *Quomodo utendum praesenti vita* which round off Calvin's discussion of the Christian man (*Inst.* III, 6–10). What does God's command mean as addressed to man in his limited time? What is the bearing on ethics of eschatological expectation? It is precisely in his *limited* opportunity that every man is the fellow-man of Jesus Christ, called to solidarity with Him. He must regard it therefore as a form of his freedom. And again there are criteria by reference to which he knows a little more clearly how matters stand in respect of his obedience or disobedience to the command of God. To be conscious of having one's own particular place brings with it the highest degree of candour and of resolution. Further, the knowledge that one has no time to lose breeds the art of making time and taking opportunities. And above all, it is a mark of obedience to remember steadily but without fear that one must eventually die. There are notions born of fear which seem to help man overcome the fear of death, but the only *Memento mori!* which brings into life that qualified sense of its significance which is the mark of obedience is the concrete *Memento Domini!*, the knowledge of who it is who awaits me at the limit to which I am hastening. Here Barth quietly reckons with the existentialism which he has now outgrown.

He passes next to the theme of man's vocation, distinguishing between God's calling of him (*Berufung*) and the "calling" (*Beruf*) in which he finds himself. Luther's influential treatment of this matter was by way of reaction to medieval monasticism and there is room for a truer account of man's station and calling as the *place* of his responsibility to God, not something in itself to which he is responsible. This place has certain marks which merit attention *vis-à-vis* the question about God's command. First there is the fact of being of a certain age, and Barth goes through the various stages of life to bring out their peculiarities as well as their interconnexion. He does it with the same powerful combination of theological clarity and pastoral wisdom which is evident on every page of this volume. Next there is the fact of being set to live at a particular juncture of history, which is to be taken not as matter of determinism but as the provision of a stage whereon man may experience the calling of God. The same approach in terms of freedom applies in the case of the special abilities with which a man is endowed, and to have a cut and dried estimate of them and assess one's duties accordingly is the mark, not of obedience, but of trying to be one's own creator and lord. The last fact to be reckoned with is the range within which one counts for something, and here more depends on man's own choice of his calling than elsewhere. The theology of Providence comes to its own here, if anywhere, and the ethical question deals primarily with the problem of being true to one's chosen calling. Luther has much to teach us at this point, though the calling (which can be repudiated in favour of another with perfect obedience) is never to be regarded as a divinised *Ordnung* with its own law. What abides is not the calling in itself but the actual calling by God.

The last theme is that of human dignity, and the esteem due to man as a creature of God and as occupant of the position to which he has been called. The casual English, alone among the nations of Britain and Europe with the possible exception of the Norwegians, would probably be inclined to let this take care of itself, but it has done this one no harm to see how the rest of the world lives. The dignity of man in his station is never to be assessed except in the light of the higher dignity which he has in virtue of God's Word and command addressed to him, and the interrelation of the two kinds of honour is close. It is a dignity in service. Since it is God's free gift it is to be enjoyed only in gratitude, humility, and humour. And though degrees of dignity are useful and indeed indispensible for men in their relationships, these degrees are not taken very seriously by God in His estimate of man's honour as the language about Christ's "little ones" serves to remind us. The protection of one's honour is something which hardly troubles the man of faith except in the limiting case where his service is impaired by loss of proper dignity. And here it is the imperilled service, not the imperilled dignity, which matters. Care for the honour of others rather than for one's own is the New Testament prescription for dealing with such emergencies.

In conclusion let me quote the closing remarks of Professor Otto Weber in his summary of the volume published in the *Reformierte Kirchenzeitung* to which, in this case, my own summary owes not a little:

> The work just reviewed may be called an Ethic in the light of free grace, that free grace of God which already in Jesus Christ allows man to live in his creatureliness, establishes him in freedom and brings him honour. Man has no other life, no other freedom, no other honour. His continuing endowment is his whole wealth. And the command of the Creator is his whole freedom.

(1952)

THE STATE AND DIVINE LAW

THE AUTHORITY OF THE STATE, THE MEASUREMENT OF ITS JUSTICE, AND its relation to the Kingdom of God, are problems raised in a more acute form to-day than perhaps at any time since the New Testament was written. That the State is an instrument of God is a doctrine derived from Scripture, and maintained in some form by all Christian thinking. But can this doctrine be affirmed with regard to contemporary States, in a form which takes account of their alienation from Christian faith and morality? The most disreputable, perhaps, of Europe's rulers declares that in his country "people get that social justice which is compatible with order and a sense of authority. We are right, and God is with us. God will not allow barbarism and brutality to rule over us." Elsewhere, men are confronted with the theory and reality of completely secular States, which make far-reaching demands on their members in virtue of an "authority" consisting chiefly in the State's possession of supreme means of power, physical and psychological. Again, in liberal-democratic countries, the idea that "authority, not wisdom, makes the law" has gained much ground. Politicians may still speak of justice, tolerance, freedom, etc., as a basis for politics; the coercion of the individual by the State may be well concealed in such countries; but the majority of democratic politicians grow increasingly unsure of their ground when they seek to base action on principle rather than on expediency. If the State is a divine instrument, it must be subject in some clear way to the divine law, and it is hard to see how this may be held as true in the case of any of the contemporary States.

Subjection to the Law of God implies, in Christian thinking, moral responsibility. No mechanical operation of a "law" in nature or history does justice to the relation which must exist between God and His instrument the State. Again, this subjection implies that no State can ever be regarded as an arbitrary expression of the will of the people or of their governors. They may have conceived it as such, but in fact they lack the power to preside over its office and destiny. Its history will bear evidence of the divine law, and at every point a moral obligation is conveyed, whether or not it be acknowledged. Again, Christians cannot but suppose that this moral obligation will issue in a service rendered by the State within the Kingdom of God proclaimed and established by Jesus Christ. We have to enquire about the existence of such a divine law, and the nature of the State's subjection to it.

It is possible to raise this question at a level where all men are equally concerned, and in terms to which all men can subscribe. Christians and non-Christians alike are concerned to re-establish the authority of law in political theory and practice, and to safeguard the morality of the State's use of power. The norm by which State activity is to be directed, on this level of thinking, has to do with such matters as the preservation and nurture of human life, the rights of man, the development of his nature and personality, the reformation and defense of the secular structure within which he lives, and the establishment of a just and lasting peace. But discussion on this level presupposes a prior understanding of the place which the State has in the purpose of God for the present world, upon which Christians are not agreed. It will be necessary therefore to look at a group of questions which lie properly within the Christian theological sphere, in order to conceive a context for the supposed subjection of the State to divine law. This matter has been brought to the fore by Karl Barth and Alfred de Quervain, both of whom speak in a new way of the political order as an order for the service of God. The question they raise is implied in the Declaration of Barmen, the standard adopted by the German Confessional Church in 1934: "We reject the false doctrine that there are spheres of life in which we belong, not to Jesus Christ, but to other masters; realms where we do not need to be justified and sanctified by Him." The primary reference of this to the National Socialists' claims for German blood and soil and for their own party-State, is clear and straightforward. But it may well have a bearing on the political doctrine of the seventeenth-century Reformers, and that of developed Lutheranism and Calvinism, as well as on the Roman Catholic theory focused in the doctrine of Natural Law. It may well appear that the authority of "God" upon which the justice of the State is deemed to rest in all these theologies, is something other than the authority of Jesus Christ made known by the Gospel. If so, recent developments in New Testament exegesis (particularly of such passages as Colossians 2:15 and Ephesians 1:9, 10) provide a ground from which to criticize traditional thinking of all kinds, and from which the context with which we are now concerned may be seen more clearly. In passing, it may be noted that the encyclical *Quas Primus* issued by Pope Pius XI on the occasion of the establishment of a new Church festival, the Feast of Christ the King, bears evidence of a like Christocentric thinking, though the Pope's development of the thesis is unlikely to commend itself to Protestant thinkers.

I. *THE STATE AND THE KINGDOM OF GOD*

Both Roman and Protestant thought about politics rest traditionally on an implicit denial that the revealed Kingdom of God has any *direct* bearing on the theory and practice of politics.[1] The reality of the State, and its office, derive from an order prior to the redeeming work of Christ. From the Catholic standpoint,

> St. Thomas bases political philosophy on natural reason and natural law, not on revelation and supernatural theology. . . . Thus it remains that the rights and duties of citizens are not changed in substance through super-natural theology or baptism. The natural motives are strengthened through supernatural motives, but they are not superseded by the latter. The divine law that issues from grace does not abolish human law that issues from natural reason. In its field the State and the citizen have therefore a genuine though not absolute autonomy.[2]

Revealed truth has its part to play in strengthening natural motives and purifying them. Further,

> it was a salutary step forward to human freedom when St. Thomas and the doctors of Late Scholasticism based their political philosophy upon reason and natural law, and took away from the State its sacred theological majesty, its divinity with which paganism had consecrated it.[3]

Nevertheless, it should be clear that this procedure rests on a theory of law and of the State which is ultimately theological. It is all very well to say that "political institutions are not to be judged by the theological errors which ideologically called them into existence, but by their conformity to natural law," but this presupposes acceptance of the Roman Church's conception of the dealings of God with the world of men. It arises from an ideology which may well be based on theological error. What is the context of this doctrine of the natural law?

God created men, and the world in which He set them, with the purpose of establishing the human race in supernatural communion with Himself. The Kingdom of God which accomplishes this purpose is realized in the relation between Christ and His believing people; that is to say, in the Church. The powers of Christ in His kingdom are communicated to His people, and though not realized in their fullness in any individual, they are completely deployed in the total hierarchically ordered life of the Church. The Kingdom may therefore be identified with the Church of

---

[1]Cf. Brunner, *The Divine Imperative*, p. 443 and note 7 on p. 680. "The Reformers have no Christian philosophy of the State, any more than they recognize a divine *jus naturale*. They take seriously the statement that the State is a secular order *along-side* of the Church, and it is at this point that virtually the idea of the State based on Christian ideas is abandoned." I dissent from Brunner's analysis on p. 443, mainly because of his peculiarly Continental Protestant use of the concept "nature."

[2]Rommen, *The State in Catholic Thought*, p. 112.

[3]Rommen, p. 116.

Jesus Christ, made visible through the ages in the Roman communion under the headship of the Pope.

The bearing of these powers on politics is to reinforce in man the active principle of natural community, which can be apprehended by the intellect, and affirmed in moral freedom in particular concrete acts which establish a State, whose end is "right order," expressed, preserved, and developed by the proper functions of the State in the community. This political life gives to all men the possibility of self-realization of their social nature, towards an end of natural self-sufficiency. The supernatural end of communion with God is attained by grace in the Church. The Kingdom of God in the Church embraces that whole life of man, and it is from the Church that the believer learns true political life, in terms of "Natural Law." He learns that politics is concerned only with the natural life of man. As a political creature, made for community with his fellows, he affirms the State as an ordinance of God which guarantees the public order, and expresses the inner moral necessity that the lives of individuals be organized in community. He learns also to require of the State, to which he gives political allegiance, that it acknowledge the supreme status of the Church as above all other communities. For the rest, the action of the State must be based on the structure of creatures as natural beings. This structure, both in its present actuality and in its perfection, so it is assumed, may be perceived by the human mind; then the will is laid under obligation to realize in free human acts the greatest possible perfection of man's nature in the natural and moral cosmos. In actual fact, human sin prevents true perception, much more true implementation of the Natural Law; and the Kingdom of God, revealed by His grace in Jesus Christ, alone is able to deal with this weakness of moral nature. But man's life in the State, even when he is aided by grace, is still strictly natural. The State is necessary to the natural life of men who are also in the Church, and may indeed operate so as to drive others to grace, but of itself it is unaffected by the order of redemption.

The State, and the Natural Law to which it is in principle subject, have here only a preliminary connection with the kingdom of God established in Christ. His Incarnation and Atoning Work have no bearing on the law by which the State's operation is to be measured. The subjection of all things to Christ (including the State), acknowledged in *Quas Primas*, is expressed in the "spiritual authority" which the State should accord to the Church.

Protestant Church thinking has not, of course, assigned such a positive and optimistic significance to what is achieved in the sphere of nature. The foundation of Church thinking about that State is to be found only in the order of creation, and the judgement of the divine law upon it, which are revealed in Scripture. The consequent tendency is to leave the State alone in the sphere of the lost world, requiring from it only such freedom for the Church as will promote the proclamation of the Gospel. If the ruler of a territory be a personal believer, he is expected to take responsibility in the community life of the redeemed Church—special responsibility indeed, in virtue of the office he holds in the State. In this case, the way is open for conceiving his political office by means of a theocratic model based on Scripture. If he is not a believer, he is summoned to hear the Gospel and believe, and to live by the forgiveness of sins rather than by self-justification. Again, there are Scriptural models from which to interpret his office. If he denies to the Church its freedom, he is still to be honoured, by the Church enduring suffering at his hands as did Christ at the hands of Pilate. In either case, his political duty is discharged on the basis of an authority delegated to the State by God in His Wrath, for the restraint of sin, the preservation of order, and (in His secret mercy) for a pedogogical function of bringing men to repentance and so to Christ. The law which he serves, and by which citizens may measure their own loyalty, is the divine positive law revealed in such portions of Scripture as are deemed to be Law rather than Gospel.

Though the Lutheran conception is of Church and State standing alongside each other in a given territory pursuing diverse interests, rather than of the Church presiding spiritually over States, and though, further, the temper differs from Roman thought, in that the Christian, knowing that he cannot "Christianize" this piece of fallen nature, accepts passively whatever it cares to do in its own sphere, still, Lutheranism has not departed radically from Catholicism on the one point that the Kingdom of God in Christ is realized only in the Church, and so the State and the divine law to which it is subject have only a preliminary connection with that Kingdom. The State is conceived as operating in a realm which is not yet subject to Christ—nor, perhaps, even can be. Christ's rule, as Bultmann has reaffirmed in his recent commentary on the Fourth Gospel, must not be called political, since Law and Gospel, State and Church, differ fundamentally in their character. The two spheres must be co-ordinated, with very little interpenetration. In Romanism, on the other hand, the State is conceived as spiritually subordinated to the Church. But, in both cases, there is a radical separation of the Kingdom of God from the earthly kingdom.

Calvinism differs from Lutheranism in declining to separate Law and Gospel so sharply. The law is a *demand* for the life which is *offered* by the Gospel. Calvin himself was aware that the Lord is the king of kings, and in his hand are the hearts of kings and the revolutions of kingdoms. "No government can be happily constituted unless its first object be the promotion of piety, and all laws are preposterous which neglect the claims of God, and merely provide for the interests of men." Quoting Jeremiah 22:3, he says that: "*Righteousness* means the care, patronage, defense, vindication, and liberation of the innocent; *judgement* imports the repression of the audacity, the coercion of the violence, and the punishment of the crimes of the impious."[4] We may unfortunately agree with him that the "nature of this argument seems to have no connection with the spiritual doctrine of faith" discussed in the rest of the *Institutes*. He sees the promulgation of the Law as an eternal act of sovereign divine grace, but this is a "general" grace, not integrally bound up with the Person and Work of Jesus Christ. As a result, he was able to conceive (in opposition to Lutheran thinking) that the natural order may, in virtue of "the rule of the saints," become the scene of Christ's open rule—a conception which proved illusory both in Geneva and in seventeenth-century England. In other contexts he conceives of Church and State existing side by side, each in its own right, each serving the purpose of God. The political order is affected by the Person and Work of Jesus Christ only in so far as State and Church must come to terms with each other. Outside that direct contact—admittedly a nerve-centre for the whole matter—the State's responsibility to God is interpreted by elements in religious thinking other than the Kingdom of God established in Jesus Christ. The statesman is a minister of God, subject to His law, and the Church's demand for freedom for its own life and witness serves to conform the statesman's actions to this law of God and guide him in the promotion of piety and justice. But only by virtue of saving faith and membership of the Church can he ever be said to be a servant of Jesus Christ. The English Calvinists had a clear conception of the world as a twofold system: a scheme of nature, to which man, as man, belonged; and a scheme of grace to which the elect belonged.

Although, as has just been implied, Calvin seems to have no clear relation in mind between the Kingdom of God in Christ, and the political order, it has recently been suggested that he is feeling after a more Christocentric account of the situation than has yet appeared.[5] He believes that the atoning work and heavenly reign of Christ have positive consequences for the State and its office. He is ready, for that reason, to speak of a political justice derived from natural law, which must be sought and upheld in the name of Jesus Christ. It is worth noting in passing that he held an Occamist view of law, as deriving from will rather than from reason. He would not, therefore, with St. Thomas Aquinas, have articulated a doctrine of natural law in terms of access to the divine Reason by means other than the mediation of Jesus Christ. In certain passages he seems to conceive the State as owing its present reality, office, and authority, by reference to the kingly office of the exalted Redeemer. Article 50 of the *Heidelberg Catechism* speaks of the ascended Christ as "the

[4]*Inst.*, IV, xx, 91.

[5]W. Niesel, *Die Theologie Calvins*.

Head through whom the Father rules *all things*" in distinction from His Lordship over the Church.

In line with this, Barth and de Quervain[6] have raised the fundamental question whether there is a theological basis for the State which is related directly to the grace of God in Jesus Christ. The State, in this Age of Grace between the times of Christ's ascension and His return in glory, has an office and operation different from those attributed to it by reference only to the Creator-God, or to the God who restrains sin in His Wrath. It does, of course, preserve the purpose of creation, and its office is still to restrain sin. In this it is a sign that the old world has not yet passed away. But, with the New Testament writers for whom the issue was raised as acutely as it is to-day, we may also regard the State as a worldly power which has been "spoiled" (Colossians 2:15), and brought into the service of Christ and the Gospel. From the New Testament, especially from the part played by Pilate in the Passion Story, it is plain that the State survives by virtue of the forgiveness of God. In its own way, and amongst all men, it serves the Lord whom believers love as their Saviour. What is achieved by the State is not inferior or subordinate to what is achieved by the Church. Its service is a service of Christ to which believers and unbelievers are alike summoned, and which both are capable of rendering by virtue of His saving work. Its significance lies in the fact that the whole creation now looks forward to the final triumph of God's Kingdom in a new *political* order, to which the nations will bring their glory. In spite of sin, and in face of unbelief, the State exists in the service of Christ, to promote the extension of the Kingdom of God, by securing the preaching of the Gospel, and by the achievement of neighbourly love. The statesman and citizen, whether they are believers or not, should discharge their political obligations in a way which promotes the cause of Christ in realms which are not the Church, nor are subject (even "spiritually") to the Church.

In deriving from this theology a conception of divine law to which the statesman *as such* is obliged, we may however learn from Romanism not to confuse theology with political philosophy, but rather to derive a true philosophy, intelligible apart from faith, from the scrutiny of reality in the light of theological perspectives. Further, traditional thinking of all varieties serves to remind us that there is a proper independence of civil government from ecclesiastical—as opposed to divine—jurisdiction. To say that the law which establishes the State in truth and justice and imparts to it its rightful authority is integrally related to the Person and Work of Jesus Christ, is not to imply that the true end of the State will be achieved when it has become the Church, or the instrument of the Church. On the contrary, the Church acknowledges a work of Christ in the political

---

[6]Barth, in *Church and State*, and in *The Knowledge of God and the Service of God*, as well as in his wartime letters to Czechoslovakia, France, and Great Britain. Alfred de Quervain in his recently published *Kirche, Volk, und Staat*, which is Vol. II of his *Ethik*.

realm other than His work in her own life. State and Church exist there-fore, side by side, inter-related and interpenetrating; but in the action of both there is positive *Christian* significance. In particular, the State, as English-speaking Christians have sensed obscurely for a century or more, is positively connected with the order of redemption.

II. *THE STATE AS A MORAL INSTITUTION*

The State has been defined as a nation organized for action under legal rules. Gladstone spoke of it as "the self-governing energy of a nation, made objective." Brunner says, "The State is a definite ordering of the nation. . . . It confronts not only every individual, but also the collective body of its 'subjects' as an independent entity, and yet it is never anything else than the will and thought of these very people poured into this mould."[7] We are dealing therefore with a factor in human life whereby authority is exercised over individuals for the sake of public order and for the achievement of a common good in a national community. To it is committed the monopoly of supreme power, and its exercise of moral suasion is backed by coercive power. What is the derivation and meaning of this factor in human life, and how can moral responsibility enter into the situation if it be conceived as subject to divine law?

The doctrine that "the powers that be are ordained of God" is suscep-tible of a simple, primitive, and perhaps inherently pagan interpretation, in terms of divine right. Authority is delegated to the rulers of a nation by that nation's divine Lord. They are invested with a theological majesty, and, in virtue of their office, they share the mind of God. The word translated "ordained" means, however, "appointed," "arranged," "set, in a certain station." All that is affirmed therefore is that States exist by the will and purpose of God. The rulers have no inherent divinity, and they hold office in virtue of their ability to share the mind of God.

If, on the basis of Ephesians 1:9–10, it is said that in faith we know the secret divine purpose for the State, it remains for us to explicate this theological knowledge in terms derived from a rational examination of the State. First, we ask whether, and to what extent, this purpose can be discerned in the natural roots from which the State grows. Rational ex-amination at once compels recognition of the ambiguous character of these natural roots. The reality of political government in national com-munities has a long history, explicable in terms of economic, psychological and strategic necessity. Positivists are content to find here the clue to the mystery, and to explain the State in terms of a balance achieved between mankind and natural forces, and between various opposing human in-terests. On the other hand, it is clear that rational human judgement has

---

[7]Brunner, p. 441.

played a great part in creating a given State. Citizens have affirmed its authority on the basis of a rational or intuitive recognition of its nature and purpose. This affirmation has been an act of moral quality, not to be confused with the operation of mystical and mechanical efficient causes such as produce order in physical and biological nature.

At this point, something must be said about the persisting consequences of the Fall of Man for this expression of corporate life. There is a tendency in Protestant thought to explain the whole existence of the State as a consequence of sin. The attempt is sometimes made to fix on some feature, such as the State's use of coercive force, as *the* place where manifestly it is irremediably involved in the Fall. To criticize this approach is not to deny that the problem of power is an urgent one—the more urgent now that modern weapons and techniques have given to the omnicompetent State a complete insurance against the threat of the citizens to rise in their might against tyranny.

In my judgement, there is no feature of the State's existence which can be wholly identified as deriving from the Fall. The effect of the Fall is subtle and all-pervasive. The authority of the State is exercised by men who are sinners. Its inherited conception of its task, the circumstances within which that task is discharged, its tradition, and its resources of power, are all the product of sinful men acting in a sinful world. This appears in the constant danger that any State will act in complete self-sufficiency and irresponsibility. It appears also in the domination of all States by vested interests, which work against such political reformation as may be necessary for the right response to a given situation. At any time, the perception of the State's duty will be imperfect because of the self-justifying blindness of sinful men—believers and unbelievers alike. The situation in which it must act is one created by past sin, and statesman and citizen alike are bound by this chain of guilt to choose the lesser of two evils. The State is therefore always liable to become the instrument of human selfishness and not the instrument of the justice of God.

The same things, however, can be said about the life of the Church. The life and office of the Church are to be distinguished from those of the State, because the life of the Church, rooted in the objective atonement wrought in Christ, is a life of liberation from sin. The Church *is* the Church by virtue of its humble *acceptance* of divine forgiveness. The State operates among all men, where forgiveness of sin is not accepted in the absence of universal saving faith. The State, therefore, if it be a minister of Jesus Christ, operates in a context where His redeeming love has not free course. But that is not to say, either that its operation is derived not directly from His redeeming love but from some neutral "nature," or that the context of this operation is wholly coloured by human sin and divine Wrath.

This being so, are we justified in saying that the State, with its ambiguous derivation and its sin-corrupted life, is derived from the will and purpose of God and in particular from the act by which His purpose is accomplished in face of human sin, that is to say, from the Work of Jesus Christ? Are we justified in regarding the State as a *responsible* form of human life, answering to the creative and now redemptive demand of God? If so, this demand is conveyed in the secular realities (or natural roots) from which the State and its work arise, and in the rational apprehensions from which men create the State in acts of free moral responsibility. This, I think, is what the Gospel bids us believe. Any State is a sinful organism, acting in a sinful situation, but by virtue of Christ's redeeming work and the subjection of the State to Him, it is possible for that State so to act that, in the name of Jesus Christ, its action may be upheld as right. When it does so, that action will also be affirmed as reasonable and just by all men of good will and right reason. This is the truth behind the classical doctrine of Natural Law.

In this context, very different from his own, we may find verbal agreement with the statement of a Roman Catholic philosopher of great wisdom:

> The universe is order, cosmos not chaos. It is the eternal law, the divine reason, which has instituted this order. Since free rational beings can intellectually grasp this eternal law, and through it the will of the divine legislator, for them this order becomes the natural law. In the light of reason, man recognizes the order as one that ought to be realized by himself. . . . Non-intellectual creatures follow their nature blindly without moral responsibility. Intellectual free beings ought to realize their free, rational, and social nature in freedom. In the last resort, accordingly, there is a coincidence of the laws of biological life and the natural law.[8]

The order instituted by God *in His act which redeems the fallen creature* may be recognized in the light of reason as the order that ought to be realized by man's free acts of moral responsibility. Thus, through the existence of the State and the discharging of political responsibilities, all men enjoy a measure of the freedom which Christ has bought for mankind. The State, in its own limited way, serves the purpose of the Kingdom of God established in Jesus Christ.

This thesis calls for a re-examination of the process whereby the duty of the State may be discerned. For this, man needs the light of a rationality set free by the work of Christ to function reliably within the secular realm. Such discernment will not come without reference to the Gospel, but that is not to say that it can come only to believers. True, only the believer can see the State's task within the perspectives of God's purpose revealed in the Gospel; and these he will see only in so far as he is willing to expose himself to the technicalities of political life wherein the demand of God is conveyed. These realities in themselves have an autonomy relative to

---

[8]Rommen, p. 181.

the Gospel revelation, and the help which experts can give in exhibiting them is independent of the experts' faith or unbelief. But when they are seen within the perspective of the Gospel, the believer is able to speak of them rationally; and there seems no reason why this rational illumination, once it is established, should not be a light in which unbelievers also may see and take action.

It may be questioned whether this task of "theonomic thinking"—as it has been called[9]—has been faithfully discharged in the past. In Roman thinking, it seems that fallen nature is too readily accepted as bearing upon itself the will of the divine legislator. In Protestant thinking, the criterion for the divine purpose of the State is taken to be an account of divine positive law, derived from the Bible but not integrally related to the Gospel. Theonomic thinking implies, for those who are affected by it, a genuine sharing in the mind of God, the ground for asserting that the State is a moral organism, and that there is such a thing as corporate conscience in a State. The nation is therefore responsible to God for what is done in its name. The State exists as a form of national life whereby certain corporate functions are responsibly discharged. As such, it is derived from the will and purpose of God, and plays its part in the Kingdom He has established in Jesus Christ.

III. *THE RESPONSE OF THE STATE TO DIVINE LAW*

This fundamental thesis must be explicated in face of the questions disclosed in political philosophy. What is the conception of divine law, relevant for the politician as such, which arises within the world order which God has instituted by creation and redemption? If, for the State to discharge its office under Christ, it is not necessary to postulate saving faith in all men or even in its officers, there must be some relation between political activity and divine law which is significant for the politician as such. It was suggested in the last section that man is given access to the mind and purpose of God in so far as he apprehends this order by living through historical situations, reflecting upon them in theonomic thinking, and acting in the light of such thinking with moral responsibility.

The divine purpose is effected in the development of history, however incomplete may be the apprehension thus made possible, or however inadequate the response to it. Pilate's betrayal of his office served in its own way towards the establishment of the Kingdom of God in Jesus Christ. The persecution of the Church by a pagan or apostate State serves in its own way to promote the Kingdom of God; and the Church, by its willingness to suffer in such circumstances, respects the divine ordination of the State. Nevertheless, the purpose of divine law is realized only par-

---

[9]A. R. Vidler and W. A. Whitehouse, *Natural Law; a Christian Reconsideration*.

tially, the possibilities of a given historical situation have an incomplete fruition, where there is not true discernment of the divine law, and morally responsible affirmation of its demands by statesmen and citizens. Therefore, as Barth says, the Christian community should expect from the State such action as will promote the interests of Christ and His Kingdom.

The promotion of Christ's work by the State should, of course, be conceived in different terms from those which apply to the service of the Church. Here is the root of the distinction between Law and Love which has produced much confusion, especially perhaps among English-speaking Christians. Obedience to law, it is supposed, must be essentially self-regarding, and therefore must be in an entirely different order from the realm of love created by the Gospel. The action of love is free self-giving. But if the moral content of love be safeguarded, then love's purpose is partially effected in a situation where the free gift is unappreciated or rejected, by means of a demand for righteousness. Law may be described as love operating at a distance. Now in the political life of mankind, God's gift of Himself in Jesus Christ is not, in general, appreciated; occasionally it is openly rejected. This is not true of the Church, whose office among believers is, therefore, quite different from the office of the State among all men. God's dealings with men through the State are works of law, but what is effected thereby is a measure, permitted by the situation, of His purpose of Love; and that purpose is "to sum up all things in Christ" (Ephesians 1:10).

The divine law by which the action of the State is measured, is communicated to it in a threefold contact with the life and thought of the Church.

First, the State must deal with the Church as with an earthly institution, existing within its territory in a certain form. It is a means of grace to the State that the Church seeks from it peace and freedom for its own witness to the Gospel by word and life. Jeremiah exhorted his captive brethren to "seek the peace of the city whither ye are carried away captive, for in the peace thereof ye shall have peace." In claiming freedom for its preaching and its own form of life, the Church contributes towards the peace and well-being of the State. It is no part of this essay to elaborate the duties of the State to the Church, or the duties of Christians to the State, but two points may be noted here. First, if this claim for freedom is to be a means of grace to the State, the Church must take seriously the form of its own life. The contribution to political life in England made by the claims of the Reformed Churches for freedom for their peculiar form of church life is an illustration of what may happen. Second, the demand for political conditions wherein Churchmen can serve the State with Christian integrity, is itself a means of grace, provided that such men are concerned to make their demand felt either by criticism or revolt whenever conformity is impossible. Barth makes the interesting suggestion that the "good" referred to in Romans 13:4 ("The ruler is the minister of God to thee for good"), is not some neutral "good" of nature, but rather the Christian "good" established by the Gospel in the lives of believers.

Second, the State has to reckon with the Church's proclamation of true religion. The responsibility of the State, if interpreted from the Ten Commandments, is not confined to the second table thereof. The Gospel proclaimed by the Church summons the State to free itself from paganism. The State cannot itself be the organ of true religion in the sense of faith in the Christian Gospel, but it may not commit itself to an official religion other than Christianity, if it is to serve its purpose in the world where the Father rules all things through the exalted Christ.

Third, there are areas of political decision which are affected only indirectly (if at all) by these direct contacts with the institutional Church. Contact with the Gospel is implicitly achieved, however, in the practice of theonomic thinking, where such technical matters may be scrutinized in the light of divine law, reason being the guide acknowledged by believer and unbeliever alike—reason redeemed for its true purpose by the work of Christ.

Before introducing the characteristic features of the State's response to divine law, let me quote an excellent account of the place of law in the Bible:

> God's lordship over the world and over the societies of men is not left in Scriptures as an abstract principle, but finds expression in concrete ordinances given for the regulating of man's relations with the material world, on the one hand, and with his fellow men on the other . . . This law is not an Old Testament conception which is, as it were, a mere approximation or moderately successful guess at the requirements of God, which is outdated by the Gospel. On the contrary, it is the instrument of God's love which ever regulates the life of men as creatures in history, and which, while it is fulfilled by the Gospel, will never be superseded until the end of the world. . . . To take this Biblical category of law seriously would deliver a good deal of Christian thinking from the confusion in which at present it stands. For example, it is sometimes put forward as a matter of debate among Christians whether they are or are not justified in compromising the law of love for the sake of justice. If we lay hold on the Scriptural insistence that God's law is an instrument of His love, we shall be at home with the related idea that justice in the communities of men is the mode by which love becomes operative. The Bible is not at home with the question of compromise, because it does not deal in ideals or principles, but with the service of God in and through the concrete conditions of man's historical existence. The service of God is the love of man, and love of man in the large-scale life of society expresses itself in the struggle to establish and maintain justice with freedom on a basis of material security.[10]

---

[10] Alex Miller, *The Presbyter*, 2 (1944).

What then, may be said about State action in these areas of political decision not directly affected by the existence of the church or by its characteristic life and concerns? Does consideration of the State's task yield the possibility of reference to the divine law through which all things are subject to Christ? It is perhaps foolish to risk making the broad general comments which alone are possible within the scope of this essay, but they may serve to indicate directions along which careful enquiry would be profitable.

The activity of the State is to create justice and to restrain evil. But this task it pursues for the sake of the citizens who, as neighbours, are bidden to love one another, and not in the interest of an absolute impersonal justice, or an indestructible world order. This service consists, it is true, in the establishment of an external order, but this order is not for the sake of the State's own prestige. In itself, it is not holy or good, nor has it any intrinsic worth. "Righteousness" has, in Scripture, a soteriological reference. It is associated with the vindication of the poor and oppressed, and can never be dissociated from mercy and grace. To philosophize about the bestowal of righteousness upon creatures, we must begin from the revealed righteousness of God and not from a rationalization of human or natural justice. In every age, and in every society, some agreed conception of justice must be reached in political thinking before the society can live together in peace and blessing; nor can it be doubted that the history of political thought and action since the time of Christ bears marks of His lordship over earthly States. This is true of Marxist developments, as much as of the growth of Social Service States. These modern developments, like the earlier development of liberal-democratic political theory, are not "Christian"; indeed their effect may be to increase the temporary danger that the State will become an instrument of human selfishness rather than of divine justice; but their significance can be most clearly discerned in relation to the Gospel, and in their own way they bear testimony to its truth. Also they bear witness to an increasing apprehension of depths in the justice commanded by God which hitherto had not been plumbed. This apprehension is faulty, and the response may in practice be perverse.

Granted the primary point that State action should be for the sake of persons, and that its major concerns are to be understood in relation to the divinely instituted order of redemption, there are four spheres wherein moral responsibility may be clarified with reference to divine law.

(a) It is the task of the State to ensure the primacy of human law over its own ideas and interests: to establish the rule of law and the impartial administration of human justice (conceived with reference to humanity rather than to impersonal natural order), so that a measure of personal freedom and integrity is preserved for the individual and the social groups within the State.

(b) The State must also ensure the safety of the community from external enemies and from internal disintegration. A national government which does not treat its Home Office and its war potential with the utmost seriousness is not worthy of confidence. But its penal methods, and its practice of warfare, involve serious moral issues which need constant and careful scrutiny.

(c) The cultivation of mental and physical health, and of civil virtues, is again the responsibility of the State. The standards it accepts must be based on an understanding of humanity, must be appropriate to the best kind of civilization which man has achieved, and must be modified wherever possible and reasonable by distinctively Christian insights.

(d) It is the responsibility of the State to strive for a right solution of the economic problems which so intimately affect civilized living. Here, as in the other spheres, the subjection to divine law of State action in regard to Labour, Industry and Trade, Agriculture, Finance, etc., needs long and careful explication. Perhaps the most important aspect of the present political situation is the possibility of vastly increased control of man's environment and conduct through the resources of scientific thinking. Is it not perhaps true to suggest that this also should be understood with reference to the purpose of God established in Jesus Christ; His purpose, namely, to elicit from men a fully moral response, in political as well as individual life, to His saving righteousness?

(1947)

CHRIST AND CREATION

SINCE THE REPUDIATION OF MARCION IN THE SECOND CENTURY, THE Church has firmly professed its belief in God as the Maker and Preserver of all things both visible and invisible. There has been little, if any, serious controversy about the bearing of this doctrine. It had to be pressed with particular force, and sometimes in new terms, whenever the Church had to meet the ancient counter-belief that the natural world springs from an evil root. For the rest, at any rate in Western Christendom, the chief interest in this part of Christian doctrine seems to lie in the possibility of establishing and illuminating the belief by way of natural science or philosophy, though errors of a dualist or of a pantheist kind have always been available as targets for the conscientious theologian. The impression given (and perhaps in these circumstances it is hardly surprising) is that the doctrine seemed to be complete in terms of the Creed's first article. The texts which speak of Christ as the mediatorial agent of creation were not essential to its statement. Their proper bearing is in the second article, where the clause "by whom all things were made" underlines the uniqueness of Christ but is not intended to have any decisive effect on the doctrine of creation. With the growth of the modern world-view, these texts have become something of a puzzle, even when the doctrine of creation has not been questioned.

This situation has altered, suddenly and remarkably. In Biblical theology the attention paid to eschatology has brought a new interest in the theme of creation as its necessary counterpart. This has entailed much learned discussion of the affinities and disparities between New Testament thought-forms and those current in the Hellenistic and Rabbinic environments. The same kind of problem has been raised about the Old Testament and the "Myth and Ritual" patterns of the Near East. The Bible is now being expounded by typological exegetes who claim to find in it a widespread "ktisiological pattern" which suggests that "the six days of creation are renewed in all the redemptive events of history."[1] In the field

---

[1] L. S. Thornton, *The Dominion of Christ*, p. 48. The phrase "ktisiological pattern" comes from the essay by Gösta Lindeskog in *The Root of the Vine* (ed. Fridrichsen). I have not

of Systematic Theology there is Barth's massive restatement of the doctrine in Christocentric terms, offered in the course of his *Dogmatik* (Vol. III, 1). There is the highly significant Roman Catholic response from H. U. von Balthasar (*Karl Barth: Darstellung und Deutung seiner Theologie*) which has much to say about the handling of the creation theme. And from Lutheranism there is a most impressive chapter in Edmund Schlink's *Theologie der lutherischen Bekenntnisschriften*. All this may be viewed as part of the Church's effort to recover the full measure of faith and of theological understanding. But the effort, at any rate in respect of the doctrine of creation, is no more than under way, as two observations may demonstrate.

First, there is plenty of room for scholarly debate about the form and the place of a specific "theology of creation" both in the Old Testament and in the New. Does the Old Testament "doctrine of creation" develop simply in the form of a presupposition which is ultimately subordinate to a central theology of election and covenant? Or is it a major theme, one which "cannot reasonably be relegated to a subordinate place" and became a twin focus for religious life and thought alongside the Exodus theme when the foundation of the kingdom in Israel brought the cult of the divine king into Yahwism?[2] Is there in the New Testament a profound and deliberate doctrine of creation, expressed in a widespread pattern of images, or does the topic occur only in a few passages whose bearing is Christological rather than cosmological? In either case, have we fully entered into the use made of Gen. 1–2, Prov. 8, and associated passages by the Christian writers? Was a Christocentric doctrine of creation a major theme of early Christian thought because "Christ's resurrection is effective not only in the redemption of mankind, but in the true and perpetual creation of the world"? If so, what precise steps were taken, and why, to mark off this doctrine from current political mythology on the one hand and from Greek philosophical speculation on the other?[3] There is no room to take up these problems in detail in an essay of this character, but the implications of accepting one kind of integrated account rather than another may appear from what follows.

A second observation suggests that matters have not yet come to a head

---

seen Lindeskog's *Studien zum N.T. lichen Schöpfungsgedanken*, but I assume from the anticipatory essay that it has affinities with Thornton's work and also with Austin Farrer's *Rebirth of Images* and *A Study in St. Mark.*

[2]Lindeskog adopts this second point of view (*The Root of the Vine*, p. 4) and brings a charge of inconsistency against Gerhard von Rad who, on my reading of his Genesis commentary (*Das Alte Testament Deutsch* 2/4), does not. Lindeskog seems anxious to have the best of all possible worlds and has hardly managed to produce an integrated account. Lionel Thornton has firmly made up his mind about the form and place of a creation-cycle of imagery conflated with the redemptive history, but like his beloved Greek Fathers he does not expose the technical weighing of pros and cons to the full light of day.

[3]The quotation is from a most illuminating essay criticizing the formula *creatio ex nihilo*, by Arnold Ehrhardt in *Studia Theologica*, Vol. IV, fasc. I (1951).

so far as modern discussion of the doctrine of creation is concerned. It is taken from the field of ecumenical discussion. The Bishop of Durham, in a somewhat disgruntled report on the Evanston Assembly of the World Council of Churches, said that in his opinion both the theologies dominant in the discussion of the "Main Theme" "lacked the right starting point in the *doctrine of creation* and the right goal in the *Beatific Vision*, with the call to holiness as the way to it. . . . It was a happy thing that Anglicans, Eastern Orthodox and English Methodists found themselves joining hands in a plea for a more comprehensive theology of creation, incarnation and sanctification."[4] It is a healthy thing that there should be injected into ecumenical debate the theme so notably stated by an earlier scholarly Bishop of Durham, B. F. Westcott, in his essay *The Gospel of Creation*. We have remarked that the doctrine of creation has not played a lively part in Christian thought and imagination for some time past. It has been formally professed in much the same way by Churches of all traditions, but it has not been explicitly related to the person and work of Jesus Christ, nor to the doctrines of the Holy Spirit and of the Church. Westcott chose to dwell upon a subject which some, he knew, would regard as "a mere matter of speculation, or a curious fancy of a past age." His conclusion was: "The thought that the Incarnation, the union of man with God, and of creation in man, was part of the divine purpose in creation, opens unto us, as I believe, wider views of the wisdom of God than we commonly embrace, which must react upon life."[5] This theme has been taken up by Anglican theologians of our own day, notably by those otherwise very different thinkers Lionel Thornton and Charles Raven.[6] We shall return to Dr. Raven's work at another point. But it will not be readily agreed, on the ecumenical scene, that here the Anglicans—or anywhere else their fellow petitioners—can supply a ready-made "right starting point" for the discussion of all other theological matters. Nor, of course, does the Bishop say so. The point, with which I agree, is that false or impoverished understanding of the doctrine of creation may be among the factors which keep the Churches apart. But when the time is ripe for this to be examined on the ecumenical level there may be much that we all have to learn.

Having noted some points at which the Church is beginning to show a lively concern with the doctrine of creation, we can turn to look at secular thought, for there too the situation has altered. It was a fairly safe assumption, until very recently, that any religious person (which means most people for some of their time) would subscribe to the first article of the Christian creed in some form or other. But when that article is ex-

---

[4] *The Bishoprick*, published at the Diocesan Office, Durham (Nov. 1954).

[5] *The Epistles of St. John* (1884), p. 328.

[6] *Experience and Interpretation*, the second series of Gifford Lectures (1953), particularly chs. IV-VI.

pounded in the penetrating terms of Luther's *Larger Catechism*, those who would still confess it with their lips can at best only faintly believe with their mind that:

> This is what I mean and believe, that I am a creature of God; that is, that He has given and constantly preserves to me my body, soul, and life, members great and small, all my senses, reason and understanding, food and drink, clothing and support, wife and children, domestics, house and home. Besides, He causes all creatures to serve for the necessities of life—sun, moon, and stars in the firmament, day and night, air, fire, water, earth, and whatever it bears and produces, birds and fishes, beasts, grain, and all kinds of produce, and whatever else there is of bodily and temporal goods, good government, peace, security.

This belief has worked almost with the strength of an intuition in the lives of religious persons, even in those who would not regard themselves as committed or instructed Christians. But now, even for some instructed Christians, it is a form of pious words which has to maintain itself with difficulty against a curious alliance of rival intuitions: first, that the things enumerated come to us through a history of nature in which inscrutable Fate plays a considerable part; and secondly, that it lies within man's power and destiny to master the raw material of history and of nature in whatever way seems good to him. Only those who have great piety can now trust God to give; the rest of us take for ourselves as best we can and put up with mishaps with such dignity as we can muster. This is not the place to analyse the acids of modernity which have corroded simple faith in the Creator and His work. Among them, no doubt, there is the new scientific view of the world. But there we must take into account the paradoxical situation exposed by Mr. Michael Foster, who has shown how much the rise of modern natural science owes to the Christian doctrine of creation.[7] This particular acid is not a recrudescence of the notion that the natural world springs from an evil root. Historical scepticism, which became the handmaid of Nihilism, is perhaps a different matter. Two main positions have been established, outside the paths of traditional Christian thinking, which offer alternative ways of dealing with historical existence. Both of them are based on a complete rejection first of Greek cosmology and ontology, and secondly of the Christian doctrine of creation. In dialectical materialism, to borrow a phrase from A. C. Craig's *Preaching in a Scientific Age*, there is "the vision of man's mind displacing God as the creative intelligence of the world." In atheist existentialism, there is a defiant acceptance of "being here" without knowing the whence or the whither. Neither of these positions involve any decision about the origin of the world, though Communist dialecticians would presumably be ready to pronounce on the matter in scientific terms if it should become important

---

[7]*Mind*, 43 (1934), pp. 446ff.; 44 (1935), pp. 439ff.; 45 (1936), pp. 1ff.

to do so. The professed Christian doctrine has been rejected as dogmatism in a field where men have no basis for being dogmatic, and this rejection cannot, as I suppose, be challenged on philosophical grounds. It is true that some scientists advance, as the more probable hypothesis, a theory of an origin in finite time for the natural universe in its present state. But some British astronomers are working out what they hope is a better hypothesis to explain the past out of which the universe has come. They are testing the possibility of a law for the continuous creation of matter. Aristotle would not have been disturbed by this; nor would Heraclitus:

> This world, the same for all of us, none of the gods nor of the humans has made; it has always been, and is, and will be, an ever-living fire, flaring up in parts, in parts dying down.[8]

It still seems unlikely, as it did to Aquinas, that any doctrine of creation can be established philosophically. The question is whether the full Christian doctrine can still be established theologically and whether it is our duty to God and to the world that we should do this again. If there is such a pressing duty, our power to fulfil it, like that of the early Christians, may depend very much on a renewed conviction that all things have been created by God *through Christ* the eternal Son who was incarnate and who suffered under Pontius Pilate and rose from the dead on the third day.

But the secular thinker, confronted by what he must regard as polemical theology, will at once make a further point which the theologian should heed for his own good. There are good reasons for suspicion about religious dogmatism in matters of this kind. We can look back to the ancient civilizations of Egypt and Babylon, where considerable knowledge about the constitution of the world and the technical manipulation of its resources was held in the form of religious secrets. There was also "an official mythology, transmitted in priestly corporations and enshrined in elaborate ceremonial, telling how things came to be as they are."[9] The scientific approach to what exists, in contrast with the religious, is often traced back to the "Ionian Enlightenment" of the sixth century B.C., and it is mentioned as a favourable circumstance "that these communities, to put it briefly, were not priest-ridden."[10] Thales was able to shake off priestly fetters and talk constructively about the world, its constitution and its origin, *without letting Marduk in.* Now the point is not to be irreligious for the sake of being irreligious, nor yet because religion necessarily makes a man a poor scientist. It is the political significance of priestly corporations and of religious mythology which draws down well-merited suspicion. The political character of the term *cosmos* (*mundus*) in Graeco-Latin thought was doubtless appreciated by early Christian writers. "The Hellenistic theolo-

---

[8]Fr. 30 Diels I, 84.1ff.
[9]Benjamin Farrington, *Greek Science*, pp. 27–31.
[10]E. Schrödinger, *Nature and the Greeks*, p. 54.

gians stated it quite plainly that 'the king is the last of the gods and the first of men,' the connecting link between the supra-lunar *cosmos* and the sub-lunar *chaos*." When the king was acclaimed as *Epiphanes* (the present god) and *Soter* (the saviour), this "was not rank flattery but religion, the result of strong sentiments based upon a genuine and, in its way, competent theological and philosophical attempt at understanding the universe as a political system with a monarchical constitution."[11]

The religious leopard does not change his spots, and Christianity has in this world the form of a "religion," often without showing any serious self-criticism in this respect. Further, a critical observer of the British scene, to go no further afield, might conclude that an official mythology enshrined in elaborate ceremonial with royal personages at its heart has not lost its religio-political usefulness. The same critical observer would also be inclined to say that the New Testament witness to Jesus Christ as Lord and Saviour of the world looks like the supreme and consummating example of religio-political mystery-mongering, an impression which seems to be confirmed by extravagant attempts to commend Him as one who acted within the Godhead at the creation of all things.

I do not suggest that these secular observations should frighten the theologian away from a clear New Testament theme, nor that they should influence his handling of it, except perhaps in one respect which does not impair the proper substance of his work. The quotation from Luther's *Catechism* shows more clearly than do most of the available formal statements that what is professed in the first article of the Creed reaches down to the simplicities of which a man is most conscious when he lives humbly in this world. But it has an equally intense bearing on the great complexities of historical and political organization. If it is to be treated as one of the great themes of Christianity, as undoubtedly it is one of the great themes of "religion," it must be expounded with care and responsibility, the emphases placed where the Bible places them, and perhaps with a reserve which matches that of the Biblical writers in both the Old and the New Testaments.

"God has spoken to us in a Son, through whom also He made the world."[12]

"He has delivered us from the dominion of darkness and transferred us to the kingdom of his beloved Son, in whom we have redemption, the forgiveness of sins. He is the image of the invisible God, the firstborn of all creation; for in him were all things created . . . through him, and for him."[13]

That is the particular theme, to be proclaimed "in faith," with which

[11]Ehrhardt, pp. 18–22.
[12]Heb. 1:1–2.
[13]Col. 1:13–16.

this essay is concerned. In the remainder of the essay I shall consider its presentation under some aspects which call for well-informed theological decision. This piecemeal approach, on the basis of two isolated statements of the theme whose exegesis I am taking for granted,[14] is perhaps excusable if I am right in supposing that current discussion of the doctrine of creation is still in the exploratory stage.

The theme has to be proclaimed "in faith" and it is "by faith" that it must first be held true. It is necessary first to explain how, when we say "by faith," we are not saying "by the speculative imagination" or "by the superstition which produced the ancient creation-myths of Babylon or Egypt or even Greece." The faith of Israel, which produced the very unmythical confessions in Gen. 1 and 2, and the faith by which Christians understand the world to have been framed by the Word of God, are not of that order. In both cases, no doubt, it is a matter of holding an intellectual opinion of grounds which lack theoretical certainty. In Israel's case, however, it is a matter of acknowledging that the whole of life has been set in a pattern and direction for which no sufficient natural reason can be discovered. The pattern, like the direction, is one of *gratitude*; gratitude to one who is not to be counted among natural factors but who calls for divine worship as Israel's *wholly gracious God*. This gratitude was evoked in Israel by the calling and the deliverance from Egypt and by the covenant relationship offered and accepted at Sinai. Historically it may be true that this characteristic faith of Israel was not fully articulated until the promised land fell wholly under the control of the early monarchy, and by that time other factors—notably the pattern of Canaanite religion— had their part to play. It was at that period most probably that the response of gratitude took concrete form in the production of an integrated tradition depicting the past out of which David's kingdom had come. This tradition included God's earlier call and covenant with Abraham, and a pre-history of that remarkable choice running back to a "beginning" when heaven and earth were created. The whole tradition expressed and perpetuated a faith which marked off Israel from all other nations as "the People of God," bound to a strictly supernatural God whose distinctive demands and promises were pressed by the prophets upon an audience all too ready to be as other nations were.

The pattern of gratitude was enriched and deepened, and this is particularly true of Israel's gratitude to God for *an originating act of creation*. It is the prophets who had to wrestle with the disaster of the Exile and the seeming collapse of the covenanted purpose, Jeremiah and Second Isaiah, who bring this theme most obviously to the fore. When all the documents of faith are taken into account—later strands in the Penta-

---

[14]For the exegesis of the second passage I would acknowledge a particular debt of gratitude to W. D. Davies, *Paul and Rabbinic Judaism*, especially ch. 7: "The Old and the New Torah: Christ the Wisdom of God."

teuch, prophetic writings, wisdom literature and apocalyptic—the total impression is clear. Israel acknowledged by word and life a God with power over all things as His creatures, and of a goodness which merited absolute trust. This pattern of gratitude had been evoked in history; it was one to be sustained in history; and the truth of it, which present history could only partly authenticate because of sin's disordering power, would appear in history at the consummation. That is the ground of Old Testament faith in God the Creator.

Behind the New Testament confessions of God the Creator, and especially behind those which speak of creation through Christ, there is a grateful acknowledgment, of this same order, that God has disclosed His power over all things and all circumstances, including now the whole gamut of rebellious devices used by creatures estranged into some wrong allegiance; that He has wrought "an act of justification that penetrates back to the very beginning and sets man's life on the basis of God's creative purpose";[15] that He has disclosed an abiding love for what He made by raising from the dead the body of the crucified Saviour "having reconciled to Himself all things, whether on earth or in heaven, making peace by the blood of his Cross."[16]

Belief that all things have their origin in a divine act of creation, done in perfect freedom, perfect wisdom, and perfect love, is thus to be accepted as one moment in a given pattern of gratitude. But the *truth* of this belief is not settled merely by finding that one's life has been set in such a pattern, nor by managing to maintain it, knowing all too clearly that the brink of chaos and despair is only just behind one's heels. Does this gratitude reflect and embody the truth? In terms of Biblical logic, the reply to this urgent question is that we must strive for an ever deeper understanding of that which has evoked the grateful faith, but there can be no final assurance until the truth appears at the end of history. On the first point in that reply a Christian will say that what was given in Israel's experience before Christ, like that which is given elsewhere apart from Israel and from Christ, does not provide adequate ground for satisfactory understanding; but the incompleteness of Israel's experience is remedied when the Christ to whom it pointed appeared on the earthly scene. He will also say, taking up the second point, that in this coming of Christ there was a veiled enactment of the consummation, so the truth about divine creation has been disclosed eschatologically in the form of an open secret.[17]

But Christ came on the earthly scene, not in the role of Creator but in the role of Reconciler. By faith He is worshipped as Lord and as Saviour

---

[15]T. F. Torrance, "The Atonement and the Oneness of the Church," *Scottish Journal of Theology*, 7 (1954), 262.

[16]Col. 1:20.

[17]I take this to be the meaning of "mystery" in Eph. 1:9–10.

of the world; the effect of His coming may be described as a "new creation." But by what right is he worshipped as "the beginning of God's creation"[18] where the reference is to Gen. 1 and 2; that is, to the accomplishing long ago of heavens and of an earth made by the word of God (2 Pet. 3:4)? It has been argued that the Fourth Evangelist (John 1:3) "turns the idea of a creation which was accomplished once for all at the beginning into that *which to the human mind appears* as a continuous process."[19] But this interpretation, despite the reservations implicit in the italicized words, tends to obscure the real distinction between the divine works of creation and of reconciliation, and I do not think the Fourth Evangelist meant to do so. It is a presupposition of Biblical thinking that there is a line of salvation-history which runs forward to the consummation and also backward to *the* creation of all things—that is, to an event where God established a theatre for the historical enactment of the covenant of grace. That which was done "in the beginning" is no doubt fairly said to have been recapitulated as an act of reconciliation in the midst of time. But there is no confusion in the Christian witness between an act of creation, done once for all, and an act of reconciliation, also done once for all. The two acts have different settings in the dimension of time, both in God's time and in our time. The act of creation brought man into existence as the responsible partner of God at the centre of an ordered world where there is room, both in time and space, for ages of history to unfold and for the Reconciler to appear as man for man. By what right is the Reconciler to be worshipped as co-agent with his Father in that original work of creation?

New Testament scholars have explained the various ways by which Jews and Greeks habitually expressed the relationship between God and the world. The explanations usually involved a Mediator, characterized as Logos, Wisdom, Son of God, Heavenly Man, active with God in the world's creation and able to intervene as the world's Saviour. When the first Christians found in Jesus a Saviour and Lord, it was an easy and natural step for them to clothe His person in this kind of imagery; and scholars have shown how the language of these explanations is taken into Christian service in passages where the cosmic role of Christ is affirmed. The religious and philosophical allusions which made such passages readily intelligible to the first readers are neither familiar nor convincing to the ordinary intelligent Christian of to-day, and I find it hard to suppose that some schooling in this technical background is either necessary or desirable for present believers, in order to assist their affirmation of Christ's cosmic role. It is important to observe that the texts in question (e.g. Col. 1:1–16; Heb. 1:1–2; John 1:1–3) are not calculated to express a particular

---

[18]Rev. 3:14.
[19]Ehrhardt, p. 40 (my italics).

cosmogony but to characterize Jesus. Further, it has been well said that it is "exegetically impossible to understand them of an eternal divine Son or Logos *in abstracto*, but solely of him in his unity with the man Jesus."[20] All our thought on these matters must therefore be controlled by what we know of Jesus in His historical work. But then it is extremely difficult to believe that He, the crucified and risen Man, embodies resources through which this universe has been made.[21] It is of no help, however, to imagine those resources under the figure of some divine cosmic magnitude, corresponding to the Logos or Wisdom of ancient religious philosophy, and then try to add this as an invisible factor to Jesus as we know Him. In any case, this is not how the Bible encourages us to think. We shall return to this problem of philosophical categories before long. Meanwhile, let us attempt to make a direct statement of the New Testament affirmation whose logic we have to reproduce in our own responsible faith without leaning on the language and thought-forms of first-century religious philosophy.

What is it that moves the believer to worship Christ as co-agent of the creation? The answer, I think, is that Jesus Christ has brought *man* into existence, historically and securely, as the responsible partner of God to whom the rest of creation has been subjected; and he has done so precisely at the point where man had incurred the doom of annihilation (cf. Heb. 1–2). This mighty work is attributed to Jesus, the Messiah of Israel, who brought his own people—and in principle therefore the rest of the cosmos—to a crisis where God's final judgement was enacted in a veiled form and the coming dispensation of a new creation was inaugurated. What issues from this crisis is man, raised from death for eternal life in a new context of heavens and earth wherein dwelleth righteousness (2 Pet. 3:13). Christ Himself, and those who are "in Christ" as in a "new Adam," have already entered upon this life, but the appropriate environment is one for which we still wait. The dominion of Christ, and of man in Christ, is presented to us in and through this eschatological detail. What it means is that Israel's faith, Israel's election by God, Israel's covenant-history with God, and also therefore the original work of creation which is presupposed in that history, are all fully and finally authenticated.

This statement raises two further problems which must also be deferred for a little while: the problem posed by the anthropocentric char-

---

[20]H. U. von Balthasar, *Karl Barth: Durstellung und Deutung Seiner Theologie*, p. 218.

[21]The difficulties as I see them will be mentioned in the last section of the essay. Having now seen the Isenheim altar in its present setting at the Musée d'Unterlinden in Colmar, I now realize that an artist can do what science and philosophy cannot do for me. The awful figure hanging from the flattened arc of the cross-beam is the very man, brought to the nadir of humiliation; but he is the one who came to what was and remains his own possession and the resurrection panel only confirms what is already evident, that he is able to subdue it all unto himself.

acter of the whole story, and the problem of whether or not there are discernible signs in the history of nature that creation has this Christocentric ordering. Before passing to the last part of the essay, to which three problems have now been relegated, there is one further point to be made.

This testimony is taken seriously only in faith, and then it has to be acknowledged that the agent of the mighty works is not a man ultimately separate from God, nor a divine magnitude ultimately separate from God, nor a divine magnitude ultimately separable from the man Jesus, but is the second person of the God who must henceforth be acknowledged as the Holy Trinity. The dominion and love which are expressed in the work are the dominion and love of Jesus Christ who is very man, but they are, identically, the dominion and love of the Father to whom He explicitly gave perfect obedience, and, identically, the dominion and love of the Spirit by whose work they are carried into effect and we are persuaded of them. It is this awareness of *God* in Christ which finally sets men free to say that in Jesus Christ they have encountered the Creator of the world. Only the divine architect and builder of history could display such perfect dominion over its disorder; only the archetypal lover of men could bring to our race the assured hope and present anticipation of faithful partnership with God. Looking to Christ, therefore, we should make the grateful confession that the ground of all existence is simply the divine claim and promise which have been made good by His ministry and resurrection and which were *His* claim and promise before ever the world was. This means, however, that some decision has to be taken as to the form in which He acted with God in the beginning. By which of the available titles can this best be expressed? We could claim, I think, the authority even of the Fourth Evangelist for saying: by the title "Son of God," the hypostatic correlate of the title "Father." He is the Son who as such fulfilled the roles ascribed sometimes to Word, Wisdom, Torah; a son destined by eternal generation to be man for us men. The deed done in time by the incarnate Son is one into which the agent's being was wholly poured before the worlds were made; what is expressed in the history of the Son of Man is the perfect utterance of what He always is as Son of God. There lies the point of the contention that it is Christ's resurrection which is effective, not only in the redemption of mankind, but in the true and abiding creation of the world. But it does not follow, I submit, that creation is to be treated as a seemingly continuous process, nor that it should be amalgamated with conserving and redeeming processes, after the fashion of pagan religions inspired by the cycles of nature.

There are certain obstacles for the modern mind which hamper any full and free expression of faith in the cosmic role of Christ, and we shall glance at three of them by way of conclusion. Faith is not achieved by negotiating these obstacles. Rather is their negotiation one of the delicate and exacting tasks to which the believer must address himself if he is to understand and enjoy that which he believes.

First among these is the fact that we approach Jesus Christ with pre-conceived ideas of what the creation is, and therefore with preconceived ideas about the resources adequate for its production, and so with pre-conceived ideas about the character of a possible world-Creator. The pres-ent philosophical climate is unusually helpful in this respect, for philosophers are now disposed to utter solemn warnings about the stu-pidity of metaphysical attempts to measure reality as a whole. Neverthe-less, there are factors which militate against Christian belief. Some kind of world-picture is in everyone's mind. Most of it may be the fruit of sheer positivist description, but the elements of description tend to be accom-panied by "explanatory notes" of one kind or another. The main trend of the "notes" can usually be labelled either "Idealist" (with an "animist" flavour) or "Naturalist" (with a "materialist" flavour). In the ancient world the "Naturalists" fought a losing battle. The cosmos, as anciently imag-ined, was one that could be explained, necessarily and absolutely, by pos-tulating the appropriate "ideas" and "souls." The modern picture, on the other hand, finds the fundamental cosmic reality in the multifarious forms of physical "energy" or "action" which are still being tracked down. The "Idealist" tradition has waged a vigorous and fruitful battle to keep "ideas" and "souls" in the picture at the most fundamental level, but the fact remains that if you talk nowadays about the creation of the world, it is no longer possible to brush aside the question of this amazing physical power and the control which lies behind its wonderful deployment. To offer an explanatory note which suggests that it is all a matter of "ideas" enter-tained by "souls" will hardly do. Therefore we tend to suppose that there is some root of absolute necessity in the ineluctable givenness of physical energy, and to this root, perhaps, can also be traced the ideal principles on which the world seems to be constructed. We hesitate to say that we have found the origin from which the world has come unless what we have found yields to our minds the reason of this absolute necessity. Jesus of Nazareth, even when He is presented in the most careful theological fullness, does not do this.

To this we may reply that what is being sought is the reason of a wholly fictitious absolute necessity. We can do this by calling on the existentialist critique of all notions that this is a stable meaningful world in and for itself. Alternatively, or by way of supplement, we can point to the growing conviction that what is most concrete, and therefore most actual, is not physical energy, nor yet souls with their traditional microcosmic status, but sheer event or eventful history. In this way it may be possible to

recover something like Luther's doctrine of creatures as *larvae Dei*:[22] entities instrinsically incomplete in themselves or when taken all together;
masks which carry an echo of the one complete Being who is using them
but which in themselves conceal Him in all His works and ways; "Dei
larvae, allegoriae, quibus rethorice pingit suam theologiam: they are meant,
as it were, to contain Christ."[23]

The second obstacle is to be found in the clearly anthropocentric character of Christian doctrine. The first two chapters of Genesis have for
their focus God's election of man; the rest of the creation is man's appropriate environment. It was relatively easy to think in this way in the ancient
world or in the Middle Ages. It is now very hard to imagine that the
history of nature can be explained, even in principle, by reference to
God's purpose with man. It savours very strongly of wishful thinking. At
the moment we are haunted by the notion that man's knowledge of the
hydrogen bomb and man's freedom to use it could destroy the species of
which we are members. But there is no reason to imagine that the Creator
would thereupon ring down the curtain and banish from the stage of
space-time the earth itself, the solar system, the Milky Way and all the
concourse of galaxies to which ours belongs. Nevertheless, the Christian
doctrine, with its emphasis on Christ not only as the Wisdom of God but
also as the Second Adam, calls for an anthropocentric view.

There is a strand of Christian thinking which has shown some awareness of what is involved. It was represented in the Alexandria of Clement
and Origen, among the Cambridge Platonists of the seventeenth century,
and now in the work of Charles Raven who finds in Christ the consummation of a principle "which enables both the highest development of the
individual parts and their full co-operation in an ordered society" and
which "seems to apply on every level from the atom to the saint."[24] For
Raven, Christ is "an adequate symbol of the divine," the perfect Son of
Man towards whom the creative process consistently points. He is mankind's example and representative, whose office it is to give the Spirit free
course and thus "to quicken sensitiveness, heighten vitality, remove cal-
lousness, and so enable response to the beauty and meaning and worth
of the world."[25] Raven has done his best to justify the belief that heaven
and earth exist for the production of human persons in community. He

---

[22]There is a useful note on this doctrine in P. S. Watson, *Let God be God*, pp. 76–81.
The doctrine is worth mentioning because it serves to give a better indication of what is
wanted than does Thomist doctrine, a point which Watson explains. Philosophers and
theologians must do a lot of work together if there is to be a new and satisfactory decision
as to what we are talking about when we say "creatures." My own view is that among the
philosophers it is Whitehead who has most to give.

[23]WA, XL.1, 463 and 469, with the German words translated.

[24]*Experience and Interpretation*, p. 145.

[25]*Experience and Interpretation*, p. 151.

has looked honestly at nature and pointed to the many ways in which it seems to carry the trademark of Christ—a suffering Christ, let it be remembered—who supremely symbolizes the creative process moved everywhere by love.

It is easy to criticize this story, by questioning its conformity to the Biblical grounds adduced in its support, or by noting to what extent Raven's world turns out to be Western man's dream of Paradise and the porch thereinto. But it cannot be dismissed like that. The history of nature is coming under man's dominion to an increasing degree; it is being increasingly permeated by man's purposes; and the effect is not wholly detrimental. Is not this a token, however ambiguous or proleptic, that it is already permeated by the mind and will which received historical expression in the man Jesus Christ? The mind and will by which mankind tends to permeate the cosmos independently must of course be transformed if they are to become the mind and will of Christ. But signs of this transformation are not altogether lacking in the changing pattern of man's thought and purposes.

The last obstacle to be mentioned is a failure in practice rather than a difficulty in theory, though it will not be overcome by practice without careful theological assistance. It is unlikely that we shall enjoy a renewed faith in the Christocentric doctrine of creation until the Holy Spirit moves men to a more distinguished practical response of gratitude and obedience in the ordinary business of living. We can look back to the practical piety of Luther's *Catechism* and recognize nostalgically that the pattern and direction of life which it promoted had a distinction which is not there in modern substitutes. We remember the *joie de vivre* of medieval artists and scholars and craftsmen. We find it difficult at present to imagine that this universe has been framed with special reference to God's purpose in Christ with mankind. Such a thesis, which may be defended on a broad view at some risk of special pleading to keep up public morale, is very hard indeed to defend when one descends to details like the domestic cat or the spiral nebula in Andromeda. The medieval Church was singularly ready to keep such eccentric details in the picture; it fitted them into its *Speculum Naturale*, carved them in stone upon its cathedrals, and thus made them media for the worship of Christ. With more reservations, we remember also the confident Christian contributions which have been made to law, politics, philosophy and learning, which in their own way expressed a firm belief in Christ's dominion. Can we look forward to a movement of the Spirit by which some men will be empowered to show in modern terms the symbols of Christ's dominion as Creator of the world? It is for the artist to release the symbols which chiefly move us to gratitude. It is for the technician, the politician, the ordinary worker, the educator, to release the symbols which chiefly point to new obedience.

The theologian, as part of his own work, can point to the poverty of our present condition and to the riches by which that poverty ought to be banished. What he can also do, in common with all his brethren of mankind, is to do right, entrust his soul to a faithful Creator, and pray, and prepare if need be to suffer, for new integrity in the humble ways of life.

(1956)

CHRISTOLOGICAL
UNDERSTANDING

I

To work in the personal service of another human being is, once more, the least coveted role in human society. Young persons may have to do this as part of their apprenticeship. Shop assistants and bus conductors must do it, but can protect themselves to some extent from the thought of indignity by "serving the management" rather than the customers. Personal secretaries can bask in the dignity of their boss and enjoy the game of managing him—and can leave him for another if they are defeated or bored. Domestic servants, and more especially those who must serve their employers or their employers' "guests" at table, are no longer in a worse position to look after themselves than are others engaged in direct personal service; but this occupation, lightly undertaken to earn money in a vacation, has revealed to many students the perils and indignities of being in personal service to their fellow men and women. They have tasted, in a greatly alleviated form and by uncommitted sampling, something which was a painful commonplace in Hellenistic society. It was scandalous for Jesus to interpret His own role, and to present the terms of discipleship, by using this model. But He did so, with the personal service of the table-waiter firmly in view.

Then, as now, the general idea of occupying oneself and expressing oneself in "service" was not unacceptable. To serve a respected householder or farmer, to serve the community in the apparatus of government, to serve God from some niche in the religious establishment, these were possible ways of enriching one's life and of giving to it value and meaning. (To serve a commercial enterprise is a quite recent addition to the list of worthy causes.) To serve one's mere fellow man who happens to be in need was not, and is not, comparably worth while. If done at all, it is done occasionally, as an act of condescension or as an act of religious obligation. Judaism conjoined love of neighbour with love of God. Indeed, any religion which expresses among other things a community's will to survive is likely to prescribe some form of neighbourly service to the needy. What is scandalous about the teaching and example of Jesus is the suggestion, embodied in His choice of model, that those who follow Him must spend themselves in direct personal service to any who call upon them, without calculation and without any safeguards of dignity. Their true dignity will emerge precisely in so doing, but it will not commend itself as such to those wise in the ways of this world. Nietzsche saw the point with rare clarity after it had been masked for centuries by the dignities of "Christendom." The disciples of Jesus will, it is true, be serving Him, serving, too, the "cause" which He embodies, and (so He assures them) serving God, by putting their resources at hazard in this way. But faith and obedience may have to do without the comfort of being able to regard Him, or His "cause," or the God whose name He invokes, as obviously adequate grounds from which to derive authentication for such a programme of living.

The scandal is aggravated when one reflects on that aspect of the public ministry of Jesus which particularly struck the theologians of "the Social Gospel" in the nineteenth century: His deliberate turning to the poor and the incompetent rather than to the able and influential. To help such lame dogs over their various stiles is a humane procedure, and indeed may be an important safeguard for the community against social collapse. But to make this the corner-stone in a policy for world-regeneration is utterly "unrealistic." Those who call for personal service most loudly and most frequently will always be "the poor." One need not hold them in contempt (though the "realistic" tendency is always in this direction), but to suggest that personal service to their manifold needs is the lever which alone will avail to transform and regenerate the world is folly. It is perhaps excusable and comprehensible and in some mysterious way right, in a Jewish religious leader, who identifies "the poor" with "the pious and therefore the oppressed"; but the actual conduct of Jesus can be neither justified nor explained in terms of that handy assumption. The "poor" to whom He turned were persons whom it is unrewarding to serve (even, one might add, on that assumption); and to give Himself to them in the humble role of *diakonos* was to lay Himself open to degradation and wasteful self-destruction. In doing precisely this, the Son of Man gave up his own life. But He did so with confidence that this would provide "for many" the means of procuring their emancipation (Mark 10:45).

Among "the many," first and most evidently, are those who hear the news about Jesus Christ, leap to lose their chains, and therefore receive it as "the word of the truth" (Colossians 1:5). In His case, they are persuaded, such spending of life in diaconal service has been authenticated, first in His own resurrection from the dead and now in His coming to them as their living Lord through the Holy Spirit to give them the freedom of faith. His lifetime of diaconal service was rooted in God. They do not, however, proceed by one short direct step to obey the injunction "Go and do thou likewise" (Luke 10:37). This would be to step aside from one religion of righteousness by works to another one—to "an impractical and inept idealism" which is even less appropriate to the condition of men and their world than whatever religion it is which they are ready to abandon. They do indeed turn to God from idols, to serve a living and true God (I Thessalonians 1:9)—a possibility to be joyfully welcomed in principle. But they serve Him first by the gratitude of faith; by acknowledging the grace with which He has emancipated them from the dominion of darkness and transferred them to the kingdom of His beloved Son "in whom we have redemption, the forgiveness of sins" (Colossians 1:13–14).

Their gratitude is for services which they can neither repay nor emulate. In the servant-manhood of Jesus they recognize the Christ of God, the authority of God's anointed Servant; they see deeper, and identify this authority as the authority of God Himself in person, the Lord of all who has come to men as a neighbour in this world to serve them in their deepest need. His service to them has turned them into accepted fellow servants with Jesus, in a service to the world which God Himself is giving in His Christ. Yet they dare not say: "I will therefore give myself as a Christ to my neighbour," until they have first suffered the judgement and transformation of human self-awareness out of which there emerges the qualifying clause: "just as Christ offered Himself to me." Vivid in their minds is the picture of Christ giving Himself to His disciples in the diaconal service of washing their feet. At the heart of that episode is the word to Peter, who had found in Jesus a cause to serve and a master to emulate: "If I do not wash you, you can have no part in me" (John 13:8). Those who are to serve must first let themselves be served. Only as beneficiaries of His unique personal service to them can they follow Jesus in freedom and light, being effectively emancipated from the darkness of this world's preoccupations. Among such preoccupations there is a certain interest in serving adequate causes or serving an adequate Lord, and the gratitude of faith includes testimony to the fact of having found such a Lord and such a cause. But the judgement and transformation in human awareness which Christian faith entails bring emancipation even from this subtle interest. In this life, believers are content to follow Jesus on the road of diaconal service whose end is the Cross. Those who make Christ's life their own believe that "when Christ, who is our life, shall be manifested," they with Him shall also be manifested in glory (Colossians 3:4); and such hope provides in them a steady source of discipline and determination without which it is hardly possible to continue steadfast on so inglorious a road. But those who are to tread it must do so as men *prepared* always to find that it is intrinsically inglorious—though dignities, graces, and gratifications *may* be added, and to reject them when offered, to tread the road grimly wearing a hair-shirt for its own sake, is as bad in its own way as to depend on service being ennobling. Those who are prepared for the road have their feet washed by Him into whose death they are baptized; and this ever-renewed foot-washing means ever-renewed emancipation from ungenerous and self-regarding preoccupations including those of a religious kind.

Discipleship therefore means actually following Jesus in the paths of mundane personal service to those who call out from conditions of need however crude. The parable of judgement (Matthew 25:31–46) speaks to men in this world whose fellow men are physically short of food and drink, actually lonely and unwelcome in society, short of clothes, in poor health, locked up in prison. Discipleship is judged by the actuality of mundane service which makes its own quite concrete and practical difference to their condition. The service must be offered in its own right and for its own sake, but it is, in fact, set by God in a dimension deeper than humanitarianism or social therapy. Those conditions of deprivation, incompetence, and bondage, are symbolically (and perhaps symptomatically) significant for the entire being and experience of every man in so far as he has not yet responded to the ministry of Jesus, Servant and Lord. He is ready to make our mundane service part of His own unique service; and what we have to offer may be viewed without presumption as a potential witness to, and vehicle for, the personal service which He alone can give. It bears witness, or may do so, in that it comes through servant-disciples who owe their freedom to services rendered; but more directly may it do so through its own intrinsic, but borrowed grace.

"As our heavenly Father has in Christ freely come to our aid, so we ought freely to help our neighbour through our body and its works, and each should become as it were a Christ to the other that we may be Christs to one another and Christ may be the same in all; that is, that we may be truly Christians." Luther's words express the hope of bringing the help of the Gospel, in, with, and under the practicalities of neighbourly help. It is not, in the last resort, for us to calculate for this; though what we can do "through our body and its works" is never dissociated from what we simultaneously provide "through our soul and its works," and we must reckon with the possibility that this will be used as God's vehicle for His own word. It is not, however, for the servant-disciple to assess what service is likely to be "spiritually profitable," nor how to make it so. Like a waiter, he is at the beck and call of everyone in that part of the room where he happens to be. Their calls for mundane service must be answered with mundane efficiency "through the body and its works."

II

So far, with assistance from Luther's *Treatise on Christian Liberty*, we have considered how the Christian is conformed to his Lord as "a perfectly dutiful servant of all, subject to all." The prospect is scandalous to anyone who wishes to conduct his life as an essay in self-fulfilment. Such a person (and he is alive in all of us) may, when he becomes a Christian, conspire with his obituarist to produce a career which both can regard as "self-fulfilment in a lifetime of service." By so doing he will have distorted in practice what he ought to have been giving. The neighbourly personal service open to an individual under the Cross is piecemeal. It lacks the self-justifying cohesion to which so satisfying an epitaph seeks to draw attention. An obituarist is professionally obliged to disregard the fact that a really Christian life is a life broken and thrown away. This is not to deny that God may grace such a life with fullness and dignity in His own way, and that hints of this may be vouchsafed even in this world's experience. It serves merely to stress the truth that a Christian "lives not in himself but in Christ and his neighbour . . . , in Christ through faith, in his neighbour through love."

But Christ whose accepted fellow servants Christians are is more than an exemplary individual. In Him, so faith acknowledges, the Son of God assumed the role of King and Priest whose office it is to make all creatures related with God and with one another in mutual grace and self-giving. Taking the form of a servant, born as man, humbled in obedience even unto death on a cross, He is now exalted, to be owned as Lord by every creature, to the glory of God the Father (Philippians 2:7–11). His service to "the many," which at present only believers accept and acknowledge, incorporates their emancipated lives into "a royal priesthood, a priestly kingdom." Of this, the Church is the visible embodiment. To live in Christ by faith is to take one's place in the community of His Church. The discipleship of each individual, called to live in his neighbour by love, is caught up into a corporate service which has direction, scope, and shape of its own. It is in this fellowship of service that believers receive their high privilege, granted by grace and secured only through the Holy Spirit, that God's own service to His world in the person of Jesus Christ should be mediated through their persons and their actual worldly service.

Before saying any more about this, a word of warning must be interposed. It is improper to treat participation in the Church's corporate service as one element, perhaps optional, in the whole service to which individuals are called. A calculated risk has been taken in this essay by adopting an order of discussion which might suggest such a view. It is more nearly true to regard the individual's personal service to his fellows as the developed expression of his Church membership—but not if this leads him to distort his service to men in life's common ways by twisting it into some kind of service to the Church and making it ecclesiastically meritorious. The discipleship of each individual is caught up into the corporate service of the Church and is constantly renewed, as we shall see, at that centre; but each service, corporate and individual, has its own distinct and proper shape. There is some truth in the impropriety of viewing participation in the Church's special and limited service as one element in the individual's total service. Luther took risks here when he fought to make plain the freedom with which a Christian man gives himself in service. It is, I believe, still necessary to do so.

The *direction* of all Christian service is sufficiently indicated by the phrase: "a diaconal service of reconciliation" (2 Corinthians 5:18, to be understood in the light of all that precedes that verse from 3:4 onwards, and with attention to chapters 8 and 9, where there is lavish and varied use of "diaconal" terminology).

The *scope* of reconciliation is the whole creation, viewed from Christ as its centre and now brought by His service under His dominion. To live in Christ by faith is therefore to have one's own small being rooted in that principle which gives cohesion to all things; in Him all fullness of God has chosen to dwell, that through Him God may reconcile to Himself all that is (Colossians 1:17, 19–20).

The first question is about the scope of the Church's own distinctive service. Its members have usually been unwilling to demarcate at all rigidly the frontiers of this new visible community; yet for some purposes it is proper to define them, and this rather precarious human decision can be safeguarded against the twin perils of arrogance and indifference if it is accompanied by recognition that the sphere of the visible Church and the sphere of Christ's Lordship do not in all respects coincide. The expression of Christian faith and life in diaconal service has for its scope a sphere of operation which transcends the apparent frontiers of the visible Church, but is nevertheless encompassed by Christ. He has defined this sphere, and He has done it not by first identifying Himself with the Church but first by identifying manhood with Himself. No human experience is alien to Him, and inasmuch as you do or do not render diaconal service to any human neighbour in need, you do it or don't do it to Him. (Matthew 25:44f.).

It is rightly said that there is a mystery here, a mystery of the presence, in the person of each actual needy neighbour, of the Lord "to whom to refuse anything is a monstrous sacrilege" (Calvin's comment on Matthew 25:40); and that Jesus wants His disciples to know about this mystery, so that their actual service may be cleansed from all taint of patronage and all will to impose. It is rash, however, to try to develop an understanding of this mystery—in terms, perhaps, of some "identity-mysticism"—lest the service should come to seem rewarding in a religious sense to him who gives it, when nothing more can be at stake than its being actually helpful to him who receives it. Yet Calvin's moralizing, however valid, may not be quite sufficient to bring out in the right way this mystery and its power to safeguard the quality of "obedient" service. Eschatological parables, as Hoskyns said, serve to strip us naked of transient preoccupations and little moral busynesses, so that ultimate facts and duties stand out in luminous simplicity. In this parable we hear how our lives are set in a fellowship of diaconal service where Jesus, the Christ of God, makes the call of the needy His own call and makes the answering word or gesture or helping hand His own as well. In Him it is all being justified, reconciled to God and sanctified, so that in the end it may be glorified.

The Church does not monopolize this fellowship of service; it knows about it and must bear explicit witness to it. It must do so by being itself a fellowship of service, in a way and a shape which are the more eloquent for being special and limited. This, however, raises a complicated question about scope which must be noticed before leaving that topic for the third one, which is shape. New Testament evidence about the Church's effort to express itself as a fellowship of service frequently suggests that such an effort, made as it is by believers, must be made in terms of the needs of believers. This is intelligible in the circumstances and it poses no great problem in a community which all the time is addressing itself with success to the task of drawing others in. With Christians for whom the whole of their society was "Christendom," no problem is raised at all. For us, however, the Church is a community whose domestic life can all too easily be shut off from the main stream of society, so that a self-contained expression of diaconal service within the fellowship of the Church has no witnessing power and is spoiled in its very character by a taint akin to incest.

In the course of transition from "Christendom" to present post-Christendom conditions, the Church has retained an interest in special activities and institutions through which, from the early days of "Christendom," it tried to extend diaconal service into the whole fabric of society. It now has to reckon with a general verdict that these are rightly conducted under an aegis other than its own. It may, indeed, concur with that verdict. The Church's special interest in these activities and institutions is not so central as it once was to its own, or anyone else's, concern. They are residual lines of penetration for the Church with its distinctive witness, but they cannot be regarded in this light without embarrassment.

This is germane to the question about *shape* for the Church's life as a fellowship of service. There is something to be said for working towards an answer beginning from need and not from willingness to serve, and beginning from need outside the Church's domestic life. Since face-to-face personal service to persons is a vulnerable and wearing occupation, the Church ought not to relax its corporate concern that teachers, doctors, nurses, welfare officers, prison visitors, be raised up from its own membership, to help in manning the relevant services and maintaining their quality. But a distinction between these vocations to service and those open to an accountant, an assistant in a public library, a saleswoman, or a garage mechanic, is not easily drawn under modern social conditions— and neither should we expect it to be, when the "waiter" model for diaconal service is kept in mind. The residual lines of penetration do not stand out with their former distinction. Alongside all such lines of direct personal service to persons, furthermore, there are the great service-complexes of the national establishment and of industry and of semi-public and private administrations—new material for theological evaluation only in the sense that this has traditionally been confined to "the State" in its varied manifestations, but now requires revaluation in a wider context and with more attention to the "personal" nature of service in these complexes. There is a give-and-take of service between the Church and all parts of this worldly network. The problems involved are treated elsewhere in this symposium.[1] They are mentioned here simply as a reminder of the rather puzzling conditions under which the Church must try today to shape its own life as a fellowship of service, and, in its *special and limited way*, be eloquent of the truth which it knows about through the Gospel of Jesus Christ. Traditions inherited from the apostolic age and from the epoch of Christendom are neither sacrosanct nor sufficient in new circumstances, though to consult such traditions, as preceding essays have helped us to do, is rewarding.

It is as a fellowship of believers that the Church must still shape its own life. In the conduct of its own peculiar affairs it can learn a great deal about human needs and can do experiments in the art of meeting them as a fellowship of believers. But as such it lives all the time in an open commitment to serving unbelievers, serving *with* unbelievers, and being served *by* unbelievers. No aspect of its domestic structure is insulated from the effects of such a commitment, least of all its structure for diaconal service.

When we move right into the Church's domestic life it is plain first of all that its members are united in a fellowship of service to God offered through Jesus Christ. This is personal service offered to a neighbour, for in Christ God has given Himself to His people as their God and as such He has become their neighbour. But He is not a neighbour who needs either man's work or His own gifts returned. He asks for faith. Faith expresses itself in worship; and worship is the surrender of human interests, in adoration, to a Lord whose influence upon the being and well-being of the worshippers they wholly accept and wholly trust. Because God blesses human beings in all acts of worship where self-preoccupation is lost in praise of His goodness, their "service to Him" is transmuted into a new experience of "being served." In this experience they are turned afresh towards neighbours on the other side, so to speak; towards their fellow men whose cause God has made His own in Jesus Christ.

Our human neighbour does need our resources; and if they are laid

---

[1][This essay originally appeared in *Service in Christ: Essays Presented to Karl Barth on His Eightieth Birthday*, ed. J. I. McCord and T. H. L. Parker (London: Epworth Press, 1966).]

open to *him* in an offer of personal service, no one can say what he will do with them—and with the person in whom they inhere. In this direction there is no question of faith in one's neighbour, no worship of humanity, no unconditional devotion even to its more worthy preoccupations. In direct association with the Church, as contributor to its special and limited service, the Christian participates in a service to men which has been distinguished since very early days (Acts 6:2) as "preaching the word of God" and "serving tables." In both respects the Church demonstrates by Christian discipleship how men can help one another, having first been helped by Christ. To divorce the two distinguishable aspects is always wrong. But it is right to observe that it is through the second motif, "serving tables," that the Church's special witness to diaconal service has been explicitly developed.

Christians who seek precise bearings from the New Testament for the shape and structure of obedience must take what comfort they can from experts in this field. It is evident that in New Testament times the Church paid explicit attention to the actualities of personal diaconal service, and shaped its life accordingly. How it did so is not very clear. Some of its members, presumably those who most obviously filled a role of personal assistants to their fellow men, attracted to themselves the title *diakonos* (Philippians 1:1; 1 Timothy 3:8–13); and *diakonia* is evidently the name (not, of course, in all cases) for one special activity among others, presumably of a "table-serving" kind. It is difficult to see what more should be made of the evidence than what stands in *A Platform of Church Discipline Gathered out of the Word of God*, presented to the Synod of Cambridge, New England, in 1649:

> The office and work of the Deacons is to receive the offerings of the church, gifts given to the church, and to keep the treasury of the church: and herewith to serve the *Tables* which the church is to provide for: the *Lord's Table*, the table of the *ministers*, and of such as are in *necessitie*, to whom they are to distribute in simplicity. (ch. VII, par. 3)

It is also difficult to hold back an opinion that something has gone wrong when such deacons are regarded as inferior personal assistants to the "priestly and ruling" ministers, with servant-status less essential to the fundamental structure of the Church than that of the clergy proper.

To be unconcerned about structure, to confine concern in the case of deacons to their clerical status, to assume that the economic realities of the Church's life (treasury-keeping) may casually be conformed to the world's current practices—all these attitudes may cloak a fundamental lack of concern for the *actuality* of diaconal service within and beyond the Church's domestic life. If so, they betray the Gospel and depart from original apostolic tradition. Less heinously, they could be merely symptoms of a high-minded attitude to sordid practicalities—which has its endearing side, though it is sinful and imperceptive. To suppose that the Church is engaged in a "spiritual service," which in principle is not impaired if its resources for practical mundane support are abused or squandered or left unused, is to work with false distinctions and ill-conceived priorities. It is tempting to say that, in this matter at least, the Church may find some significance in the lack of adequate help from tradition, and should let the contemporary situation structure its theology and its practice. After all, the whole point is to *serve*; and usually this means to be imposed upon, without imposing. But tradition, critically consulted, may help to renew and inform a concern for structure within the Church; and though, in diaconal service, it must be prepared for being imposed upon by men in their actual needs in the world as it is, its action must everywhere bear the stamp of standards imposed from a kingdom not of this world.

III

Luther's *Treatise on Christian Liberty* was a Christological demonstration that God's truth about His world and about human living shines out in Jesus Christ, but had been obscured and opposed in mediaeval ecclesiasticism. Luther helped it to shine out again as light; light in which men may find and develop genuinely human lives. To do this work of theological clarification is to give personal service to persons—and to invite obloquy by doing so, whether it be done with Luther's epoch-making incisiveness or with Barth's daunting thoroughness. Barth has provided the same positive help, but with thorough-going attention to the ways in which this truth is obscured and opposed in modern humanitarianism. In his *Church Dogmatics*, Volume IV, Parts 1, 2, and 3, he demonstrates how men live as beneficiaries of the Lord who became Servant, the Servant who became Lord; and how, by our engagement in diaconal service, His justification of us and His sanctification of us are concretely shown forth in prophetic declaration. Faith working through love expresses the hope in which man as such is called to live. This hope is true to a world where man is to live as the accepted partner of God, purged from the pride and healed from the sloth which corrupt his authentic humanity; and in this hope, truth prevails over falsehood. The truth shines out as a light in which all may live, and to the hidden realities of righteousness by faith and sanctification in love there is added the visible testimony of wisdom—knowledgeable practice. Authentic humanity comes to us from its source in Christ Jesus, whom God made our wisdom, our righteousness and sanctification, our emancipation (1 Corinthians 1:30); and in us, as in Him, the substance of knowledgeable practice is diaconal service.

"The true community of Jesus Christ is the society in which it is given to men to see and understand the world as it is, to accept solidarity with it, and to be pledged and committed to it" (*Church Dogmatics*, IV, 3, p. 780). Experience of this will vary with time and with place. Those who at present speak about it from a place in radically secularized societies tend to stress (cf. Hromadka) the unhelpfulness of "high-sounding doctrines, lofty ideals or moral demands and aims" and ask for greater readiness "to follow Christ's example of serving at the lowest levels of humanity." Readiness so to do should not, perhaps, entail complete neglect of service on other levels, including those where doctrines, ideals, demands, and aims are very much to the point; though it is right to observe that men sick from the effects of an ideological diet are not helped by having a rival ideological diet served up to their tables, particularly one which they have already rejected as debilitating. In every cultural situation at present wise diaconal service must have a more helpful content than that.

Barth's balanced and penetrating account of the world as it is, and of humanity pledged with Christ to solidarity with it and to service, rests on preparatory work done in Volume III, Part 2, the theological account of man as the creature of God. Those who are ready to be helped by Barth, but are not prepared to let him do their thinking for them, must make an effort to relate what he has to suggest (in Volume IV) about the actualities of life in service to his earlier analysis of manhood as being-in-encounter. To understand how man *is with* his neighbour and in limited ways *can be for* his neighbour, is to know the conditions of service. It is also to appreciate how, in diaconal service, the Church and the Christian should be *at their most human*.

Secular humanitarianism, like mediaeval ecclesiasticism, bears its own witness to God's truth, even while suppressing it by pride and wickedness. And secular humanitarianism may help the Christian community to learn (if it will learn from no other source) that it must come out from behind the protective masks of religiosity and self-interested ecclesiasticism and act with the unadorned integrity of generous men. The eleven-page discussion of possible confusions between "humanity" and "Christian love" (III, 2, pp. 274–85) gives salutary help in this matter. Christian diaconal service, though proceeding from love and renewed by love, is *essential humanity*; it stands or falls by that criterion, a fact easily obscured when it is conceived explicitly as the outworking of Christian love.

God's truth shines out and prevails in the wisdom of diaconal service; and, in a special and limited way, this fact can be focused in Church Order, which itself should at all points be eloquent of the Gospel. Church Order expresses the full life of the Body of Christ, and the expression of this particular aspect has to be related to the total structure by which that is done—a total structure which may be shaped by a central Papacy, an Episcopal Bench, a hierarchy of Church Courts, or a network of localized Church Meetings and Synods. My own experience falls within the last of these areas, and, unlike most professional theologians, it includes service as a deacon (and vivid youthful impressions of the diaconal practice observed in the village church where I grew up) in a pattern of Church Order derived by way of seventeenth-century Congregationalism from Calvin at Geneva. The practice involves the "social diaconate" of an elected group of men and women, whose humanity is certainly unadorned, but displays in rough and ready ways varying from person to person some integrity which warrants election. These men and women prepare the Table for the Lord's Supper, carry the food on it to the congregation, receive the collection, and entrust to one of their number the charge of giving quiet help from that money to anyone known to be in particular distress. In the village church where I grew up breaches in human relationships within the congregation were healed more often by the deacons than by the minister, and it was they who cared most effectively for the lapsing and the lapsed. It was they who saw to it, often in the absence of a minister, that congregational activities were maintained and financed. They knew better than any minister how to deal with local mischief-making, a matter of some importance when the congregation, along with two others of a different Church Order, was a focus of village interest. They also knew how to deal with patronizing or imposing interventions from higher ecclesiastical sources, intent, in most instances, on marshalling financial and economic resources in their own way, which often seemed to be neither Christian nor consistent with human dignity.

From this special and limited domestic Church experience, deacons were equipped to go out, as many did, to public positions of social responsibility and to care in a humanly acceptable way for persons and their affairs outside the Church. Such special diaconal service was also a help to all Church members who went out in their company.

(1966)

PART TWO:

Exploring
Divine Authority

SANCTITY AND WORLDLINESS
IN THE BIBLE

IN THIS PAPER I SHALL DRAW ATTENTION TO PASSAGES, CHIEFLY FROM THE
New Testament, where the condition of Christians is represented as a
condition of sanctity and is set in contrast to another condition which may
be loosely described as worldliness. This is a limited theme within the
New Testament and the statement of it is associated with a select vocabulary which must be noted in order that we may detect the theme when
it occurs and grasp the background of thought which it suggests. It is a
theme which may very well stand in tension with other themes, such as
Christ's objective Lordship over the world or a proper Christian interest
in the world as the good creation of God. Taken in isolation as a domi-
nating theme for an understanding of the Gospel, it has led to sectarian
enthusiasm which is a distortion of Christian obedience but which may,
nevertheless, have something to contribute to a new ecumenical understanding. This theme, because of its strength and centrality in the Bible,
may be regarded as an obstacle which has to be measured carefully before
we collect from other strands of Biblical thinking some conclusions about
Christ's Lordship in world and Church. I shall therefore try to offer a
fairly full and direct statement of this obstinate theme with some suggestion of the points which ought to govern our interpretation of its statement in Biblical passages.

I

*The designation of Christians as "saints" means that the Old Testament Torah
about the condition called "sanctity" is relevant for the Church. It is a condition
associated with the love of the sanctifying God; it is secured for His People by an
act of reconciliation and an outpouring of the Spirit.*

Whether St. Paul uses the designation "saints" or not, it is clear in all
his letters that he regards his readers as destined to be saints with the
Lord Jesus at His Parousia, their hearts (and "spirit, soul and body")

having been established unblamable in holiness (1 Thess. 3:12f; 5:13). The Church's association with Jesus was understood as the intimate association of the "saints of the Most High" in Dan. 7 with the Son of Man, whom in turn they regarded as God's right-hand man whom He had made strong for Himself (Ps. 80:17). They called upon Him, not indeed as Son of Man but as "our Lord Jesus"; the Kurios who now determines their way before God in His world is their Sanctifier and their way is the way of eschatological sanctity.

In this matter as in others the Church found guidance in the Torah and the prophetic oracles by which God had formed Israel for His own purposes. A new exegesis had to be undertaken, however, distinct from that of scribes or Pharisees, because the People formed by this Torah had in the last days misjudged Him whom God had made both Lord and Christ and had forfeited their sanctity in the very act of trying to secure it. From a rapid review of the Old Testament undertaken with Christian eyes we might collect the following points which have a major bearing on our theme.

Israel was called through Abraham. From Abraham the Lord does not hide what He is about to do, notably to overthrow Sodom and Gomorrah for lack of ten righteous men, "for I have known him to the end that he may command his children and his household after him, that they may keep the way of the Lord to do righteousness and judgement" (Gen. 18:19).

Israel was carried out of Egypt and brought unto the Lord. "Now therefore if you will obey my voice and keep my covenant you shall be a peculiar treasure unto me from among all peoples, for all the earth is mine; and you shall be unto me a kingdom of priests and a holy nation" (Exod. 19:5). But Israel are a stiffnecked people, liable to be consumed if the Lord should go up in their midst to the promised land. Therefore He refuses to go with them, but in response to the intercession of Moses He gives them commands which mark off their conduct from that of the world into which they go (Exod. 33:3; 34:9). By this event of reconciliation, the Lord's presence with His people is secured, and this presence is the root of their sanctity. In the New Testament, the language of holiness, backed by the conviction that we have access to the Presence of God, is deliberately joined to the interpretation of Christ's work as "reconciliation."

An elaborate organization is then prescribed by which Israel may meet the Lord's claim and come under His disposal; and a pattern is prescribed for the preservation, and where necessary the restoration, of sanctity in daily affairs. The rubric is that they are not "to do according to the doings of the land of Egypt wherein they dwelt" nor "according to the doings of the land of Canaan whither I bring you" (Lev. 18:2). The Levitical Torah of Holiness has the appearance of an emergency measure appropriate to this people with its special destiny, but in later Judaism it came to be invested with a wider cosmic significance and there were some who suggested that to live in the beauty of holiness under the control of this Torah was in fact to live the natural life of God's creatures, and those who do not are in effect "*dead* through the trespasses and sins in which they walk" (Eph. 2:1f.).

Codes and prophetic oracles reinforce one another in providing an ethical, humane exegesis of the way of holiness rather than a magical one. In Deuteronomy we find stress on the special connexion between sanctity and the *love* of the sanctifying God and the destiny of the sanctified to *love* him and one another, a connexion which again is stressed in the New Testament. (The emphasis in Deuteronomy may owe something to Hosea who had rescued this element in the rationale of holiness from its squalid associations in non-Israelite religion.)

From the beginning, however, Israel is a mixed multitude which is vulnerable to the danger of "lusting," and its leadership has to be strengthened by taking the Spirit which was upon Moses and putting it upon the elders; and Moses is moved to wish that "all the Lord's people were prophets, that the Lord would put his Spirit upon them" (Num. 11:16–29). This consummation is envisaged in later prophetic oracles (Isa. 4:2–4; 63:7–19; Joel 2:28–32). In the same oracles, and earlier in Deutero-Isaiah, we find the conviction that God's holiness cannot be reflected in the life of His people until He creates a new heaven and new earth as a possible context for it. Then all flesh, including the seed of Israel which remains, shall come to worship before Him (Isa. 65:17; 66:22f.). The Spirit of holiness, which alone can create eschatological sanctity, and the Spirit of God which is the vehicle of creation in Gen. 1:2, are therefore brought together in the New Testament as agent of a new creation; and again the connexion between the Holy Spirit and the expression of love among the sanctified is emphasized.

This Spirit, according to the New Testament, has come upon the saints of the Most High, by their association with the Son of Man to whom dominion, glory, and a kingdom have now been given, that all peoples, nations and languages shall serve Him (Dan. 7). We note, however, that saints and Son of Man alike are to be "worn out" by a King who "speaks against the Most High and thinks to change the times and the law," before they enjoy the Kingdom in its fullness. The choice between the way of God in which the saints walk and the way of Babylon is set out in Dan. 10:1–6, as preface to the apocalypse of the saints' destiny.

II

The Church enjoys eschatological sanctity by the effective calling of God (1 Thess. 2:12, etc.). Self-consciousness about this condition (and about an alternative condition of "worldliness") is part of the knowledgeable faith by which it can be sustained without relapse into worldliness. It is recognized, however, that the Church's sanctity, the significance of that sanctity, and the plight of those who do not enjoy it, are matters which rest in the hands of the exalted Lord. The Church has a share in His self-consciousness, because the Spirit's presence is that of an Instructor, and we enjoy a wisdom which is "not of this world, nor of the rulers of this world which are coming to naught" (1 Cor. 2). What the Church has to say about its sanctity is said with restraint and is controlled at every point by its testimony to the Sanctifier.

A statement of the Gospel in these terms of eschatological sanctity is most obviously to be found in the Epistle to the Hebrews, though the terms lie on the surface of many Pauline letters, of the Pastorals, of 1 Peter and James, and of at least two Gospels—the first and the fourth.

According to Hebrews, God has spoken at the last and His utterance is a Son who reflects His glory and upholds the universe. This Son has made purification for sins and is seated at the right hand of majesty. He is the Sanctifier who is bringing many sons to glory (1:2f.; 2:10f.). As pioneer of their salvation He is "holy, blameless, unstained, separated from sinners, exalted into the presence of God" (7:26). By His performance of God's will once for all through the offering of His body, we, by that will, have been consecrated (10:10). Again, "the blood of Christ, who through the eternal Spirit offered himself without blemish to God, shall purify your conscience from dead works to serve the living God" (9:14); and it is clear from the context that the phrase "dead works" is intended to bring Judaism into the category of "ways of the world" in which the sanctified may no longer walk (cf. Paul in Gal. 4). There follows, in 10:19–31 a summons to "draw near with a true heart" (the mainspring for adequate obedience which is the substance of sanctity); "hold fast the confession of our hope without wavering, for he who promised is faithful"; and "stir one another up to love and good works." In this passage we may note also the criteria of relapse from sanctity, viz. to "spurn the Son of God," to "profane the blood of the covenant" by which consecration was effected, to "outrage the Spirit of grace." Upon this, in turn, there follows in chs. 11–12 an exhortation to endure in faith under discipline "that we may share his holiness"; and in ch. 13 there are directives for the regular life of the holy people which must be considered later in association with similar material.

Paul's references to the sanctifying Lord and His work are usually marked by deliberate use of the verb "to reconcile" (cf. Rom. 5:1–11, followed by the delineation of Christ as the Second Adam with whom there comes a new creation). The argument in Romans advances through ch. 8 to the appeal in 12:1–2 that Christians present their bodies as a living sacrifice, holy and acceptable to God and recognise a condemnation of the flesh for which provision should no longer be made (13:12ff.). The language of sanctity comes to its own in the passages about Christ's cosmic significance in Colossians and Ephesians (Col. 1:19–23; Eph. 1:3–14; 2:16–22; 3:16–19; 4:22–5:20), which is what one might expect when one remembers the cosmic perspectives of priestly writing. Sanctity is an accomplished fact. We have been taken into God's possession by an effective work of reconciliation. The Father has qualified us to share in the inheritance of the saints in light. The reconciling obedience worked out by His Son is extended into us by the Spirit to produce from us a personal offering to the will and disposal of God which we may expect to sustain, through all affliction, to an end which we do not yet see (Col. 1:12f.).

Wherever this language is used (cf. Rom. 5:1–5) a reference is likely to be found to God's *love* and to the love of the saints for God and for all beloved of God. This is most clearly the case in the Johannine writings. It is in those writings also that the rejection of sanctity and love receives explicit treatment as something characterizing "the world." For Paul (2 Cor. 5:19) the love of God takes concrete form in an act of reconciliation which has the world for its object (cf. also Rom. 11:15 where the rejection of the Jews means "the reconciliation of the world"). The world under its present ruler, with its own spirit and its own wisdom, must pass by judgement and recreation into a condition which Paul describes as the "age to come." Cullman may be right in thinking that an epoch is envisaged, called "the kingdom of the beloved Son" (Col. 1:13), where the possibility of being conformed to an unreconciled cosmos still exists. For John, the Son has been sent because God so loved the world. He bears the sins of the world. He is the light of the world. He comes as manna to give life to the world. But the world does not believe the truth in Him and meets Him with hatred. Therefore the ruler of the world is judged and shall be cast out. But meanwhile, it is envisaged in the Last Discourses that the world will persist as the great opponent of its Saviour and it is he who hates his life in this world who will keep his life in the age to come (John 12:25). The Spirit which believers are to receive is one whom the world cannot receive (14:19). Believers, loved by Christ and commanded to love each other, are liable to be hated as the Son is hated by the world (15:19). But the Son takes leave of His disciples with a summons to be of good cheer for He has overcome the world (16:33). The ruler of this world is about to engage with the Son in a decisive encounter: "He has no power over me, yet I do as the Father has commanded me so that the world may know that I love the Father" (14:30f). In this situation Jesus sanctifies those whom the Father has given Him by prayer offered in the plain language of sanctity:

that they be kept from the evil one;

that they may participate in the self-consecration of the Son;

that they may be taken into the unity of Father and Son;

that they may receive glory in and with the Son;

that they may come to be with Him where He is, to behold the glory which the Father has given to the Son before the foundation of the world;

that the love with which the Father has loved the Son may be in them and the Son Himself may be in them. (John 17:14–26)

In the First Epistle of John, Christians are assured that they have been anointed by the Holy One and the anointing abides in them and teaches them about everything (2:20; 2:27). In virtue of the Father's love, expressed in this sanctification by the Son, they are called "children of God." "It does not yet appear what we shall be, but we know that when he appears we shall be like him. ... And everyone who thus hopes in him purifies himself as he is pure" (3:1–3). False spirits have been overcome, even that of antichrist which is in the world already. To confess that Jesus is the Son of God, sent by the Father in the flesh to be the Saviour of the world is to know, to believe and to abide in the love which God has for us; and "in this is love perfected *with us*, that we may have confidence for the day of judgement, because as he is, so are we in the world" (4:1–5; 4:13–17).

Sanctity is a condition into which some of God's creatures have been brought *and know they have been brought* by the human obedience of a Son adequate to the divine Father, with whom they have become joint partakers of the Holy Spirit. In this eschatological fulfilment it is clear that the condition is not an abnormal one, appropriate only to some creatures for emergency purposes. It is the proper condition for God's creatures as such. The concept can be used to draw attention in a special way to the truth that all things have been created in love and for love. Sanctity has been secured to those who believe that Jesus is the Son of God, and it can be maintained in dependence upon Him within the ecclesia of those who, by the Holy Spirit, can say "Jesus is Lord."

III

The "worldliness" of those who are not confessing Jesus to be Lord is diagnosed and rebuked in a restrained and incidental way; first, as a condition out of which Christians have now been lifted; secondly, as a condition in which many still are and into which some have been more deeply plunged by rejecting the call to holiness in Christ; thirdly as a condition devised by powers opposing God, with a natural attraction for men, which makes them instruments for "wearing out the saints of the Most High."

The condition out of which Christians have been lifted is depicted by Paul as one of slavery to the "elements" *(stoicheia)* of the world, beings that by nature are no gods. Men are born, and are liable to walk, in accordance with the flesh, and are given to persecuting what is born and walks according to the Spirit. To "gratify the lusts *(epithumiai)* of the flesh" is the conventional description of their natural motivation. Their doings, in consequence, are those listed in Gal. 5:19–21, and "those who do such things shall not inherit the kingdom of God" (Gal. 4:3; 4:23; 4:29; 5:16–21). The same story is told in Rom. 1:18–3:21, with the additional point that the Law known to the Jews leaves every man speechless in his own defence and this brings the whole world under the judgement of God. Jews who seek sanctity through the Law and in this quest pronounce Jesus to be anathema find that the Law operates upon them precisely like an enslaving "element of the world," and so do Christians who look for sanctity from Christ *and* Judaism.

Men in this condition are ruled by "archons of this age" who do not understand the policy of God and are doomed to pass away. These archons impart a "spirit of this age" and a "wisdom of the world" to every psychical man. Such a man "does not receive the gifts of God, for they are folly to him"; these gifts are discerned pneumatically, and he is in the grip of an uncomprehending and incidentally a hostile pneuma (1 Cor. 2:6–16; cf. 2 Cor. 4:4). This Pauline teaching is summed up in Eph. 2, addressed explicitly to Gentiles: "You were dead through the trespasses and sins in which you once walked, following the course of this world, following the prince of the power of the air, the spirit that is now at work in the sons of disobedience. In this context we all once lived, in the lusts of our flesh, carrying out the inclinations of the flesh and of the reasoning mind *(dianoia)*." The change which has been wrought is then expressed in the language of sanctification.

In 1 John 2:15–17 there is an explicit warning that to love the world and the things in the world is not consistent with the existence offered by holy love. In Titus, where the matter is presented in terms of straight moral exhortation, we are told that to the corrupt and unbelieving nothing is "pure"; they are disqualified for any good deed. The grace of God which has appeared for the salvation of all men trains us to renounce "irreligion" and "worldly lusts" (Titus 1:15ff., 2:11ff.).

In another group of passages the worldliness of the unsanctified is depicted in a more polemical interest. They are explicitly regarded as enemies of the Church's sanctity and are the more dangerous when found within the Church's own ranks. Their condition is one into which apostate saints will fall irremediably if the references to Cain, Esau, Baalam, and Korah are taken seriously, not forgetting the dominical word about the sin against the Holy Ghost. In Jude they are plainly identified for us: "grumblers, malcontents, following their own passions, loud-mouthed boasters, flattering people to gain advantage. . . . These set up divisions, worldly people devoid of the Spirit. . . . They revile whatever they do not understand and are destroyed by the things which they know by animal instinct" (Jude 16, 19, 10f.). They are to be found in the Church, indeed at its love-feasts, and the language of sanctity is used to arm the faithful against them (cf. also 2 Pet. 2:20–22). Paul provides some precedent for these lurid passages in 1 Cor. 3:18ff., where the wisdom of this world has invaded the Church and produced divisions; also in Phil. 3:18f., and in the great summons to separation in 2 Cor. 6:14–7:1. We can add, at this point, the warning against those who would "make a prey of you by philosophy and empty deceit, according to human tradition, according to the elements of the cosmos" (Col. 2:8).

A slightly different background for such material is exposed in 1 Pet. 4:1–6, with its intimate picture of the pressures upon the Church from pagan neighbours, who are addicted, we gather, to living in licentiousness, passions, revels, carousing, and undisciplined idolatry. This profligacy disturbed pagan and Jewish moralists no less than it distressed Christians, but the Christians saw the phenomenon in greater depth as something conscripted into the great assault upon the holy community now established by God. This community must continue to distinguish itself by living, not in terms of human passions but "by the will of God"; an expression of the contrast which is conventionally familiar to all strands of this material.

IV

The Torah of Christian sanctity, while containing much that is common to parallel moral teaching, Jewish and Gentile, embodies an attack on all policies of carefully contrived security, religious or political. Sanctity which is conformed to Christ in this respect is a uniquely effective witness to the world of His Lordship.

It can be said with much truth that nothing is put into the diagnosis of worldliness and sanctity which cannot be found in the best moralists of contemporary Judaism and Hellenism. There is, however, one feature of the material, one emphasis in its presentation, which may tell against this. It is in the Gospel traditions that it can be most readily studied. In the Gospels, the manhood of Christ is presented systematically. It is the manhood of the King of Israel who is also the High Priest, who has realised *in His own Person* but on Israel's behalf the covenant communion of God with His people. His words and works are the utterance of that personal achievement and stand in place of the Torah for the new humanity. The first Gospel is more explicit about this and uses the language of sanctity more obviously than do the second or third Gospels.

The Holy One of God, anointed at baptism with the Holy Spirit and recognised for what he is by the unclean spirits whom He ejects, is tempted to receive all the kingdom of the world and the glory of them by an act of submission to Satan, but He replies "you shall worship the Lord your God and him only shall you serve" (Matt. 16:13; 4:8–11). He defines the blessed who are to be the salt of the earth (5:1–12), and gives them their mission, which is to be attempted but not completed before the Son of

Man comes (10:5–25). In the day of judgement it shall be more tolerable for Sodom and Gomorrah than for cities which reject the mission. The mixed response is foreshadowed in parables (13:22f.; 13:36f.; 22:1–14). The reason for rejection is a kind of worldliness which is more to be pitied than blamed. It is a careful, and sometimes high-minded, preoccupation with the right conduct of affairs in this world which betrays a blindness to the eschatological drama now being enacted. In the Parable of Judgement (25:31–46) the goats are disqualified from community with the Son of Man by unconscious failure in simple human compassion. The Son of Man himself becomes notorious as a companion of outcasts (9:10; 11:9).

What is to be done among the saints is contrasted with what is done among the religious (ch. 6), with an explicit warning not to lay up for yourselves treasure upon earth, nor to be anxious, nor to serve two masters. There is clear protest against the search for security in this world in the story of the Canaanite woman and in the diatribe against the Pharisees (ch. 23). There is another contrast, though the worldly conduct of political authorities is upheld in its place as something to be respected, though not emulated, by the saints.

"The Son of Man came not to be served but to serve and to give his life as a ransom for many" (20:28), and when Peter questions this way in which the Son is walking he is rebuked as a hindrance who is not on the side of God but of men (16:23–27).

The apostolic letters, and the codes which they are said to incorporate, do not always reflect this challenge to any policy of carefully contrived security as clearly as one might wish. Emphasis tends very quickly to fall upon the moral aspect of sanctity as a pattern of life in this world, at some cost to the true heart of the matter which is sheer self-abandonment to the vision of God granted to us through the manhood of the Sanctifier. There remains, however, a proper suspicion of boasting and aggressiveness. Paul himself admits at one point that this zeal in the cause of Christian integrity has laid him open to the charge of walking according to the flesh even in this holy calling (2 Cor. 10).

V

In the codes which indicate how sanctity may be sustained in this world, a "cultic" reference is not obliterated, but the core of the matter is trustful obedience by those who are clean in heart. The codes echo various traditions about holy and good living, and there are hints that the way of sanctity can be advocated as the way to good life here and now for all men. But it is by God's sanctifying action in Christ that His creatures, made by love and for love, are alone free to enjoy life. And the form of this enjoyment is one of watching, praying, patiently enduring, and rejoicing in every sign of the new creation.

It has been suggested in recent works of N.T. scholarship that the directives for sanctity found throughout the epistles come out of a common store of catechetical material whose characteristics have been analysed by Carrington, Selwyn, and others.

Neo-Levitical codes of freedom from defilement play their part, notably in Thessalonians and in 1 Pet. 1:14–2:17. The teaching is to *abstain* from lusts which had power within men in virtue of their ignorance of God and to act instead with noteworthy *agape* and *philadelphia*. The piety of the Hasidim, who speak in some Psalms in somewhat *un*worldly fashion of their desire to dwell in Yahweh's house and behold His beauty, has left some traces, because kindness and generosity were taken to be the chief symptoms of this attitude. From the same source there is clear emphasis on "knowledgeable holding-out" *(hupomena)* as a mark of the saints: waiting, watching, suffering, and praying, for the kingdom of God. There is also material which has affinities with the literature of the Jewish sects; and here, if Daube is right in his controversy with Klein, we may include the *Derekeretz* literature among the sects. This material rests on the conviction that a new covenant has been established and faithfulness to it brings into the heart a love for God which is adequate response to His love as finally and peculiarly expressed. This faithfulness implies the rejection of those notorious worldly ways: idolatry, fornication, murder, and unjust acquisition of gain.

It is not so clear, but it is at least arguable, that the N.T. Torah of sanctity includes a suggestion that the way of sanctity is not an emergency measure for the elect only but is in fact a way for all who want a good life here and now. "Well-doing" (a technical concept) is urged upon Christians, and "evil-doing" is rebuked, in terms which show some influence from Psalm 34 and Proverbs 3, passages which express what might be called the "acceptable worldliness" of the Wisdom tradition. Conduct based on deliberate truthfulness, humility, subordination, and thus kept clear from sins of speech and temper, is sound wisdom for the upright. And the Lord who has imparted this wisdom "is a shield to them that walk in integrity, that he may guard the paths of judgement and preserve the way of his saints" (Prov. 2:6–8). The Epistle of James is written in this key, though in 4:7–5:6 there is the same passionate protest against arrogant worldliness which we find in Enoch 94–103 and which there was provoked by Sadducean prostitution of the earlier Wisdom tradition.

There is one feature of this instruction in all its strands which it shares, apparently, with Tannaitic instruction of the same kind. These catechetical codes

> appear to have attempted, not so much to give a systematic account of dogmas and duties, or even of the major dogmas and duties, as to convey an impression of the atmosphere of the new life. Lighter and weightier matters, easier and more burdensome duties, stand side by side. The can-

didate was led very gradually towards the goal; ... he was given milk before he could receive strong nourishment, just like the Israelites in the desert or the converts to Judaism.[1]

What is finally urged upon the saints is a "patient continuance in well-doing" (Rom. 2:7). This is important because Christians, as men adoring God "in Christ," have to act with non-Christians to achieve many limited human purposes in the world. Responsible "worldliness" is required on their part if the life of God's creatures is to be kept human, kept within bounds, and kept open for God's covenanted work. But this responsible worldliness is essentially a matter of watching, praying, waiting in patient steadfastness for the new creation to be manifested, and rejoicing in every sign of it. It means "standing" and "withstanding," as well as "submitting for conscience sake." And all this is sustained within the Spirit-created "koinonia in Christ," a Body whose testimony to His holy Lordship is offered by obedience even unto death.

(1981)

---

[1]Daube, *The New Testament and Rabbinic Judaism*, p. 125.

THEOLOGY
AND
"HUMAN RIGHTS"

A MORE ACCURATE TITLE FOR THIS LECTURE WOULD BE "CHRISTIAN THEOLOGY and the *topic* of Human Rights." This topic is canvassed and pursued with interest and determination in many contexts, with passionate concern in many distressing situations, and with some acrimony on the part of people of intelligence and good will who suspect that the words and the concepts employed are being invested with a weight they cannot bear. The words are degenerating visibly into a high-sounding *slogan*, the slogan of a *"movement."* The task posed for Christian theology, as I conceive it, is to offer a critique of the interest expressed by Christian churches in "the Human Rights movement"—including, of course, lack of interest where that is evident. The topic comes on to the theologian's agenda, already developed and articulated, with technical hazards, discrepancies and obscurities, from the broad "secular" human agenda. What happens when Christian churches are seized of the topic, take it up as a topic to be adopted as their own, and contribute to the current canvassing and pursuit of it? That is my theme in this lecture; and after this brief introduction I will ask you *first* to look from a Christian perspective at the secular soil from which the topic has arisen; then, *secondly*, at ecclesiastical responses to its currency; then, *thirdly*, I will sketch the lines along which theological comment might aptly run; and then draw the whole survey together as best I can.

It is tempting to say[1] that the Church, Christian congregations, and ecumenical organizations, can join in the struggle for human rights with less prejudice than other institutions, since, in principle, churches are neither private associations nor statutory authorities. If so, ecclesiastical interest may have some useful spin-off for general discussion of the topic. As for churches themselves in their ongoing quest for Christian integrity, a theological critique of their interest in the struggle will certainly provide useful spin-off for the integrity of their general thought and practice.

---

[1] As Jürgen Moltmann does in the symposium *A Christian Declaration on Human Rights*, ed. Allen O. Miller (Grand Rapids: Eerdmans, 1977), p. 130.

Karl Barth said in a letter written in 1932 that "the proclamation of the church is by nature political in so far as it has to ask the pagan polis to remedy its state of disorder and make justice a reality."[2] In broad and simple terms *ius* is the art of living well, with and for others, since "all human beings are fellow human-beings." In the simple confessional language of Christian theology we can therefore ask: What is Jesus Christ saying to his Church *from* the Human Rights Movement? That "movement," in its contemporary manifestation, stems from the promulgation in 1948 of the Universal Declaration of Human Rights by the United Nations Organizations; but to treat that document as normative for the topic has come to seem naive and partisan in this thirtieth anniversary year. The broad secular agenda from which the topic comes must be surveyed more widely.

I

The "Universal Declaration of Human Rights" was "adopted and proclaimed" by General Assembly Resolution 217 (A. III) on December 10, 1948. On December 16, 1966, two "International Covenants" were "adopted and opened for signature, ratification and accession" (2200A.XXI)—the first on *Economic, Social and Cultural Rights* and the second on *Civil and Political Rights*. The separate packaging of these two parcels should draw our attention to a source of disagreement about perspective and priorities which was barely acknowledged in 1948 but which runs deep into the soil of "broad secular" human concern out of which the "human rights" talk springs and has sprung. The "final act" of the 1975 Helsinki Agreement (signed by 33 European states, by the U.S.A. and by Canada) is the most recent document in the case. In the "Western" tradition of views on human rights, the rights, dignity and prerogatives of the individual citizen, in the face of established political and ecclesiastical institutions, had priority. Declarations from this perspective "defend the interests of citizens as free individuals, free producers, free proprietors"[3]—with elaborations of the right to life, to liberty, and to participation in public affairs (phrased, misleadingly to our ears, as "the pursuit of happiness") spelled out in terms of "bourgeois" culture. The American Constitution, with its Bill of Rights and Supreme Court, is the historical *locus classicus*. The *French* "Declaration of the Rights of Man and of Citizens" (and Tom Paine's defence of the Revolution in France which put the phrase on the map in 1791) are usually bracketed with the American gesture as the source from which has come "a growing consensus of opin-

---

[2]Eberhard Busch, *Karl Barth: His Life from Letters and Autobiographical Texts* (Philadelphia: Fortress Press, 1976), p. 216.

[3]Jan Milič Lochman, "Human Rights from a Christian Perspective," in *A Christian Declaration on Human Rights*, p. 15.

ion" about the principal rights and duties essential for membership of an "enlightened" society. In 1963 Pope John XXIII joined in the consensus, without misgiving, in the Encyclical *Pacem in Terris*—but of course with a "Catholic" accent. These eighteenth-century "progressive" political developments (and their seventeenth-century antecedents and nineteenth-century elaborations) were directed towards "liberating" persons from the "oppressive" pretensions of traditional political and ecclesiastical assumptions and institutions and to enlarge their "franchise" as citizens. "Progressive" developments (revolutionary or reformist) in our own century have displayed by contrast a "totalitarian" disposition. "Freedom" is hedged about by sanctioned *confiscation* of personal goods and of personal identities, and by sanctioned resort to incarceration and to torture, where "emergency powers" are ritually invoked against the awkward citizen in the interests of "national security" or of "national economic development."

I have learnt (from Hannah Arendt, *On Revolution*) to distinguish between the American and the French eighteenth-century gestures and to see the twentieth century in the light of that distinction. America spoke up for men "created equal" and "endowed by their Creator with certain unalienable [human] rights, . . . [to] life, liberty and the pursuit of happiness." France substituted anthropology for theology, and spoke up for men who are "born and always continue free and equal in respect of their rights"; but, more significantly, said that "the end of all political associations is the preservation of the natural and imprescriptible rights of man; and these rights are liberty, property, security and resistance of oppression." Thomas Paine's exegesis pleads for:

Democracy (to safeguard the "poor" against the alleged capacity of those not "poor" to represent their interest)

Independence (ethnic self-determination, with territorial integrity and sovereignty over wealth and resources)

Economic growth: Revolutionary war: Social security
(the main planks of the Chilean Junta's platform and that of their Friedman trained technocrats, as they contend with restive "moderates" and awkward bishops).

Miss Arendt argues for the presence in France of a factor not pressing in America, the "Social Problem" of citizens exposed to intractible forces making for poverty, want, raw and basic need. Hence the distinctive emphasis on rights more raw and basic than those of individual civic dignity. Economic growth, with more fairness of distribution is the reigning value, and human rights (viewed "collectively" rather than individualistically) depend upon *governmental management*, improved for the purpose by ridding itself of archaic involvement with religious preoccupations and institutions. The Marxist appraisal of our human condition has, of course, brought these eighteenth-century seeds to their twentieth-century harvest. And it becomes clear why in 1960, the "socialist" states in UNO set far more store by the Economic and Cultural Rights Covenant than by the Civil and Political Rights parcel.

Last December the Assembly adopted two so-called "priorities" for future work by the 32-member Commission on Human Rights. "UN Swings to Collective Rights" was the *Washington Post* headline; and the article under it referred to a Soviet delegate exulting in a "significant development" which lays down "a new UN approach to human rights." It is the approach for which Andrei Vishinsky spoke up, a lone voice, in 1948, with the concept relating (for implementation) to "the prerogatives of governments" and with individual freedom seen as relative to the interest of society and state. The first "priority" in world-concern is now to combat violation of the "human rights of peoples"—with apartheid, racial discrimination and colonialism as violations in point. The second "priority" is "the realisation of the New International Economic Order." It is fair to observe that the language of human rights has been taken over from the "world" of "liberal capitalism" and of "Marxist socialism" and adapted to contend with the collective emergencies of "Third World" societies. "In comparison with these collective emergencies the rights of individuals, whose prominence is relatively foreign to the social and cultural traditions of most nations of the Third World, tend to fade. In such a situation human rights mean primarily a demand for life-sustaining conditions for work and nourishment, for an improved balance of life-opportunities between the poor and the rich, for elimination of exploitation within national and international frameworks."[4]

Talk about "human rights" has spread over the landscape of politics with the speed of a virus infection, and some regard it as truly virulent, not least because disagreement about perspectives and priorities breeds acrimony and so darkens counsel. Yet, with the Helsinki Agreement of 1975 and the Carter administration, it has become a major motif in hard politics. The disordered condition of the human body politic, which such talk serves as a symptom to disclose, differs from one locality to another and from one interest-group to another. Is there an acceptable common denominator for such talk, and for the elephantine measures devised for implementing it, even within that "world" formed by Western traditions of liberal democracy—for what the Charter 77 group says and does in Czechoslovakia and for debate at Strasburg about the birching of Manx delinquents of appropriate age and sex, with or without trousers.

With care it is possible to frame a rhetorical statement about the landscape of politics in that world and in those contiguous with it on the same

---

[4]Lochman, p. 15.

planet of our Earth. Let me borrow one from an expert in constitutional law at Tübingen, Ludwig Raiser:

> We live in a world echoing in all directions with reports of poverty, hunger and misery, of exploitation and oppression of great masses of people, of the arrests, tortures and assassinations of politically undesirable persons, of the abduction and extortion of innocent victims by politically radical revolutionary groups or by greedy robbers, of the suppression of any freedom of expression by dictatorial regimes, including freedom to confess one's own religious belief—of any number of incidents, in other words, which reveal a frighteningly widespread disdain for and degradation of human personhood. In such a world, deep disturbance of conscience drives us to seek possibilities for the protection of fellow men and women who are being threatened or are being physically and psychologically injured in these ways.[5]

II

"Deep disturbance of conscience": I turn now to the efforts being made in Christian churches to produce an *instructed* conscience, among Christians as such, but in a form which is open for consensual sharing with people of other faiths and of none. At times it seems that these efforts have served chiefly to add new reaches to the elephantine sprawl of talk and of measures to implement it which the topic everywhere provokes. There is, however, a record of salutary and costly activity across the globe from Korea to South Africa, from the Philippines to Brazil, and the pursuit of interpretation by integrated attention to theory and practice is no longer a Marxist monopoly. Since, like the fool, my eyes are more frequently on the ends of the earth than on the local parish pump (an amenity for which a pump room still exists in Ravenstonedale where I live), I am not well informed about patterns of active interest among our British Churches; and elsewhere I can only speak with close acquaintance of work pursued in the family of churches to which my own communion belongs—the World Alliance of Reformed Churches stemming from Calvin's tradition of reform in Geneva.

I have mentioned the Papal Encyclical of 1963. I wish I were better

---

[5]Quoted in Lochman, p. 13. The phrase which associates "greedy robbers" with "radical revolutionary groups" is a reference to "Terror International"—"creatures of a political underworld whose leftist rhetoric barely conceals its moral emptiness." Can one regard them with "liberal" sympathy, as people for whom social inequality breeds frustration which can only lead to a determination to smash the system without futile argument? Or must one recognise that the leading spirits among them do it for *pay*, for *power*, for *pleasure*, because they are *bored* by a world which offers to them less dramatic "self-expression" than the violence to which their "feelings" impel them? And should one not add, in either case, that there, but for the grace of God and natural timidity, very many more among us would be ripe to go?

equipped to draw upon material from the subsequent work of the Papal Commission, *Justitia et Pax*. My impression is that where prelates, clergy, and laity in the Roman Catholic Church have been moved to make common cause with victims of "disdain for and degradation of human personhood"—and that story is world-wide and dramatic—they have heard and responded to "what Jesus Christ is saying to us from the Human Rights movement" in a fashion which goes well beyond the conflation of Natural Law tradition and the United Nations Declaration which John XXIII offered.

Activity in the World Council of Churches has displayed deep sensitivity to the actual landscape of politics—much too readily so for the taste of many of its constituency.[6] The Report of the Nairobi Assembly (1975) provides in Section V, "Structures of Injustice and Struggles for Liberation," the *locus classicus* for this area of concern.

The Lutheran World Federation has been at work on the topic since its last full Assembly in 1970. One of its German theologians remarked that deep aversion from the topic was discernible in German Lutheranism, but "reports" (of typically Germanic thoroughness) have emerged from the Lutheran churches in Eastern and in Western Germany. It is worth remarking that in the Federal Republic, as in Italy, and in Czechoslovakia and Russia, the idiom of human rights has been used in the drafting of modern constitutions for the State, and this has supplied Christians and other potential dissidents with political opportunity for arguing to some purpose.

The effort pursued in the World Alliance of Reformed Churches since its last General Council in 1970 is now documented for English and American readers in a book *A Christian Declaration on Human Rights*, edited by Allen Miller and published by Eerdmans in 1977. The United Nations documents and the final act (Principle VII) of the Helsinki Agreement about Security and Cooperation in Europe are printed as appendices. A document entitled "The Theological Basis of Human Rights" is included, and the essays by two of Europe's most vigorous theologians (Jan Lochman, on loan to Geneva from Prague, and Jürgen Moltmann) show where the tone and leadership in this enquiry has come from. Despite its quality, I do not myself think that this enquiry has so far provided a really satisfying answer to the question about what Christian theological exegesis will best serve to create an instructed Christian conscience and afford critical but positive support for the thesis that human beings, by creation or by nature, are endowed with "rights."

At a World Council of Churches Consultation at St. Polten (Austria) in

---

[6] Cf. Philip Potter, *Ecumenical Review*, 30 (1978), 42ff., and the account on p. 59 of the Report of the Second Colloquium on the Churches' Role in the Application of the Final Act of the Conference on Security and Cooperation in Europe, held at Montreux, July 1977.

1974 an effort was made to select and to focus priorities among all the exigencies where human dignity is at risk. The six headings, for what they are worth, are as follows:

(a) There is a basic human right to life—inclusive of the entire question of survival, of the threats and violations resulting from unjust economic, social and political systems, and of the equality of life.

(b) There is a right to enjoy and to maintain cultural identity—which includes issues such as national self-determination, the rights of minorities, etc.

(c) There is a right to participate in the decision-making process within the community—which comprises the entire issue of effective democracy.

(d) There is a right to dissent—which prevents a community or a system from hardening into authoritarian immobility.

(e) There is a right to personal dignity—which implies, for example, the condemnation of all torture and of prolonged confinement without trial.

(f) There is a right freely to choose a faith and a religion—which encompasses the freedom, either alone or in community with others, in public or in private, to proclaim one's faith or one's religion by the means of teaching, practice, worship, and ritual.

This list is the fruit of an effort to collect and arrange priorities from the whole range of experience in First, Second and Third Worlds, which the Christian Churches acting together are peculiarly well qualified to do.

As a footnote to this survey of ecclesiastical responses let me allude-to work in hand at the Irish School of Ecumenics in Dublin which will, I believe, bring further light on how to pursue this topic in the world as we find it.

In that world "trouble with the Church" is apt to come on to the agenda of government business at almost any point in the political landscape (England, Scotland and Wales always excepted) and it is important that "traitor-priests," the epithet hurled recently at three Chilean bishops, should create trouble only with proper Christian integrity.

III

"Human rights," placed thus as a topic on the theologian's agenda from the broad secular agenda of the world in A.D. 1978, has to be accepted, with its conceptuality and language, and with considerable uncertainty about the foundation of its language and about how such language may focus past experience and create new experience in this situation or that. What may a wise theologian see fit to do about it?

(a) Since his expertise has a deep respect for "reason" at its heart, he will ask first what language about "rights" means when used seriously and not as a vehicle for rhetoric. Briefed as well as possible in the cultural and political areas we have visited, he should turn to jurisprudence. There talk about "rights" stems from social contexts where a *right* is created or granted from an established source of authority; and so establishes for the recipient the basis for a *claim* which the recipient may make if occasion arises; the granting of the right, furthermore, creates an *obligation* upon someone to give him his due. Professor Hart, in his Oxford Inaugural Lecture of 1953, elucidates this social device and shows how it may have derivative forms, "liberty," "immunity," "power"—with "privilege" as an exceptional "right."[7] The layman had access to current discussion when Lord Hailsham reviewed in *The Listener* (March 24 1977) an argument between Professor Dworkin and Professor Rawls, with reference to Dworkin's book *Taking Rights Seriously*. The detail is not germane to my main point. The wise theologian, I am suggesting, will emulate in his own way, predecessors who spoke in Christian terms about "Natural Law"—without invoking all that they said about it as though it were eternally true and useful. Their fundamental thesis was that in human affairs, moral, legal, political and economic, the correct procedure in disorderly situations would appear when *reason* discerns the "nature" of the case and the "nature" of the parties involved. Reason is able to discern the nature of the human animal, the nature of our social relationships, the nature of that *bonum commune* which promises fulfilment. Reason will derive from the nature of any case and from the human nature of the parties involved the precepts; *honeste vivere, neminem laedere, suum cuique tribuere*, and will clarify their immediate bearing. And reason will instruct the will with the injunction: *naturam sequi*. This doctrine set limits to the sovereignty which states enact as "positive law" and provided a basis for criticism of all such enactments. We may have doubts about following the clue of "nature" in those traditional ways, but we do well to emulate our forbears in careful but confident deployment of *reason*.

It seems to me that whenever "self-expression," so deeply cherished by modern persons, brings our pampered humanity up against "objections" thereto, there is aggressive talk about "rights"; and language is often corrupted from sober to satanically pretentious use. But often, too, it may be apt. The theologian must learn to look for right reason in this matter.

(b) Then, of course, the theologian will consult the documents of his faith which express the conviction that the world in all its aspects, and every human life within it, exist by "right"—right created and granted

---

[7]H.L.A. Hart, *Definition and Theory in Jurisprudence* (1953), pp. 16f.

from the authority which is God, whose voice we may and must hear and obey with faith, love and hope. Here the theologian must listen to objections from his own constituency. The voice of God, it will be said by some, does not come with the accents and emphasis of the Human Rights Movement; *au contraire*, indeed. "What does the Lord *require* of thee . . . ," not "What rights does he confer on thee?" If, furthermore, his speech provides emancipation and founded freedoms by divine adjudication, the content thereof has little if anything in common with the St. Polten theses.

In reply to the first point I would argue that the God who *requires* of men that they do what Micah (and President Carter) say, *promises* first of all to secure for humans as his covenant-partners what in Hebrew is called the *mishpat* of each and all—the third term in the trilogy "commandments, statutes, *judgements*" announced in Deuteronomy 6 and similar texts. He promises to do this in covenant-loyalty ("loving-kindness") which spares no effort to make common cause with "the fatherless and widows" and, more widely, with the alienated in all their limitations and awkwardness and offensiveness. To do justly, to love loyalty, to walk wisely before your God, is to act with him in this respect.

The second objection is more plausible. New Testament theology reflects the salvaging of human dignity vis-à-vis the assault of Satan, working through accusing Law, human sinfulness and the appointment which finite creatures must keep with death. Under this assault, faith (the "courage to be") is corrupted into pride, love is soured into sloth, and hope is corrupted into false pretension. Yet through the advent, the sacrifice, the resurrection of Jesus Christ, human dignity is rescued and healed for a life to come, with God in a renovated creation, and the fruits can even now be tasted in advance. If Human Rights crusaders are guilty at times of exploiting ill-founded language sloppily used, one might ask in their company: against what, against whom, is the claim constituted by these so-called rights directed? The answer which Christians have in mind will be: against everything that opposes God and the manhood he has made for his own, and against the persons and structures in which such opposition finds expression, in fashions of traditional authority and traditional superstition deriving from the empire of Satan, that dark mystery of power and authority corrupted by its own pretension. The categories of religion must not, of course, be applied naively to worldly phenomena, and turned into metaphor apt to trivialise phenomena and religion alike. But some effort to uncover the empire of Satan and treasonable human subservience to it, where others may see only political expediency and self-will, may serve to deepen and clarify all struggle for human rights. The document worked out by churches in Eastern Germany finds a "structural parallelism" between the civic values of freedom, equality, and social participation, and the realities of justification, baptism, and a priesthood of sonship general to all believers, and suggests how the analogy can be fruitful in both directions.

(c) Theology, in the third place, might contribute from its own anthropology a certain freshness as well as wholeness to *the substantial agenda* of the human rights campaign. "Our biblical faith" says the Reformed Churches' Declaration (following Moltmann) "commits us to a view of human life in its wholeness expressed in three basic complementarities:

male and female

the individual and society

human life and its ecological context."

When Karl Barth proposed a schema for the conception of humanity to which the Word of God is addressed in Biblical tradition he used two other complementarities not included in these three:

"soul of a body"—psycho-somatic complementarity

"for God and for the world"—the complementarity of sacred and profane.

Is there strong theological ground for a fresh drive against torture without attending to the first? Or for a possible drive towards clarifying a right to work and to rest from work without attending to the second?

I do no find it easy to give a neat and impressive reply to the question about a special and distinctive contribution which Christian theology can offer to the topic of human rights, for lack of which the pursuit of that topic will miscarry. Perhaps it is not a matter of providing any special Christian or theological ingredient at all, but rather of demonstrating how, using the ingredients available to everybody, the topic can be pursued with Chrisitian integrity. Where its pursuit is coloured by what, to Christian eyes, is false religion or pseudo-religion, the Christian will offer his critique of this. Where it is distorted or vitiated by localised cultural or statutory interest, the ecumenical experience of the Church may serve to enlarge interest and vision. Where it is bound too rigidly to past achievement, the theologian may help to strengthen the morale of hope with Christian assurance that the Lord has yet more light and truth to break forth from his holy Word.

It has become evident that the most serious and problematic inhibition on the development of an *international* concern with human rights (as distinct from concern within the several nations in their diverse and sometimes incompatible variety) is the current realism about national self-determination, written into the first articles of both the 1966 Covenants. How "realistic" this realism will continue to be in conditions where the distinction between some affairs as "domestic" and some as "universal" is being rapidly out-moded, remains to be seen.

Stimulated by a colleague in Florence, Enrico Chiavacci,[8] I am inclined to recognize, in the history of human rights as a cultural concern, a new departure at the Renaissance, when *ius*, the art of living well, with and for others, was reconceived by thinkers who tried to extract from the social whole of humanity the "subjective" *rights of liberty* proper to human persons (the right not to be hindered by the state or by any third party, with a corresponding duty of suffering the behaviour of other persons), and then to found the complementary *rights of solidarity* (the right to be helped by the community as a whole, with the corresponding duty to work and make sacrifices for other persons) upon that subjective core. Society, then, is turned into an *instrumental* good into which the individual enters because of fear and, more positively, of convenience. This liberal enterprise of experimenting with humanity has provided valuable correctives against misguided conformity both to the exigencies of physical nature and to the edicts of political sovereignty. Mankind in our own time is evidently struggling to move beyond the terms of that experiment into new forms of social experience, with a new ethical consensus of which, in their imperfect ways, Human Rights manifestos are eloquent. Churches which are excited by this do well to encourage their theologians to share in the excitement and to help with the shaping of it, so that Christians, moving with the times, may do so with the freedom of a properly instructed conscience.

(1979)

---

[8]In a paper communicated to the European *Societas Ethica* at its annual meeting in Goslar in September 1978.

R. B. BRAITHWAITE AS AN APOLOGIST FOR RELIGIOUS BELIEF

PROFESSOR BRAITHWAITE'S EDDINGTON LECTURE IS NOT AN ESSAY IN CHRISTian Theology, nor, technically, is it an Apology for Christian Belief. It deals with a strictly philosophical problem: "The kernel for an empiricist of the problem of the nature of religious belief is to explain, in empirical terms, how a religious statement is used by a man who asserts it in order to express his religious conviction" (p. 11). The substance of Braithwaite's explanation is set out in Professor Britton's article[1] and so is the case for tackling the philosophical problem in these terms. Like all essays in philosophy the Eddington Lecture is open to criticism, either on the ground that something else could have been said even from the point of view of a logical empiricist, or on the ground that what was said, and fairly said, reveals the inadequacy of logical empiricism as a philosophical standpoint.[2] Any contribution which I have to make to this philosophical criticism will be at best an indirect one, for my approach to the matter is from the point of view of a Christian theologian with apologetic responsibilities. Braithwaite's analysis manifestly has repercussions in the Christian theologian's field which both parties might find it profitable to explore.

To the Christian theologian (and therefore to the Christian believer whom he in some sense represents) the philosophical standpoint known as local empiricism has attractive features as well as disturbing ones, and Braithwaite's analysis throws them into focus. It is attractive because it offers a prospect of re-casting the dispute between believers and unbelievers into a different and more promising mould. It is disturbing because a very questionable status is accorded to the propositions upon which this dispute has traditionally been deemed to turn, for to an empiricist many of these propositions tell stories whose efficacy for a Christian does not depend upon their being believed to be true.

---

[1] Part I of the joint Britton—Whitehouse discussion in *The Durham University Journal*.

[2] E. L. Mascall's criticism in *Words and Images*, ch. III, is of this latter kind. The chapter title, "Theism without God," shows that Mascall has little sympathy with Braithwaite's effort and he is not inclined to grant that what was said was fairly said.

In the first place, it would be useful to declare the theologian's interest, as I see it, in such a piece of philosophy. Christians suppose that their religion is an acknowledgment of God's reality, made in terms of human life. In principle, the forms of this acknowledgment may include all the forms of human life itself; in practice, the acknowledgment is fragmentary and everywhere inadequate. Christians also suppose that there is an activity of self-disclosure on the part of God, which suffices to elicit this acknowledgment, and the locus of this self-disclosure is the man Jesus Christ. Since the time of his death, this locus may be found by way of prophetic and apostolic testimony to him which produces echoes in the human activity of churches. A crucial moment in this activity was the production of authoritative Scriptures to serve as the canon for this prophetic and apostolic testimony. God's self-disclosure takes place where Jesus Christ is understood, proclaimed and represented in the churches' human activity. It is against this background that Karl Barth defines the task of theology and of dogmatics in particular (*Church Dogmatics*, Vol. I, Part 2, p. 743).[3] He asks whether there is an identity, however indirect, of God's Word with the utterances of the Church. His answer is that

> the Word of God is God Himself in the proclamation of the Church of Jesus Christ. In so far as God gives the Church the commission to speak about Him, and the Church discharges this commission, it is God Himself who declares His revelation in His witnesses. The proclamation of the Church is pure doctrine when the human word spoken in it in confirmation of the Biblical witness to revelation offers and creates obedience to the Word of God. Because this is its essential character, function and duty, the word of the Church preacher is the special and immediate object of dogmatic activity.

The theologian's task is to deal with the religious utterances of the Christian church, utterances made by all its members and not all in verbal form, by a critical and systematic discipline which attempts to answer the question of whether this alleged identity is so, and to what extent. Now Barth is well aware that everyone has some sort of philosophy, "i.e., a personal view of the fundamental nature and relationship of things— however popular, aphoristic, irregular and eclectically vacillating" and "it is really quite impossible for us to free ourselves from our own shadow, that is, to make the so-called *sacrificium intellectus.*" What he says (op cit., pp. 727–735) about the use of specific modes of thought and philosophy brought to the task of Scriptural exegesis applies to the whole theological task. He makes five points. First, all Christian utterance is venturesome, and there is always a distance between that of which we speak (even if it

---

[3]English theologians do not regularly use the term "dogmatics" or "dogmatic activity" to denote the discipline by which the integrity of Christian belief and practice is probed critically and systematically, nor in general do they envisage it with Barth's clarity. They do, however, practice it in various ways to which the work of philosophers is highly relevant.

be the determinative thought of Scripture) and our own imitative thought determined as it is by our own philosophy. Secondly, one must be prepared to move, in an exploratory, experimental, and provisional manner, from one philosophy to another, in the interest of the theological task. Hence, to put the last three points together, the debates and inner conflicts of philosophy concerning human modes of thought are germane to the theologian's task. There is no question of

> replacing philosophy by a dictatorial, absolute and exclusive theology, and again discrediting philosophy as an *ancilla theologiae*. On the contrary, our concern is that theology itself, which in itself and apart from its object can only be the fulfilment of a human way of thought, and therefore a kind of philosophy, should not forget its own hypothetical, relative and incidental character . . . or become guilty of opposing or resisting its object. (p. 734)

This is likely to happen by infection to theologians who, knowing that "everyone mingles the Gospel with some philosophy," suppose that there is autonomous value in the complete articulation of any one scheme of thought, or who suppose that in principle there is only one philosophical scheme of thought, or who suppose that in principle there is only one philosophical scheme fit to be so mingled. The theologian's interest, therefore, will be in gains and losses which seem to follow when one examines Christian utterances (both directly religious ones and more technical theological ones) with Braithwaite as the guide to understanding rather than Plato, Plotinus, Aristotle, Hegel, or Kierkegaard, none of whom necessarily deserve the privileged status which they have sometimes received.

The gains, as I have already hinted, may usefully be assessed in the context of the dispute between believers and unbelievers. Many theologians would subordinate their interest in this field to a prior concern that the believer should understand and enjoy his own freedom and responsibility in believing, but I do not think that anything is lost by attending here to the apologetic context. I offer three observations.

Christian belief (like any religious belief for that matter) has become an inexplicable way of thinking, and Christians themselves are puzzled, as never before, about the significance of their expressed belief. To deal with this situation it should be possible to give an intelligible account of religious conviction which is open to be discussed in the contemporary terms of debate. Braithwaite offers positive advice about this. Let us first agree about the meaning of religious utterances before we ask questions about their truth or reasonableness; and let us make sure that the meaning we propound will not lead to confusion or mystification. The empiricist recipe for doing this requires that the meaning should indicate to what extent and by what steps the utterances in question may be brought to the test of experience. Braithwaite has applied the recipe with an enterprising but sure hand. It could be argued, though not I think successfully, that this recipe already presupposes a philosophy or world-view which is calculated to discredit Christian belief; but if one agrees with Barth about philosophy and recognises in empiricist practice as well as theory an allergy to world-view very similar to Barth's own allergy, it is clear that this matter is not one to be pre-judged. In this connection it is worth noting that meaning, as required by an empiricist, does not serve to enshrine the whole truth about—in this case—religious belief. I suppose, however, that it does serve to represent what there is to be discussed, so far as it can be discussed to any purpose. Braithwaite makes the clear proposal that the discussion be about "the assertion of an intention to carry out a certain behaviour policy, subsumable under a sufficiently general principle to be a moral one, together with the implicit or explicit statement, but not the assertion, of certain stories."

All that Christians say about God and his activity is placed within "the implicit or explicit statement, but not the assertion, of certain stories." This deals in a most radical way with a fertile source of confusion and mystification in religious disputes. The case for this radical treatment is a strong one and it is a gain for modern theologians to realize how strong it is. Many Christian scholars seem happy to proceed on the assumption that such statements can be explained and commended by discussing the conditions, historical and psychological, under which Christians have come to talk as they do about Jesus Christ, about God, or about themselves and their world in relation to God. What matters is that such talk should faithfully echo "Biblical realism." This assumption, which could be called "Biblical positivism," must find some natural counterpart of a philosophical kind if it is to be carried successfully into the field of practical apologetics. Braithwaite's account of "stories," which are to be taken seriously as stories but not as propositions reporting empirical fact, is a congenial counterpart. As it stands, of course, it seems to lift from the believer (and so to lift out of the apologetic debate) all concern about the correspondence between the seemingly empirical propositions presented by the stories and empirical fact. There are, however, important respects in which the concern, if it is expressed in that form, is wholly unmanageable. This becomes true whenever the stories refer to God in ways which transcend human experience. Where this is not recognized, and it has not been recognized in traditional apologetics, religious utterances tend to be regarded as propositions within a super-science (or perhaps within two super-sciences, theology and metaphysics), which can be rendered more or less adequate and more or less plausible by the traditional kind of apologetic discussion. When the empiricist asks his key question: "What sort of arguments or observations tend to confirm or refute religious statements?", he uncovers aspects of the relationship with God called "faith" which many traditional theologians have known to be at the core of their problems, but to which they have drawn attention (I think particularly of Luther and Kierkegaard) in ways that are not very helpful at present—at any rate in England. I do not think that argument about the factual content of the stories can be dismissed so completely from the apologetic debate as Braithwaite's proposal may seem to suggest on a first reading. But in so far as it promises to lift unmanageable burdens mistakenly shouldered it is a welcome proposal.

It is to be observed, thirdly, that the centre of attention in the believer's debates with himself and with others must be shifted from theoretical understanding to behaving. From the point of view of experience Christianity may usefully be described as an ultimate decision to accept a way of life, and the discussion of other elements in Christian experience may be related to that core. Whatever be the case in other religions, it is true, I think, of Christian faith that to acknowledge God means to acknowledge a claim upon one's own life and upon the world. There is more to be acknowledged, but I think it can be summed up under the notion of promises which relate to the fulfilment of the claim. Therefore to examine Christian utterances in deliberate relationship to questions about human behaviour is a good programme for theological discussion. The churches, through most of their history, have displayed a most regrettable intellectual inertia in this matter. There have been times of liturgical vitality and concern; and a discipline called "Christian Morals" is one of the traditional appendices to ministerial training. The theological masters who are most respected today (Aquinas, Maurice, Forsyth, Barth, for instance) all saw the propriety of treating so-called Ethics as an integral part of Dogmatics, but the point is only rarely taken. Christians, in fact, are not well prepared for apologetic discussions framed in the light of a good analysis of the relationships between language, thought, and action, where it is clearly understood that action arises from intentions and not by inference from matters of fact. I take it that such a debate would not serve to produce theoretical justification for belief, any more than Kant's *Critique of Practical Reason* yields a theoretical proof of God's existence. The debate could, however, produce criteria for religion of the highest quality. Whether it should proceed on the particular lines of Braithwaite's moral philosophy is a matter which I gladly leave in Professor Britton's hands; and those who see in this a symptom of ecclesiastical intellectual inertia are doubtless justified.

There is an occupational disease against which English theologians ought to keep constant guard. It takes the form of applauding a fashionable movement in philosophy, explaining that it is thoroughly consistent with Christianity, tailoring it to fit such an explanation and then claiming that Christians have known about it all along. I hope that I have not succumbed to that disease. Braithwaite is in fact saying something new and disturbing and it is by no means obvious that one can think with him consistently without treason to Christianity. (It is by no means obvious

that I have enough of modern philosophical skill to think with him consistently, and since the exchange of autobiographies may have some role
to play in discussion about religion [p. 33] I can perhaps mention the
possibility that a Protestant background, a respect for science nurtured
by way of mathematics, and an indelible philosophical debt to Kant, may
count for a great deal in shaping my response to Braithwaite. Barthian
rather than Liberal Modernist affinities in theology may be an additional
factor, particularly in what comes next.) There are points where one must
note the possibility of serious loss. I can think of three such points, which
have a rough correlation with the observations already made.

First, the proposal to translate religious utterances into statements of
intention is peculiarly appropriate in present circumstances, where people
are living by Christian morality and Christian imagination and yet are
profoundly uneasy about the propositional statements to which the language of worship, say, commits them. But it is not immediately obvious
that this situation is characteristic of a "higher religion" and should therefore provide the main clue in the search for meaning. It can be argued
that the peculiarity of the situation obscures something of importance,
although in general it is most revealing. The obscured source of dissatis-
faction with Braithwaite is still in view if one goes back to Matthew Arnold's version of the way out of modern difficulties. Arnold is prepared
to say that " 'Trust in *God*' is, in a deeply moved way of expression, the
trust in the law of conduct."[4] An analysis of the word "law" used in this
sentence would show, I submit, that there is a reference to *authority*, which,
were it tracked down, would go to the root of the matter. I will not venture
to say, on the evidence of this lecture, what place Braithwaite would give
to authority in religion. In Christianity, to my mind, it has an ultimate
place. So, oddly enough, has the freedom to which Braithwaite gives magnificent testimony. But this ultimate place can be found for freedom only
in virtue of what, as a theologian, I call the authority of grace expressed
in the freedom with which God loves. This reference to authority can be
taken into account by an empiricist, no doubt in better ways than the one
I have suggested. If it worked out as I suspect, it would supply meaning
to my conviction that Christians acknowledge—perhaps, though this is
difficult, without always intending to acknowledge—the authority of the
God who is "there" in some more matter-of-fact sense than Braithwaite
can see his way to allow.

Secondly, Braithwaite's treatment of the propositions which refer to
God in ways which transcend human experience is, as I said, a radical
one. It may, however, be treason to Christianity to despair of attaching
sense, recognizable by an empiricist, to such utterances by less drastic
means. I appreciate the danger of short cuts and have dallied along those

---

[4]*Literature and Dogma*, Popular Edition (1883), p. 35.

which Braithwaite ploughs under with a few well-chosen words; lines of advance, that is to say, which suggest that the reality of God is an empirical fact known in a "self-authenticating" experience of "encounter," or that "God" can be treated as an empirical concept entering into an explanatory hypothesis (pp. 4–9). Nor can I see firm ground for attempts which are made to establish an ontological reference for these statements about God by the traditional ways of metaphysical theology. With no contribution of my own to make at this point I can only refer any interested reader who is dissatisfied with the view that discourse about "God" is fictional in character to the article by Mr. I. M. Crombie in the volume of essays *Faith and Logic* (ed. Basil Mitchell). The article proposes that this discourse is constructed out of "faithful" or "authorized" parables, which it is logically possible to *affirm*. Only the theist, of course, will affirm them and Mr. Crombie can identify himself only with the Christian theist (p. 68). The Christian theist is bound to affirm them because he is "impelled to regard the events recorded in the Bible and found in the life of the Church as the communication of a transcendent being" and the parables are "an essential part of this communication" (p. 81). Such statements are intended "not as improving fables about the things in this world, but as divinely given images of the truth about a transcendent being" (p. 73). I should myself exercise Barthian reserve in relation to "divinely given images of the truth" and recognise firmly that these images are also humanly contrived for the purpose of this non-fictional discourse. That being so, Mr. Crombie has met the need which I feel, but whether he has met the empiricist's case is another matter.

My third point bears on the programme for "moralizing dogma" (Forsyth's phrase) which in general I would support. I find it difficult to get rid of the idea that God gives himself to be acknowledged by statements whose reference to behaviour policies is more complex than Braithwaite seems to envisage. I have in mind more particularly statements to the effect that God's claim upon men has been fulfilled in Christ; that something has happened to the foundation of experience which has shifted human life from an old basis, to which a legalistic religion of works was appropriate, to a new basis where the substance of religion is well described as evangelical gratitude. "God has done what the law, weakened by the flesh, could not do; sending his own Son in the likeness of sinful flesh and to deal with sin, he condemned sin in the flesh in order that the just requirement of the law might be fulfilled in us, whose lives are determined not by the flesh but by the Spirit" (Roman 8:3–4). There is an exegetical problem about all such statements, the problem of doing justice to the "Pauline indicative" whereby salvation is affirmed as something given before conduct not achieved through conduct. It is fair to say, I think, that "catholics" and "liberals" take care in their exegesis to preserve the point that "Christ provides, but does not give, salvation." This principle is used in theological discussion to keep the doctrine of the Atonement in a morally respectable form. But the distinction which it makes may, in the judgement of some theologians, be expressing a religious conviction which falls short of complete deliverance from egocentricity and can be criticised as inadequate to the possibilities which have been established and whose actuality can be tasted even in this life when men live by faith. The effect of such a restrained exegesis is to leave Christianity as a highly refined religion of works. I am not concerned here to go into this dispute but I am anxious that it should not be ruled out of court *ab initio* on the ground that no meaning can be found, except in Braithwaite's terms of encouraging stories whose factual content cannot be asserted, for the great objective assertions upon which the "evangelical" challenge rests. I am by no means sure, of course, that the scales are weighed against "evangelical" theology in the way I fear, by this type of philosophical analysis. And of course I agree that the "evangelical" challenge must be purged of muddle and superstition before it can be sustained to any good effect in the theological field. The question is whether the purging and the sustaining can only be done by theological procedures which rest on the assumption mentioned at the beginning of this paragraph. When criteria for a religion of the highest quality emerge from a debate conducted on Braithwaite's terms, I suspect that they will offer new and subtle protection for man's natural forms of religiosity against the radical impact of the Christian Gospel. I know enough about what Paul was after when he campaigned against legalism (including unevangelical moralism) in religion, to make me hesitate before going all the way with Braithwaite.

Professor Braithwaite, let me repeat, did not stand up to lecture as a Christian Apologist. He is a philosophical critic, but unlike some, he does not treat religion as a disease of which men can, in principle, be cured—or if they can't be cured, they can at least be brought to understand the course of the disease so that it no longer inhibits their well-being! He deals with religion seriously and has put religious persons, including Christian theologians, into his debt.

(1958)

THE MODERN DISCUSSION
OF ESCHATOLOGY

In 1935 Professor C. H. Dodd published *The Parables of the Kingdom*, which was followed a year later by *The Apostolic Preaching*. These books had a remarkable influence on students, teachers and preachers in this century. With unmistakable clarity and cogency they uncovered the logic of New Testament affirmations about Jesus Christ and the connexion between His coming and the Kingdom of God. In the thought of the time, the Kingdom which "comes" in and with "the Coming One" was an "eschatological magnitude." That is to say, it comes upon men in an encounter where they are brought face to face with "the last things" in crucial decision. The effect of its coming is to disclose the true, elect Israel of God, united with the Messiah; to disclose the true God as the invisible partner who has brought about the fruition of the promised covenant relationship between Himself and men; and thus to disclose within history the end to which history is destined under the sovereignty of God. Jesus appeared as the destined Messiah. The meaning of His words and works during His earthly ministry was to establish the solidarity of His followers with Himself as Messiah. His Church conducted its subsequent mission on the assumption that all men are destined to encounter the risen Lord in and through the witness of His preachers and that this encounter will have the same eschatological character and must therefore be mediated and interpreted in the same eschatological terms. Professor Dodd's work, reinforced by that of other scholars, brought about a partial reformation of theology and of preaching in the light of New Testament emphases. But the problems raised by the eschatological interpretation of the New Testament were not ventilated in this country with the same thoroughness as was evident on the Continent. In particular, it became clear that the New Testament hope of a second advent of Christ had been accommodated rather too easily to the more congenial exposition of "realized eschatology," and it was not until 1950 that Professor Dodd came to terms with this challenge in his Advent broadcasts, published later as *The Coming of Christ.* In passing it may be mentioned that Sir Edwyn Hoskyns's exposition of "fulfilled eschatology," offered in sermons in 1926–27 and published in *Cambridge Sermons* in 1938, provokes a similar disquiet, though it affords a stimulus as great as that given by Professor Dodd to renewed seriousness about the eschatological weft and warp of the Gospel.

If the encounter with Christ is of an eschatological character, the "last things" with which man is thereby confronted may be taken to be death, resurrection, final judgement and "restoration of all things" (Acts 3:21). But modern discussion has not been directed towards producing an account of these matters in and for themselves. The practical and urgent problem whose main outlines I shall try to expound in what follows is the far wider one of how the Church today may grasp and reabsorb into its life the eschatological emphases which characterize the Gospel in its entirety. I shall leave out of account one fruitful line of discussion, the historical question of how and why the Church has failed to do so at particular crises in its development (if that indeed is the case). I am concerned only with the actual recovery of this eschatological interpretation, in the measure to which it has taken place in the complex and fruitful discussions conducted by Biblical scholars and systematic theologians during the last two decades. And even so, my interest is not to chart the fascinating paths of scholarship and of theological construction with historical objectivity, but rather to ask what has been given to us, and what are we to do about it.

The essay has three sections. First I shall glance briefly at the field where exegesis is the primary weapon and ask to what extent we have recovered the full integrity of the Biblical witness. Secondly, I shall examine the achievements of systematic thinking, the clarifications of meaning and the fruitful lines of attack which help to uncover the interior logic of eschatological faith. In the third section I shall try to work out some of the relevant theological decisions to which the Church of Christ is called at the present juncture of its life in history and in the present intellectual climate. I shall do this with particular attention to the alleged necessity of translating the substance of its faith into terms less crudely mythological than those with which the exegesis leaves us.

I

In his essay *Christ and the Christian Principle* (1911), P. T. Forsyth asked, "Can an historical person be the object of an absolute faith? Can a human personality at once express absolute Godhead and exercise a true humanity?" For lack of a positive and secure answer to this question, he maintained, the thought and devotion of the Church had come to rest, not upon Jesus, but upon ideas and principles for which Jesus stood either as sponsor or as symbol. It was in the same year that Schweitzer's words first appeared in English:

> The historical Jesus of whom the criticism of the future will draw the portrait, taking as its starting point the problems which have been recognised and admitted, can never render to modern theology the services which it claimed from its own half-historical, half-modern Jesus. He will be a Jesus who was Messiah, and lived as such, either on the ground of a literary fiction, or on the ground of a purely eschatological Messianic conception. In either case . . . the historical Jesus will be to our time a stranger and an enigma. (*Quest of the Historical Jesus*, pp. 396f.)

Schweitzer's prophecy has been largely fulfilled. The strange and enigmatical portrait has been redrawn. The discussion of particular features, such as the hiddenness of the Messiahship, the precise conception of Christian eschatology in terms of the Son of Man, the persistence of Parousia hopes after the events which supervened upon the resurrection and the lack of embarrassment on this score, the interpretation of the efficacy of the atoning death with its hard core of election and substitution, and finally the presence within the New Testament of what may be called de-Judaizing categories, is all serving to produce an integrated and self-authenticating account of the claim and promise of God as witnessed by the documents of the New Covenant. We are reasonably sure that what Schweitzer called the "dogmatic" element in the written history was put into the actual history by Jesus Himself. But it is not clear that we are better able to re-establish "the absoluteness, the finality, the cruciality for the soul's eternity of the historic Christ as the saving revelation," despite the clearer perspectives in which we see Him. We are satisfied that Jesus, His apostles and His evangelists, confront us with an integrated account of the claim and promise of God; and at the core of that account there lies the thesis that in Him "we have a new creation, the new humanity round which the old dies like a corn of wheat; we have the turning point of human destiny for all eternity; we have the presence and act of God decisive for that purpose; a final salvation—but not the final science of saving truth; a final faith—but not a final theology" (Forsyth, op. cit.). It is true and important that we have no final science of saving truth, no final theology, and this in the nature of the case. But is it not proper to ask, and to pray and to work, for a definitive exegesis, to which we can commit ourselves without any disquiet about our intellectual integrity, and which will serve, for some time to come, to inform all Christians about the Coming of the Lord as Scripture testifies to it?

The first point which I wish to make about the exegetical achievements is simply to plead for caution in the estimate of what has been done. Some would say that the progress made in the last forty years is epoch-making. I shall believe in the new epoch when I see a working version of the Gospel events, free from superficiality and from "modernist corrosion," being used in ordinary preaching and discussion with the same facility as was the old "liberal" version. The phrases are in circulation, and so are the "living images." But the foundations do not yet seem to be sufficiently secure to support an adequate and effective popularization. Schweitzer identified the "dogmatic" with the "historical" and found it to be most evidently present where the tradition was "unintelligible." He meant, I take it, "unintelligible to those who do not have the mind of the strange and enigmatic historical Jesus, engaged on his peculiar mission, and saturated with the thought-forms of Palestinian Jewry in the First Century." It may be asked whether the sayings and acts of this Jesus can or should become wholly intelligible except to the scholar. My own answer would be that if, through the Spirit, the humble believer is to be fed from the words and works of Jesus (and this, surely, is the substance for effective preaching), then the eschatological warp and weft of those words and works must be woven into his twentieth-century mind. This is a task which calls not only for greater skill and application but also for greater consensus of understanding than is yet apparent.

My second point affects the substance, rather than the form, of the exegetical results. It is valuable to have at one's disposal a clarified account of the expectations gathered up in the phrase "the Kingdom of God"; to have a clarified notion of the status and work of the eschatological Redeemer; to have a clarified understanding of Christian existence, sustained by the Spirit within the eschatological community; and to have a clarified version of the consummation of history. These themes are integral to the New Testament. But no one is carried to the heart of the matter by exposition of these things in themselves. In themselves they can function merely as another and clumsier set of "Christian principles" composing a very obscure "science of saving truth." They enable the scholar, and the intelligent layman, to follow the plot of "the greatest drama ever staged" with sound intellectual satisfaction and to achieve a sympathetic understanding of the early Christians' belief that they were living in the Messianic days. But I am not persuaded that the recent exegetical developments have liberated the New Testament writings for their essential task of confronting the modern reader with the awful reality of *God*. It may be that I am unduly sensitive to difficulties which seem to beset our best attempts to use the word "God" seriously in the modern context. It may be that the word carries more meaning, and more true meaning, to those who hear it or use it than I am inclined to think. But when orthodox expositors patronise Schweitzer for his agnosticism, suggesting in effect that for one so well instructed as he and they are it is easy to apprehend God in Christ, I am disposed to wonder what their language about God really means. Here, I think, is the chief stumbling-block in the path of any modern attempt to underpin the Church's life with a theology at once Christocentric and also profound, subtle and sure-footed after the manner, say, of Calvin's. Let me put the point like this. Modern discussion of eschatology on the exegetical level has enabled us to see *what* the words and works recorded in Scripture *purport to be*. So much is obvious. It is less obvious that it has helped us to realize *that they are* what they purport to be, and thereby confronted us in a new way with the reality of God.

I am concerned here with one moment only in a problem which is as wide as human existence itself, namely with our intellectual grasp on the content of Scripture in its integrity. Exegetes and theologians alike are aware that this content must be grasped in its own right and that it is intolerant both of dilution and of accretions. This intractable "autonomy" is intimately bound up with the eschatological marrow which pervades Biblical thought. It is therefore of crucial importance for faithful exegesis that we should wholly grasp the interior logic of this eschatology. The point of substance which seems to need rather more attention, if this aim is to be fulfilled, is illustrated by a recent Swiss controversy, and is brought out by the Roman Catholic exegete Eugen Walter in his book *Das Kommen des Herrn*. A great deal of attention must be paid to Jewish eschatology if we are to understand the interpretation within which the Gospel events are presented to us. But it is clear that the words and works of Jesus do not bear a simple relation to any Jewish scheme of thought. This was Schweitzer's point, when he said: "The case in which the Messiah should be present prior to the Parousia, should cause the final tribulations to come upon the earth, and should himself undergo them, does not arise in Jewish eschatology as described from without. It first arises within the self-consciousness of Jesus" (*Quest*, p. 385). This, no doubt, prejudges the question of a Messianic interpretation of Isaiah 53, but in a general way the point is valid enough. Schweitzer, followed now by Martin Werner, puts his own interpretation on this. The Swiss theologians who have criticized Werner (Kümmel and Michaelis) recognise the disparity between Jewish apocalyptic and the Messianic ministry of Jesus, but they have come almost to the point of suggesting that every instance of the disparity throws us back on the ultimate mystery of the Kingdom, namely that He who brings it to the earth is not merely an agent of God but personally or hypostatically God Himself.

It is generally agreed that the subject of the New Testament is an enactment of the *Eschaton* in a curiously veiled form which permits of further history. It is clear, rather, that this is what it purports to be, and the theme is presented in an integrated and coherent fashion. The question is whether the exegetes can do more to help us read the New Testament in such a way that its eschatological theme, with all its peculiar characteristics and difficulties, becomes eloquent of the mystery that the central figure who enacts the *Eschaton* is very man and very God. Systematic theologians, like humble believers, are apt to find in the New Testament the roots of the Nicene doctrine of the divinity of Christ in ways which do not always commend themselves to the scientific conscience of the Biblical scholar. It may be that the scientific scholar cannot commit himself to the thesis that the logic of the eschatological theme has its source and root in the mystery of the person of the eschatological Redeemer, and that here is a thread to be followed deliberately in the exegesis of all the passages which are saturated with eschatology. It seems to me, however, that until we have found our way through that logic to that source and root, we have not taken the measure of New Testament faith in Jesus as Word and Son of God.

II

I come next to the task which is laid upon the systematic theologian, to correct, clarify and safeguard contemporary statements of the Gospel and of the issues which it raises; in particular, to probe the interior logic of the eschatological language and concepts which are of its essence. The theologians who, as I think, are doing most for us here are concerned to avoid two extremes: the first, that of fantastic literalism which is characteristic of *Schwärmerei*, a solution with which the Bible itself leaves us discontented; the second, that of a species of *Entmythologisierung* which goes beyond any necessities imposed by the New Testament data.

The main themes which enter into any statement of the claim and promise of God; and which set the theologian his task, are these.

(1) The Kingdom of God is a decisive reality, really present in the world both in heaven and earth. Its presence on earth has been secured by the action personally wrought by God within the fabric of nature and history at a particular centre and in a particular form.

(2) The form of this action was an enacting of "the last things" in a curiously veiled manner.

(3) The presence of the Kingdom, though real, is not a presence in open glory, but a presence by signs which make recognition possible but not compulsory.

(4) God in His Kingdom claims from men their grateful acknowledgment. One moment in this acknowledgement is their cultic celebration of His reign, in all its past, present and future actuality; another moment is their active conformity to its gracious provenance in the immediate experience of life.

(5) The claim is imposed where men are brought face to face with "the last things" in crucial decision. This is the content of every encounter with Jesus Christ; and every encounter with Jesus Christ has this content. He is the *Eschatos* and the enactor of the *Eschaton*.

(6) The decisive action wrought by God within history at a particular centre in some sense accompanies history and bears decisively on all the process of historical connexions by which the cosmos moves to its consummation.

(7) God, reigning thus as King, secures for eschatological salvation those who meet the claim in faith, and does so by crisis of judgement and renewal. Already, therefore, they can live as men who are "justified," "free," "the new creation of God." In faith they are conformed to the Son of God, and their passage through the last things is the one which He has already undertaken for them. In hope they have their joyful place already in the eschatological metamorphosis of God's creation, though this exposes them to a present experience of straining for the end, coupled with a patient enduring and discipline. But in the present reality of love they live by the powers of the Kingdom and share in its overcoming of the alienated world.

(8) This Kingdom of God is best conceived as one which "comes"; that is, it is not to be regarded as a static reality either in the present or in the future. It comes in and with Christ, who is always to be thought of as the "coming" Lord.

(9) His "Lordship" is that of the cosmic Judge, by whose work sin is uncovered and annihilated, power is aligned with right, and the meaning of cosmic history is laid bare. It is also that of the cosmic Redeemer, who saves God's creation from the wrath to which it is manifestly exposed and establishes it in its original goodness.

(10) His "coming," however, is in the form of the eschatological Man, and is both an earthly and a heavenly act. That is to say, it is an act performed by the Son of God,[1] but it is an act with its appropriate "times" and historical forms. It happens when the Son of Man lives and dies as Israel's Messiah, rises from the dead, appears to His elect, and withdraws His physical presence from the historical scene, having accomplished, in a mystery, the end *(Eschaton)*. It is to be expected again, in a form where the veil of mystery is lifted, at the end *(Telos)* of history. And in the interval it happens, by what may be called an eschatological repetition, and in virtue of the work of the Paraclete, when His people gather at the Lord's appointment to meet Him.

(11) For the Son of Man is the gathering point of a new community,

---

[1]Forsyth, *Person and Place of Jesus Christ*, p. 282: "The thought and passion of the Church, its experience and not its philosophy and theology alone, has been driven to postulate behind all the acts of Christ's will on earth, behind all his pity and power, an act of *his* (not merely of his God and ours) eternal in the heavens; an act which held all these earthly acts within it."

and His mission to the world is fulfilled in and through that community. The presence of the Kingdom in the Church is the presence of the crucified and risen Son of Man who is to come in glory.

What is proclaimed in these themes, taken together, is the *real presence* of One who is *really God* and *really in history*. In his attempt to do justice to their eschatological character, the theologian has to attend to problems on two levels. On the first of these, the scope of the problems is wide. His task is to indicate the shape of our present historical experience of this real presence; to describe the eschatological present, the νῦν of New Testament speech, and to show how it is established by the historical revelation and action of Jesus Christ. The situation in "the years of our Lord" is alleged to be different from that in the years "before Christ." But what is the precise difference which is made by His presence in history? It is sometimes supposed that the theology of Christ's person and work involves so many factors which have little or nothing to do with discussion of "the last things" strictly and narrowly conceived that it would make for clarity if the term "eschatological" were not used with reference to issues raised on this level. The term *heilsgeschichtlich*, with its magnificent lack of elegance and precision, would better serve to indicate the new facets which distinguish modern discussion here. On the second level the problems have a narrower scope. They are raised when, perhaps under Schweitzer's prompting, we try to understand the unexpected lapse of time between the resurrection and the Parousia of Jesus, or when we try to examine the Biblical hope in respect of the incomplete fulfilment of the last things. They are raised by our efforts to state clearly the relation or tension between "having" and "hoping" which is at the heart of peculiarly Christian eschatology, and by our further efforts to exhibit its consistency with the logic of the Gospel and at the same time to uncover its practical bearing on the problems which vex the Church and mankind at large. Experience seems to be showing that it is not possible to isolate these narrower problems from those of the first level. Discussion on either level must be with an eye to what is entailed elsewhere. This is the justification for using "eschatological" as an umbrella term. If I may repeat the formula which seems to focus the issues, the reason why it is so necessary to discuss every problem "eschatologically" (in this irritating umbrella sense of the term) is that everything in Christian theology turns on the real presence of One who is really God and really in history; and the form of that real presence is the coming of ὁ Ἔδχατον, who is also ὁ πρῶτος; and His coming is always and everywhere το ἔσχατον, an enactment of the end where man is justified even in his ungodliness by the death and resurrection of the Son of God in the role of Son of Man.

I have already said that the deepest problem is, and always has been, that of knowing what we mean when we say "really God." It is by attention to the other two phrases, however, that I hope to indicate something of what is being achieved in the modern discussion of eschatology. In this report I shall not make use of the distinction between the two levels.

I begin with the phrase "really in history." Like so much else in modern discussion, the work done on the subject of time-concepts in the New Testament had its origin in a simple desire to understand what is written.[2] But it soon became apparent that here was a lore in which all must become versed if they would think the eschatological thoughts of New Testament writers. Sometimes, indeed, this lore is raised to the rank of a new Gnosis before which all problems melt away. I do not rate it quite so highly, for in truth there is no philosophy of time, nor indeed a single integrated and fully articulated conception of time to be derived from the Bible. What is there, and what has been successfully uncovered, is a method of handling the temporal context within which our life is set which is very different from the one to which we are accustomed by the scientific attitude. For us, time is a condition of existence in which we move inexorably out from a chronologically measured past into a chronologically measurable future. To live thus by passage through a duration of time makes it possible for us to engage as we do in responsible action; it sets our existence within a nexus of historical connexions as well as physical ones; but also it carries into our life many haunting overtones—the sense of perpetual perishing, radical uncertainty about the future, futile mockery by the elusive present—which cannot be lightly dispelled. If the "days," the "hours," the *kairoi* of which the Bible speaks, are merely moments within such a conception of time, it is impossible to take seriously the things said of them. At any rate we can only begin to do so by providing for them a rich background of Hegelian *Geist* and dialectic. No one suggests that we ought to repudiate the notion that our lives are lived in this kind of time. The temporal setting of our life is not totally misapprehended in these thoughts. What is required in faith is that we should see this against another kind of time, which is not the timeless *totum simul* of Greek eternity, and recognise that time as we know it in this chronological sense is "fallen time," a form of existence which imperils the fruition of God's purpose with man, but to which man it not hopelessly condemned. Indeed, by reason of God's decision to engage His creatures in a covenant-history, their life is also and already cast within a time which bears some analogy to the time in which God lives His own life of perfect fruition. This may seem an unnecessarily clumsy way of saying that the moments of time are impregnated with eternity. But this apparently clumsy form is important if we are to avoid importing into Scripture an alien metaphysic and an

---

[2] Cf. Cullmann, *Christ and Time*. I am sorry not to have had the chance of seeing J. Marsh, *The Fullness of Time*, though I have been able to draw on the outstanding article contributed by Professor Marsh to *A Theological Word-book of the Bible* (ed. Richardson), which shows him to be more philosophically minded than Cullmann.

alien notion of God as timeless perfection. God lives, and *acts*, in conditions of existence which we may distinguish from our own perhaps by saying that past, present and future are in one another without being identified. There is no escape from this mode of speech if we are to preserve the truth that He gives to His creatures a life in history by living as their partner. The time in which they are thus constrained to live is a meaningful succession of moments, or better, opportunities, established under the over-ruling direction of God in whose hands the cosmos is flexible to a degree we hardly credit, where they are required to make the response of appropriate action. The duration in clock-seconds of a *kairos* does not affect its momentary character. That character derives from the thing which is wrought as between God and man in and through that particular *kairos*. Each *kairos* is decisive for the future, though the pastness of the past, like the futurity of the future, is not in the least impaired. The *kairoi* taken together stand under some decisive "beginning" (ἀρχή) where an "age" (αἰών) is inaugurated, and move towards an "end" (ἔσχατον) where the content of the age is rounded off and established in its completeness or fulfilment as something eloquent of the glory of God.

This is a version of time, and of the times in which human life is lived, which has entered deeply into the Western European mind. We are familiar with it, but we have come to treat it with a certain suspicion lest it should perhaps be no more than a subjective illusion which flatters man's sense of his own importance. The recent scrutiny of its Biblical origins has disclosed a forgotten factor, namely that this conception of time can only be maintained when it is rooted in the belief that this is *God-created* time. It presents the time-conditions of our existence as the particular creation of a reigning God with active subjects whom He has adapted to His dominion. This in turn means that our whole conception of God hinges on His being the Creator and Filler of this kind of time.

It is with this background of thought that we affirm the real historicity of Jesus. In the first instance, this means His real presence in all the concrete particularity of that occasion in the past to which the Gospels bear witness—their witness, which stems from a time which is past, being itself part of the particularity of that occasion. But God, in His freedom and love, God in His threefold operation as Father, Son, and Holy Spirit, made that *kairos* to be an enactment of the last things, and therefore it is a *kairos* which "abides." Jesus, present in all the concrete particularity of that occasion, "abides" in the Father, and His disciples "abide" in Him. In that concrete particularity He is present in history wherever He "comes," and that makes the difference which is signified in the "now" of New Testament speech.

The theological questions which arise at this point are of the most profound and far-reaching significance, and some of them will come under consideration in the next part of the essay where we ask what we are to do with what has been recovered for us. The real presence of Jesus is His presence in the act of that "finished work" where men are brought face to face with the last things in crucial decision. Where He "comes," that is to say, we are in the presence of past events which have the finality and objectivity which characterizes all that is past. Our encounter with Him involves historical judgements, and the question of how one makes historical judgements in this, and in every other, case is a vexing one. We are also in the presence of future events, the enactment of the last things in open glory, and their real futurity must not be denied. Their veiled enactment has been woven into the texture of nature and history, but the question of how their glorious disclosure is related to the texture of nature and history is again a vexing one. And beyond these intellectual problems there lies the further task of achieving a deeper understanding of the promised occasions of His "coming" in the life of the Church and in the obedience of the Christian man.

My immediate concern is with the recovery of these insights, and there is one more thing to be mentioned, or perhaps one more way of putting the fundamental point, which throws some light on the intellectual puzzles. We may say, perhaps, that Jesus, present thus in history and in our human time, is present as One who lives also in the proper time of God, and that in virtue of His presence we are with Him in His time. We are also held down still in the necessities of fallen time, as He is not, and never was, this being one element in the truth laid bare by the resurrection. We may therefore describe what has happened in these terms. Let us grant, first, that man's time has been maintained for him by God acting in faithful covenant towards a faithless partner. His humanity has been upheld by this gracious action and Chronos has no final dominion over him. In the fulness of this God-given series of *kairoi*, God achieved His purpose of love by an *Eschaton*, an atoning and incorporating act which He wrought personally by taking the form of the Son of Man. The Son of Man therefore lives in the time of God, and comes to man in His time. Man, held down in fallen time, summoned always to live in his proper human time but failing so to do, finds that his life is set in something which is entirely new to him, namely the time of this Son of Man. The question is whether this new standing-ground should be construed in terms of quality—a new quality in life which brings an eternal status, or, with Heim, in terms of a new dimension of life—whatever "dimension" means in this context, or in terms of a non-temporal eternity conceived in some Platonized fashion. There is no need to Platonize at this point. A "Christ-filled magnitude," which is John Marsh's definition of the "eternal" in the New Testament, is not a realm of "eternal Ideas." I cannot, however, report that the provisional agreement which has been reached about the use of time concepts extends as far as a formal description of this new duration (αἰών) of which men have been given the freedom in Christ, nor of the ζωη αἰώνιος in which they exercise that freedom. The test comes when one tries to preach from such a text as:

> Repent therefore, and turn again, that your sins may be blotted out, that times of refreshing may come from the presence of the Lord, and that he may send the Christ appointed for you, Jesus, whom heaven must receive until the time for establishing all that God spoke by the mouth of his holy prophets from of old. (Acts 3:19–21)

We must pass now from terms of formal description to the treatment of content, and we have already come within sight of the questions which gather round the second of my two phrases, that He is *really present* and with Him the eschatological reality of the Kingdom of God. The difficulty is to define the difference which this makes and to take due account of what must still be treated as a matter of future expectation. To what extent has it been possible to transcend the conflict between those systems of eschatology which we call "consequent" (cf. Schweitzer), "realized" (Dodd) and "fulfilled" (Hoskyns), and affirm an eschatology which may perhaps be labelled "inaugurated"?[3]

In his reaction to the evolutionism of the nineteenth century, Professor Dodd emphasized the present realization of the *Eschaton* to a degree which almost banished any teleological element in our understanding of God's works and ways. Professor T. F. Torrance points out, however, that,

> in using both terms, *Eschaton* and *Telos*, the New Testament clearly refuses to teach an eschatology of judgement and new creation that is divorced from a teleological conception of creation and history. . . . Therefore while the Kingdom of God means that the fashion of this world will pass away before the eschatological rule coming from above and beyond, yet that rule actually enters into the course of history and its saving action cannot be divorced from God's original and eternal purpose in creation.[4]

The recovery of teleology is associated with an attempt to take seriously what the Bible says about the framework of nature and about the factors which enter into the making of history, for in its account of the content of all *kairoi* these things play an essential role. At the same time, its assumptions are a source of embarrassment to those who live with a modern scientific attitude. The questions raised at this point about deliteralizing and de-mythologizing must be deferred for the moment for we are still concerned with the recovery of Biblical testimony.

It is misleading, I think, to say that the Bible is tied to a particular cosmology, or to a particular mythical representation of historical process. But it does speak, in the first case of "heaven," and in the second case of κοσμοκράτορες and στοιχεῖα τοῦ κόσμου, and theologians cannot meekly

---

[3]The credit for this label belongs to Professor Florovsky, but Calvin had the idea first.

[4]From a privately circulated memorandum (1949). See also *The Evangelical Quarterly*, 25 (1953), 102.

acquiesce in a cosmology or a philosophy of history which leaves no room for such concepts.

Karl Barth has done more than most to help theologians to press the point that the "world" which is open to scientific observation is not to be identified without remainder with the created cosmos. This is not to deny the Copernican Revolution, with all its blessings. It is merely to say that the cosmos has its invisible side, heaven, and to claim the right of using spatial terms with reference to heaven. It has been the custom of many to fall back on the more profound insights of Greek thought at this point and to affirm the reality of heaven, and of the God whose dwelling-place it is, by using the category of "spirit," a non-temporal non-spatial concept reached by way of negation. By this recourse it becomes improper to speak of heaven as the *place* of God's habitation. It is difficult to give any meaning to the notion of its relative role within the created cosmos. In the Bible, heaven is an element in the created cosmos with a limited function. It is the seat within the cosmos of God's throne, a throne which He determines to occupy within His creation for the sake of His covenant purpose, but to which He is not confined. Heaven has its own denizens, the angels, whose office is not irrelevant to the mystery of the Kingdom of God as it comes to earth. To express all this by the category of "spirit"— meaning thereby a non-temporal non-spatial reality—may mean that the way of negation has been carried so far that statements which are essential to the Gospel cannot be made at all. The whole notion of Jesus as the "Coming One" is at once riddled with equivocation.

It may be that the New Testament itself invites us to take this line, but whatever its language about "spirit" is judged to mean it is important not to overlook the positive term which is used to characterize the realm where God's Kingship is openly displayed. I mean the term "glory." Nor should it be overlooked that heaven is involved in the cosmic metamorphosis which is part of eschatology. We are encouraged to believe that it will be integrated in a new way with "earth," so that our citizenship, which is secured there in the present with Christ, may be fully exercized in the future both in heaven and on earth. Here, of course, I am taking for granted the point that "earth" is man's appointed dwelling-place within the cosmos and that there is no ground for supposing that this will not be true in the apocalypse of glory. On the contrary, indeed, there is every reason to suppose that it will.

Whether scientists can be brought to respect such language is a problem to be solved by practice. There is nothing in it to aggravate the much advertised "problem of communication," provided it is used boldly (though with proper reserve) by theologians who feel no constraint to substitute something else for it in the secret recesses of their intellectual respectability, and who have first overcome within themselves the difficulties and embarrassments occasioned by the modern world view. The bearing of all this on theological discussion is that it keeps us face to face with the problem of creation's teleological end in its full magnitude, and warns us against facile accounts of the coincidence of eschatological and teleological ends.

The Biblical account of the factors which enter into the making of history has been worked out with particular clarity in Stauffer's *Theologie des Neuen Testaments*. First among such factors is the decision of God expressed in a Word which is also an Act. This decision falls in harmonious patterns of *Leitgesetze* (Stauffer's word), the ὁδοι τοῦ Θεοῦ of New Testament speech which he equates with Augustine's *leges providentiae*. It falls on men who are capable of a personal human response, but also on the lower animate creatures and on those which are inanimate; and the response they make, in all their material concreteness, is indistinguishable to our eyes from mechanical or instinctive necessity. It also falls on the "cosmocrats" and "world-rulers." All these, by their action under God's decision, enter into the making of history. Now it is history whose making is thus conceived which comes to its teleological end, in Christ. Its *Telos*, lit up for us now by the advent of the *Eschatos* and His enactment of the *Eschaton*, will not be achieved without events in which God and His people will be gloriously vindicated and creation be renewed according to His original purpose. These events may therefore be confidently expected in the future, and their real futurity is not a source of embarrassment to the faith of the New Testament. But they cannot be regarded quite simply as future; that is to say, as though their "time" were one from which we at present are totally excluded. This would be to impair the "real presence" of Christ as we are obliged to affirm it. So regarded, they must be deemed to make no difference in our present, apart from that which is produced by intelligent or unintelligent anticipation on the part of men. This is to rob the present encounter with Christ of its complete eschatological character. We are not, in that case, yet face to face with the last things in crucial decision. It is an error parallel to that of supposing that we are temporally excluded from those events in the past where the eschatological decision of God became historic fact and of treating them therefore merely as instructive allegories.

The question which has to be pressed at this point is whether, when we speak of these further events, we should affirm the real, though veiled, presence of Christ, of the whole Christ and therefore of these expected events, within the fabric of history which constitutes our present *kairos*. In that case we are committed to belief that there has been a real alteration of history, not only in virtue of what lies in our past, but also in virtue of what lies in our future. Those who know that they have been caught up into the time of the Son of Man know that they have the responsibility of understanding this. They must lay hold of the God-given teleology which has been woven into history at the *Eschaton*, and act and think in the light of it.

Questions which are of the utmost importance in the Church's mission are opened up by this notion that cosmic history has been altered in the present from an end which to us is still future. One which stands in relative isolation from the rest concerns the present state of those who have died in Christ. A doctrine which speaks in purely teleological terms of their having entered on a further stage of probation appears to be deficient in eschatology, as does the antithetical doctrine that they "sleep." The important question is not "What happens to me after death?", but how is my life in Christ at present enriched by communion with those dear to me on earth "who obtained the prize"? Here there is room for considerable developments in teaching and theology.

Other questions arise in closer relation to the assertation that something within history, which can be indicated, however obscurely, by the terms "cosmocrats" and "world-rulers," have been effectively subordinated to the righteousness of God, so that the struggle for the peace of God's creation wears a significantly different aspect from any that appears by mere scrutiny of experience. Is it the case that the fabric of nature is open in a new way to powers of renewal and reparation, whose operation serves at least to prepare the way for a cosmic metamorphosis into glory? Is it the case that the history of human thought and activity bears marks of a reconciliation wrought by God for men which is bearing fruit in actual redemption unto God? Karl Heim has been prominent in the pursuit of these themes, as have George MacLeod and the Iona Community in another way. Though much that is said and done may seem to our sober minds to be rather extravagant and unwarranted, it may be the earnest of a rich harvest from modern eschatological thinking which will be reaped in fields less crudely ecclesiastical than those which are often the centre of attention.

But these covenanted mercies of God in respect of the lives of His saints and in respect of cosmic nature and history must always be interpreted by norms which are supplied from our understanding of the Church and of the presence of Christ to the Church in all the power of His finished work. It is of prime importance to see the Church as a magnitude which derives not only from the past and present but also from the future, because it derives from Christ. The Church is the classic instance of "being what we are in virtue of Christ's real presence," but knowing that this real presence is also an advent presence. All that we have in Christ is real but not yet manifest. We have it by a security which does not depend on its being presently manifest. But the time of its manifestation presses upon us at every point. We must speak of realized teleology, however limited in scope we allege the realization to be, only with the greatest reserve. And this is particularly true in our language about the Church, for there the eschatological tension between having and not having is felt most acutely. A re-thinking of the Church, its marks, its practices, and its mission, in the light of eschatology is the way forward to a more faithful future over the whole range of life. But such a future will not give us any development beyond the Christ who is really present now, for He is the *Eschatos* in whom ever now, though in proleptic fashion, we have the consummation of God's creation.

III

It is in the Church that the claims of God's Kingdom are explicitly acknowledged and this acknowledgment takes place amid the vicissitudes of history. It has its liturgical forms where the Kingdom is acknowledged by cultic celebration, and it exhibits an active conformity to the demands of the Kingdom in the immediate experience of life, first in the ordering of its own activity and then in the corresponding behaviour of its members in all the walks of life. The intellectual acknowledgment which bears upon this practice shows evidence of different intellectual contexts in which it has been wrought out and this is part of its destiny which is one of straining towards Christ in His glory through the process of history. Its theologians must not, therefore, be dismayed because their decisions have to be formulated in new intellectual contexts, but neither must they expect them to be adequate anticipations of that final intellectual satisfaction which is reserved with the Parousia. Today, as at previous times, we are urged to "translate the Gospel into modern terms," or better perhaps, to "discover the truth which the Biblical terms ought to convey to us," and this is taken to mean that we must once more extract the hard core of the matter from the shell of out-moded technicalities and give more congenial expression to it. Let us grant that the form of man's all-decisive encounter with God is that he is brought face to face with the last things in crucial decision, and that the complex associations of this thesis have been indicated with tolerable faithfulness in the preceding parts of this paper. The problem is that we can hardly hope to weave all this into the thinking of modern believers unless we discover ways of presenting it which do not offend the modern mind but which do not go so far in the way of accommodation as to cut the vital nerve which is safeguarded so aptly by the Biblical language. There are two points to be made about this before we turn to consider immediate proposals.

First, the theology by which we take the measure of this eschatological *kerygma* must have its root, like the *kerygma* itself, in a history in which God has participated with men. But this history has never been directly accessible to men, as is history in our common understanding of it—and even there, of course, the access is not direct in any simple sense. Here, however, the events are not accessible along channels of objective factual experience, nor by channels of psychological experience, nor by channels open to the "supernatural," nor by those explored in speculative thought. The action of the living God is hidden beneath all the levels to which such channels lead and at the crucial point it is completely withdrawn from any direct grasp. But the proclamation of it depends on its being nonetheless a factual event, primarily "ontic" in character rather than "noetic." It may be, therefore, that all our attempts to adapt to our intellects the mystery in which the *kerygma* is rooted are doomed to frustration. That which happened, happens, and will happen "for us," "among us," and "in us," is not domesticated even in principle within the range of operation of the human *Geist* so that it can be rendered fully intelligible. The testimony of Scripture itself bids us halt at the outskirts of key moments in the event—the incarnation of Jesus and His vivification after death—which have no human witnesses. But in so doing it never means to deny that these things happen in this most secret place, nor to present its testimony as a mere expression of the Church's faith in the divinity of the Incarnate or in the saving efficacy of the Crucified. This insistence on the ontic reality of the history, despite the way in which it eludes our direct grasp, means already that we are not dealing with "cunningly devised fables" when the power and coming of our Lord Jesus Christ is made known. We have already turned our back, in the only sense that need worry us, on "profane and old wives' fables." We are dealing, not with a myth of a Greek god whose casual visit to earth reveals something of "the eternal," but with a coming of God to be naturalized on earth as a man and thus with a real entry into earthly history. The notions and concepts employed in the *kerygma* have already been "de-mythologized." The notion of "coming," for instance, is not to be whittled away as though it were mere instructive allegory. This, and the other concepts, are terms whose use is permitted and enjoined for those who stand in the succession of the apostles, the "eye-witnesses of His majesty."[5]

Second, what has been said about the action of God applies with even greater force to the reality of God Himself. What makes it so difficult for us to speak properly about God is that He always treats with men in terms of what is *not* God. This, indeed, sheds some light on the fact that man's crucial encounter with Him takes place in and through His eschatological handling of all that is not Himself. The resources of nature and of human personality, the authority of law and of inspired Scriptures, the security of communities, even of the most manifestly elect, are taken to the limiting point where their otherness from God is laid bare, and He is left supreme in majesty and grace. But again this is not to deny that He takes these things into His service. In particular, though our language and concepts

---

[5]Cf. *Kerugma und Mythos*, a lecture by Heinrich Vogel printed in the *Jahrbuch der Kirchlichen Hochschule Berlin* (1951), and also printed as a separate pamphlet.

are inadequate to the reality of the Word of God, that Word takes into its service our human words and human world-outlooks and prevails over them in a fashion which brings men within earshot of God's utterance and encloses them within the world of His creation.

When we have recovered the convictions of New Testament writers we have to wrestle with the question of their truth. We must have good reason for believing that the voice of the New Testament is a reliable voice, and we must find ways of stating and upholding the truth as that voice conveys it to us. The two points which have just been made have a considerable bearing on the Christian answer to such questions of epistemology. They serve as a warning that the analysis of man's rationality in itself will not afford a basis for the security of theological convictions. If Christian utterance is to be truthful, and if it is to be upheld as true, the affirmation of how God is God and how He makes Himself known to men is of even greater significance than the affirmation of how man is rational. This is not the place for an essay in epistemology, but it is clear that a concern about epistemology lies very close to the current proposals for a mode of speech about God, His words and His ways, which is not a literal reproduction of Biblical language and which is free from the mythological imagery which is alleged to obscure the Biblical message.

The term "mythology" draws attention to one feature of certain statements, namely that they are cast in a story-form which is not to be treated as though it offered an exact transcription of historical or scientific fact. It is a form which inevitably comes into use when assertions are made about divine participation in the events of human history. It is governed by current presuppositions of a particular age and place. In Bultmann's definition: "Mythology is an imaginative way of expressing the other-worldly and divine in terms of this world and of human life, the things on the other side in terms of this side." Bultmann is clear about the distinction between myth and allegory. That which is expressed mythologically is not necessarily a timeless truth, nor is it a process in the soul, both of which can only be objectified by imagery. He might, I think, agree with Thielicke that it is important to work out a conception of myth which "conveys the factuality of the *history* it enshrines." This is of special importance in the case of the Biblical material where creation, the Fall, "the eschatological event of salvation" (Bultmann), and the end of history are all things which *happen*, and which partake in the character of history. Schniewind and Thielicke have both criticised Bultmann's own essay on de-mythologizing on the ground that it disregards the finality of Jesus, both in regard to the essential past-ness of the Gospel events and in regard to the completeness of the "finished work." Schniewind says that "if Bultmann understands the event of Christ merely in terms of our present historical and personal existence, does he not reduce the history of Christ to a bare symbol or a stimulus to devotion?" Thielicke asks: "Is the New

Testament history merely a vague reality at the back of Christian experience, a reality which can hardly be recovered as it actually happened in past history?" I do not intend to expound the details of particular proposals and criticisms which come out of Continental Existentialism. They represent, in an extreme form, the kind of attack which men feel obliged to make upon the abiding usefulness of that machinery by which the Bible safeguards its eschatological message.

It will be sufficient here to take the measure of attacks which are made in the interest of de-literalizing, rather than de-mythologizing, and these occur in two forms, one Idealist and one which is perhaps better described as "Personalist" rather than "Existentialist" and is associated with writers like Buber, Otto, Oman, Farmer, and Tillich. Dr. Galloway's book *The Cosmic Christ* is a remarkable exposition of this second line as it bears on eschatology. Over both lines there stands the presiding genius of Hegel and it is still true that there are few Protestant Christians in the world today, certainly in the West, for whom Hegel does not speak more truly and profoundly than they are able to speak for themselves.

Hegel found a way of characterizing the "living ground of all existence" when he spoke of *Geist*, Spirit, the achieved identity of knower and known, which requires all the dialectic of nature and history and human experience in order to come to itself. He launched his massive protest against any conception of God which implies the subservience of man to what is extrinsic, for this means "elevating into an absolute what is only a fragment of the whole human heart" (*The Spirit of Christianity* in *Hegel's Early Theological Writings*, ed. Knox and Kroner, p. 238). This like all the dichotomies which mar our finite being, is a rending of life from life. All opposition represents a thwarting or denial of the living ground of all existence and must be abolished in a reconciliation where Spirit comes to itself in love and life. To come to God, therefore, we must pass beyond the crudity of historical happenings. "Man can believe in a God only by being able to abstract from every deed, from everything determinate, while at the same time simply clinging fast to the soul of every deed and everything determinate" (op. cit. p. 254). Everything turns on the knowledge of spirit through spirit. "The relation of spirit to spirit is a feeling of harmony, is their unification; how could heterogeneity be unified?" (p. 266). "In the Kingdom of God what is common to all is life in God. This . . . is love, a living bond which unites the believers; it is this feeling of unity of life, a feeling in which all oppositions, as pure enmities, and all rights, as unifications of still subsisting oppositions, are annulled" (p. 278). These observations, which have now become commonplace, indicate the real ground of disquiet about Biblical language, once we have realized that they have only a slight basis, if any at all, in the Biblical language from which Hegel claimed to derive them. To convey its eschatological message, the Bible talks about the fabric of nature in ways which seem at first sight to be inadequate and perhaps incredible. But that is a trifling difficulty compared with its insistence on the otherness of God and with its way of talking about the fabric of history. We are not at home with an eschatology which forbids us to run away from the physical into the realm of "spirit" and which demands, for an adequate statement, some kind of emphasis on "times." We cannot rest content until justice has been done to the magnificent profundity of Hegel's theology, or rather to the finest insights of Greek philosophy which he preserved and embellished for the modern mind.

From this point of view, the essence of the eschatological encounter where man is brought face to face with God and with the last things in crucial decision is

> that a Man should appear, the very essence of whose consciousness should be the reconciliation of the antitheses, and who should manifest this consciousness to the world, and lead the religious mind to the sole point from which its difficulties can be solved. Jesus accomplishes this mighty work ... by gradually making known the thoughts which filled and entered into the very essence of His mind. It was only in this indirect way that His person, which He freely offered up in the cause of His historical vocation and of the idea for which He lived, continued to live insofar as the idea was accepted.

This is Bruno Bauer, quoted by Schweitzer in *The Quest of the Historical Jesus*, pp. 143ff. Schweitzer's own conclusions are well enough known but deserve to be repeated:

> Not the historical Jesus but the spirit which goes forth from Him, and in the spirits of men strives for new influence and rule, is that which overcomes the world. ... Jesus as a concrete historical personality remains a stranger to our time, but His spirit, which lies hidden in his words, is known in its simplicity and its influence is direct. ... The names in which men expressed their recognition of Him as an authoritative ruler, Messiah, Son of Man, Son of God, have become for us historical parables. We can find no designation which expresses what He is for us. He comes to us as one unknown, without a name, as of old by the lakeside He came to those who knew Him not. He speaks to us the same word: Follow thou me!, and sets us to the tasks which He has to fulfil for our time. He commands. And to those who obey Him, whether they be wise or simple, He will reveal Himself in the toils, the conflicts, the sufferings which they shall pass through in His fellowship, and, as an ineffable mystery, they shall learn in their own experience who He is. (op. cit. p. 400f)

This is the finest expression of the way in which very many liberal minded Christians have come to terms with the eschatological issues. This language about "the spirit of Jesus" and our "contact with it" acquires its proper powers only against a background of rich Hegelian character, but it may be that it will acquire new powers from modern Biblical scholarship and from a theological re-thinking of Hegelianism which will make it an adequate vehicle of Christian utterance. As matters stand it is not necessary to underline its deficiencies.

Dr. Galloway, like all the "Personalists," does not substitute for the Biblical preoccupations others of a more "modern" (or perhaps "Greek") kind as Idealists tend to do, though the fundamental contrast of "personal" with "impersonal" does not, I think, carry all the Biblical credentials which it is supposed to do. He is concerned with the reality of cosmic redemption, and wishes to avoid the awkward choice between "a full-blooded interpretation which looks for some objective change in the material constitution of the universe" and a more anaemic interpretation which claims "that the subjective alteration in man's outlook, wrought by his inward experience of redemption, so alters his estimate of the world around him as to be tantamount to a renewal of the world" (*The Cosmic Christ*, p. 239). He asserts, therefore, that "a change has been wrought in the *form* in which our experience comes to us; that is to say, it is a change appearing in the correlation of self to the world." The change has come because Jesus "disclosed," in the sense of "interpreted and fulfilled," the *intrinsic* meaning of the cosmos. The "meaning" of something is "that which refers beyond its own particular existence"; "intrinsic meaning" is that carried by a symbol which evokes a personal response from us. The problem of existence is to correlate personal self with an impersonal world—a world whose impersonality is a token of the demonic. "Man's world must *claim* his personal response and claim it absolutely before he can fully give himself to it and find the ultimate security of his personal being. This is precisely what we find to be accomplished in the work of Jesus as the Christ" (p. 257). Eschatological language, therefore, points to the fact that an absolute anchorage has been given for our personal life, for all our encounter with the world becomes now, in some sense, also an integral part of our personal encounter with God. The bondage of men outside the Church to the demonic—the meaningless "It"—gives to the Church's mission the same urgency as did their bondage to the arch-demons of sin and death in St. Paul's day.

It could be argued that all these proposals for a mode of speech about God and His eschatological act fail to meet the requirements of New Testament data on which they are based because they pay little heed to the moral, as compared with the intellectual, moment in the decisive encounter; that is to say, to the fact that in that encounter man is *justified* by faith. The justification of sinners is an act which can only be wrought within a framework of eschatological magnitude, and it is perhaps true to say that the eschatological themes are not elaborated in Scripture for their own sakes so much as for the sake of this central assertion. This is something of which theology cannot afford to lose sight in its efforts to grapple with the machinery of that elaboration. Here is a thread running through the interior logic of Biblical eschatology which is closely entwined with the other thread that He who brings the *Eschaton* is very man and very God.

Because the eschatological theme is woven round this dual centre, the Biblical statement of it has a measure of intractable autonomy which theology must respect. It is not safe for the Church to seek a statement of its message which is only *suggested* by the New Testament, and which for the sake of accommodation to the "modern mind," exhibits dilutions and accretions of which in fact Biblical theology is intolerant.

On the other hand, the plea which I am disposed to make for a bold use of Biblical language is not without its difficulties. It has been pointed out to me[6] that theological decisions rest, in part at least, upon historical judgement, and it is part of the eschatological story that this should be so. Because history is what it is we cannot say: "This is said in this way in the Bible, and I must accept it precisely in the same way." Instead I am always obliged to say: "This is how I accept responsibility for interpreting what is said in this way." It cannot be taken for granted that historical judgement will mean literal acceptance. In point of fact I think that this discussion (certainly in its expository part) is a practical exemplification of the second of these statements, and if that is so it is a small contribution to theology even though it looks dangerously like a mere reproduction of Biblical words.

Theology, like the preaching which it nourishes and safeguards, ought to carry evidence of what Hegel called "a sense of the whole depth of man"; but this is only one moment in a wider "sense" of the unsearchable riches of God and the majesty of His works and ways. The Church's handling of its eschatological message has often been deficient in any such "sense," and the mere study of the theological meaning of Biblical words and concepts gives no guarantee against tragic misrepresentation of the majesty of God. Such study sets up conflicts in the modern mind which must be taken seriously if the depths are to be suggested. There is some ground for believing that these conflicts move towards fruitful resolution precisely insofar as theology pays humble respect to the awkward data, and takes particular pains to understand and appreciate the less congenial features of eschatology as stated in the Bible without feeling constrained to explain them away. I think, therefore, that theology should proceed from a conviction that the Bible's statement of its eschatological theme is a necessary and an adequate one, and that it should strive for an understanding where everything is integrated round the central themes of the hypostatic union of God and man in the person of Christ and the justification of man by God's grace alone which has been wrought out in Christ. It is not difficult to discriminate between what is metaphor and

---

[6]By Principal H. Cunliffe-Jones of Bradford.

what is assertion of physical or historical fact in the Biblical data; e.g., between the picture of a "coming on the clouds of heaven," on the one hand, and the assertion that "earth" has its place in the ultimate theatre of glory. The deepest modern problem, I would repeat, is that of knowing what we mean when we say "God," and of being satisfied that what we say of His acts is worthy of their majesty. I can see no amelioration of those difficulties except by paying humble respect to the form by which, according to Biblical testimony, God has chosen to give Himself to men and to draw His creation to Himself in Jesus Christ.

(1953)

THEOLOGY
AND THE
NATURAL SCIENCES

THEOLOGY HAS ITS OWN SUBJECT MATTER. THE TASKS IMPOSED BY THAT
subject matter are many and various. To each of them there is an appropriate disciplined approach. These tasks all arise from the fact that men
make acknowledgments, in speech and in conduct, of the "God" to whom
they aspire in religion and to whom they are related in "faith." To criticize
these acknowledgments and to help with their revision or reconstruction
is the general task assigned to theology. In discharging it, theologians have
always been influenced, and rightly so, by the prevailing cultural context.
The present context is one where people are liable to feel uncertain in
professing any belief which is not supported by those expert in scientific
knowledge and speculation. Direct support from these experts is not to
be expected in matters of religion or theology, but there will be uneasiness
if their own expertise contributes to religious scepticism or to contempt
for theology as an ill-based and misguided pursuit.

During the last four hundred years, scientists have produced physical,
chemical, geological, and biological accounts of our world's structure and
of the functioning of all its components; accounts which do not easily
harmonize with accepted versions of religion, more particularly of Christianity. A harmony of cosmological and theological outlook was a feature
of Christendom in earlier days. It was the product of intense intellectual
and cultural struggles, and it was never securely established so as to be
immune from criticism. There is nothing strange about the fact that the
struggles have been revived, in new forms and changed circumstances,
and good theologians have always tried to do more about it than merely
to defend inherited resources, accepting such modification as are forced
upon them. But theologians no longer dictate the terms of the struggle.
In the present cultural climate it is the scientists who have come to rank
as authoritative guides to human needs and possibilities. The irrelevance
of God, except as a therapeutic idea of debatable value, and the reduction
of religion to a psychosocial phenomenon infested with immaturity—

169

these are working convictions for a large proportion of mankind. The concerns of theology have come to seem peripheral; and many able persons are quietly suspicious, or openly disparaging, about its credentials as an intellectual discipline.

The scientists themselves have not, as a rule, actively promoted this change in human self-awareness, though they have generally acquiesced in its growth. The evangelizing voices have been in apostolic succession from Marx and from Comte, names which remind us that the extension of scientific claims from the physical to the sociological fields has been of crucial importance in shaping the present cultural situation. In 1844 Marx wrote that "natural science will in turn incorporate the science of man, just as the science of man will in turn incorporate natural science"; and Communist culture is the apotheosis of this conviction. Social science, Comte declared, would complete "the upward flight of our contemplations of reality" and impress upon those contemplations the systematic character they previously lacked "by providing them with the sole universal link of which they admit." Theology and metaphysics, former pretenders to the role of universal integrators, "will have for our successors only an historical interest."[1] The relation between theology and the physical sciences is therefore a limited theme within a wider concern. Yet it is a matter about which no theological worker can afford to be ill-informed.

I

First let us consider how best to envisage the interaction of these intellectual enterprises. Their independence is now generally appreciated, and a metaphor frequently used is that of "territories," with frontiers, frontier engagements, and diplomatic relationships. It is a metaphor to be used with caution, for important common ground may be obscured by attempts to map out the provinces of science and of theology so that the two kinds of enterprise may enjoy peaceful coexistence. Each enterprise takes off from the ground of common experience, all aspects of which are within its scope. Both enterprises direct our attention toward the same structure of actualities and possibilities, which, in the opinion of both scientist and theologian, is not ours to create in some arbitrary fashion, but rather is to be sought and recognized for what it is. For science, it is true, the primary target is the physical universe; or, more precisely, those relations in it which, when intellectually grasped, bring its structure and functioning within man's theoretical and practical range. But this target is pursued within boundary conditions: man in his personal sub-

---

[1]These citations are borrowed from W. G. Runciman, *Social Science and Political Theory* (Cambridge: The University Press, 1963), p. 4. For Comte's view of "social physics" as the legitimate heir which will displace theology and metaphysics, cf. also *The Fundamental Principles of the Positive Philosophy*, I, 31–33.

jectivity and corporate historicity, on the one hand; and on the other, the mystery which envelops the ground of being and of reason. The development of scientific thought casts incidental light upon these boundary conditions, and attention may be explicitly directed toward them at crises in the struggle for scientific advance. For Christian theology, the chief topics are God and man; but the physical world is not outside its purview, first because it is in this world that man is constituted and set to function, and secondly because the God to whom men aspire in Christian faith is acknowledged to be the ground, and in some sense the explanation,[2] of the world.

Retaining the "territories" metaphor, but only in so far as it draws attention to distinguishable enterprises, we can begin to explore frontier relationships by asking next whether the state of affairs suggests conflict or truce or synthesis. It is conflict, or the threat of conflict, which generally draws attention to frontiers, and in this case there has been plenty to observe. In recent years the course of traditional conflicts has been plotted by cool historical study, and the real issues have been eased and time-conditioned misconceptions undermined. It is, however, unrealistic to suppose that no occasion for conflict remains. Dr. J. S. Habgood's recent essay entitled "The Uneasy Truce Between Science and Theology" ought to disturb the equanimity of those who "assure us that there are now no grounds for conflict between the two disciplines, and that they should never have been fighting in the first place."[3] In any case, a truce—even one based on the genuine eradication of latent conflict—can be sterile and thus uninteresting. Interest shifts quickly from prospect of conflict to prospect of fruitful synthesis. But in this respect, exhortation and pious hope far exceed achievement. Some essays in integration are, of course, available. Scientific humanists, Sir Julian Huxley for instance, make proposals which take up religion into an integrated pattern of explanation with cosmic scope, but how the discipline of theology should be practiced (if at all) in this context is difficult to envisage. Teilhard de Chardin's synthesis, with firm if limited roots in science and in Christian theology, is of disputed worth. A. N. Whitehead's contribution to metaphysical construction, though temporarily eclipsed, is still in the air. The notorious gulf which at present separates the world of science not only from the world of religion but from the worlds of politics, poetry, and day-to-day living, is a standing challenge to bridge-builders. Yet synthesis may be much too strong a word for depicting what one may reasonably hope to see along the frontier of science and theology. The felt need, as expressed

---

[2]Cf. G. F. Woods, *Theological Explanation* (Welwyn: J. Nisbet, 1958), or H. H. Farmer, *The World and God* (New York: Harper & Brothers, 1935).

[3]In *Soundings*, ed. A. R. Vidler (Cambridge: The University Press, 1962), p. 23. This essay contains detailed allusions to exploitations of the "territories" metaphor. Cf. also M. B. Hesse, *Science and the Human Imagination* (New York: Philosophical Library, 1955), p. 155.

by many acute and sensitive persons, is not for a synthesis, but for a theology standing in its own right but expressed with greater openness toward the physical sciences.

Christians often say that they would welcome every improvement in men's understanding of the physical universe, and argue indeed that the framework of distinctively Christian convictions provided an unusually congenial and liberating context in which empirically based sciences were able to develop.[4] Let us, then, take an optimistic view of the frontier situation and consider the case of a man who is reasonably at home on both sides of the frontier and who would claim, if asked, that he is living a reasonably integrated life. He knows where his integrity is exposed to strain, and is aware that mental indolence may be concealing from him the desperateness of his plight; but he would regard it as wild exaggeration to say that he is a commuter, engaged in schizophrenic shuttling between two cultures. Such men exist, in larger numbers than we are led to suppose by some who write on this topic.

Such a man will not be tied by his Christian faith either to Biblical patterns of cosmology or to traditional ways of affirming human dignity. Human living, he might say, is properly viewed as a biological phenomenon: a response, generated from inherited and acquired resources, to an environment which is being lucidly and comprehensively mapped by the sciences. Human functioning, as every human agent knows, has its "inner aspect," and it is from one feature of that inner aspect—conceptual thinking—that these sciences, and theology, have alike emerged. They are among the great constructs of spoken discourse in which men engage in order to express and improve the human condition, and also to raise it to ever higher stages of conscious self-direction. Conceptual thinking gives to men a grip, both upon inner condition and upon outward environment; a grip in virtue of which they enjoy significant independence both of internal basic drives and of external stimuli. It has turned human speech into a means of communication impressively rich in nuance and amenable to the communicator's control. Further, the interplay of human lives, entrenching upon one another and upon the common environment, has produced organized social settings, which in turn have become subject matter for legal, historical, and sociological thinking. Again, no human community has failed to develop activities (games, visual arts, music) and types of discourse (metaphysics, ethics, literature) which express views and aspirations about how personal richness of life is best attained. To suppose that this mystery of human life has no more ultimate ground than a "system of nature" is implausible—if by a "system of nature" is meant a cosmic phenomenon capable of over-all description in

[4] This latter thesis is especially associated with the name of Michael Foster, allusions to whose work will be found in most of the books written on this subject since 1939. Cf. Hesse, pp. 43–45.

physico-chemical terms supplemented as appropriate by biological or
historic-sociological terms. Human experience is, of course, rooted in such
a "world." But from the earliest days of myth-making it has been a major
matter of human concern to scrutinize the fabric of experience for inti-
mations of "otherworldly" Deity. This religious quest has led in some cases
(though not all) to a conviction that man, and the natural world in which
his life is rooted, are also rooted in God. From experience of living by
Christian faith it is evident that this age-old concern is not misguided;
that its theistic conclusion is not misconceived; and that the concern is
being sustained, appropriately and fruitfully, in the discipline of Christian
theology.

The claims made in the last sentence of the paragraph above provoke
questions and comments, in minds broadly described as secularist, which
no Christian can afford to disregard. To the dogmatic secularist, "religion
(and morality) are nothing more than illusions to which men have had
recourse to sustain and inspire them in the unceasing struggle for power."
Other persons, less dogmatic, see no ground on which to proceed beyond
some kind of agnosticism. Human science, they say, now so describes the
character and constitution of the world, and man's life within it, as to
obstruct all ways through the world to the God toward whom men have
aspired in Christian religion, and whom they have tried to talk about in
Christian theology. Whether or not a student of theology chooses to join
in the public argument about what is at stake, he will to some extent have
to argue with himself. From time to time he needs a revised view of what
there is to argue about and what should be done to help matters forward.
What follows in the remainder of this essay is necessarily selective but may
provide useful clues about where to turn for more adequate briefing.

II

Science, it has been said, is "one of the greatest spiritual adventures
that man has yet known." For many of us there is an initial problem about
how to look at the territory of the physical sciences and appreciate what
goes on there. Unless those who work on the theological territory have
actually done some scientific research, their view must be that of interested
spectators who can never know the ground in the same way as do the
men who do scientific work. They must learn what to look for and must
listen patiently to warnings about inadequate appreciation. The facade of
"results," theoretical and practical, presented to the spectator by physical
science has long since transcended the grasp of any single mind, and what
the layman must try to appreciate is the solid core of achievement behind
that facade. This comes into view, but only haphazardly, through the work
of popularizers; for better appreciation it is useful to consult the historians
and philosophers of science. Practicing scientists are apt to make dispar-

aging remarks about the familiarity with their territory which is open to laymen through these channels. These remarks are justified when the layman proceeds to operate with a neat abstract story about the "essence" of scientific achievement, a story so framed as to contain the scientific enterprise within a net of generalities any one of which may be falsified by what is in fact happening in some laboratory or other. Warned, but not frightened off, by such remarks, let us observe what we can.

The most obvious, but crucial, aspect of the achievement is that through scientific research men have acquired fuller, more penetrating, and better-organized awareness of the physical constitution—and the operations—in virtue of which things are as they are. Science has improved our stock of explanations. The improvement is evident in both theoretical and practical respects. New accounts of the world's more interesting features have established themselves because they have greater *clarity* and are filled out with explanations of greater *cogency* than those hitherto available. No one claims for them the virtues either of finality or of completeness, but this makes them more, and not less, attractive. This theoretical achievement goes hand in hand with the development of new techniques for the more masterful manipulation of physical possibilities. These innovations, like the theoretical ones, are liable to be superseded by others which are still more promising. In both cases, however, many of the innovations look like permanent additions to the stock of human wisdom.

At this point voices are raised to warn us of impending danger. The innovations have already had a disruptive effect upon human awareness and upon the fabric of social life. Further disruptive effects, indeed the absolute disruption of human life, loom before us as lurid possibilities. Clarity in an account, or cogency in an explanation, are relative to a particular epoch and depend on presuppositions which have gained currency in that epoch; just as on the practical side it can be argued that masterful manipulation is not a self-authenticating achievement, nor indeed a matter for rejoicing unless the purposes of such manipulation can be established and imposed with adequate wisdom. Scientists themselves, like the observers who try to get the feel of their achievements from outside, have realized that their enterprise must be maintained within a humanist framework if it is to be kept from becoming demonic. The Christian-classical humanist framework has, however, been undermined in ways which should be in the forefront of a theologian's mind when he considers what his contribution might be to this situation. "The greatest spiritual adventure that man has yet known," has had its repercussions upon his capacity to contribute.

The culture of Christian Europe, itself the womb of modern science, was one where considerable religious capital was vested, so to speak, in prescientific accounts of the world and in age-old acknowledgments of limits to human competence. With the success of theoretical and practical innovations, much of the invested capital lost its market value. Verbal currency deriving from the earlier situation has nevertheless remained in circulation, its cash value becoming more problematic with every fresh challenge from critical philosophers alert to science. An elementary example is the motion of influence from heaven upon mundane affairs. Each month, as the moon comes to the full, the tides of the sea rise higher and weak-witted men have fits of madness and a monthly cycle is evident in the physiology of women; and all this suggests a mysterious correspondence between happenings in the heavens and happenings on earth and in human beings.[5] Stimulated by Galileo's demythologized concept of motion, scientists made the distinctions which led to clearer knowledge about which objects in the heavens act directly upon which terrestrial beings—by what means and with what effects. Or again, consider one aspect of the struggle to rationalize chemistry. Men of the eighteenth century who were learning to view the world with Newtonian eyes looked at the fascinating spectacle of what Newtonian matter could do by way of displaying energies and undergoing transformations. The great abstractions of Sir Isaac's physical theory afforded no explanation of this spectacle, but by sustained effort and struggle men extricated their thoughts about it from the traditional but confused idea of a world charged with "spirit." Once energies were distinguished (kinetic, thermal, electrical) and the transformations were plotted by means of a new theory of "elements," this "spirit" notion—which, like the "influence from heaven" notion, had hitherto linked physical and religious thinking—was stripped in physical usage of all the overtones which established the link, and indeed lost its scientific usefulness altogether. The use of these notions in religious discourse was not discredited, but henceforth that use had no rapport with the fuller and more penetrating awareness of the world to which men had attained. The Christian-classical humanist framework into which these notions entered became less obviously applicable to men's real situation.

Another factor in the process which has undermined that framework has been graphically depicted by C. C. Gillispie's thesis that aspects and areas of natural occurrence have been steadily swept within the realm of "objectivity," a realm whose advancing "edge" covers more and more of the world's interesting features.[6] Once inside the realm, these features are displayed in the light of an inherent autonomy which calls for no explanatory factors beyond those brought into the scientific account. They do not have to be rooted in "God"; and where previously they seemed to have an intimate connection with man's deepest interests, their "objective"

---

[5] The example has been borrowed from Stephen Toulmin and June Goodfield, *The Fabric of the Heavens* (New York: Harper & Row, 1962), p. 18. This is Vol. I of *The Ancestry of Science*.

[6] Cf. C. C. Gillispie, *The Edge of Objectivity* (Princeton: Princeton University Press, 1960), ch. VI.

presentation leaves man "alienated" in his subjectivity from his objectified environment. Pious men failed at first to discern the full implications. With Newton, and with "natural theologians," they believed it possible to "argue the existence of God from what science had discovered, and his government from what it had not." New territory embraced by science could still be deemed eloquent of creation, though not of personal Providence. The resistance put up in the nineteenth century to geological and biological theories based on the principle of uniformity is, from this point of view, instructive and illuminating;[7] but these disciplines, too, have established their right to clarify natural processes in terms of autonomies, and to dispense with any room for appeal to cosmic personality as a necessary explanatory factor present in some form or other in the mysterious background.

A third factor, more difficult to assimilate than the other two, has come into play within scientific experience and has made people talk in recent years about a final break with Christian-classical presuppositions about the quest for truth. The quest for truth matters because truth is all that men may safely trust. The criteria by which to distinguish truth from falsity have been differently conceived at different epochs; scientific enterprise has lent weight to criteria of an empiricist flavor and discredited any that savor of authoritarianism or traditionalism. But until very recent times these disputes about criteria have not affected a persistent conviction that truth is "known reality," a fusion of intellect and being in a reliable mind. The quest for truth has been broadly seen as the approximation of theory (and of practice in the wake of theory) to predetermined reality, whose "principles" are displayed in any achievement fit to rank as truth. Scientists work with theoretical constructs, but these are no longer deemed to serve as ever closer approximations to true statements about what the world is like, or ought to be like, in some absolute sense. They are "tentative formulae for doing things." The quest for truth has become an experimental and creative pursuit in a sense not hitherto conveyed by those objectives. Truth is what emerges in the act of testing theory against experience. It is marked essentially by *novelty*. It may not be regarded as there to be merely uncovered—there "in principle," waiting as in a womb to be delivered by the midwifery of thought. It requires for its *creation* our manipulation of the world. It has been suggested that the hard core of what emerges can be expressed wholly in the negative form of limitations—statements of what we cannot do. If this is so, no question arises about why it merits trust. But in fact the products of scientific enterprise are aggressively positive, and some answer must be given to the question of whether or not they merit trust. No clear answer is forthcoming except by means of the positivist criterion that they merit trust when "the good

---

[7]Cf. R. Hookyaas, *Natural Law and Divine Miracle* (Leiden, 1959).

of persons" is manifestly being promoted—which is the line taken by "scientific humanism." Scientists are content to work with a "modest positivistic epistemology," with implications for the human situation not yet fully explored. Further exploration[8] may help to clarify for the next generation a new humanist framework which will be open toward the territory of theology—as so-called scientific humanism is not, since an appeal to "the good of persons" does not call for theological clarification when it can be amply clarified by other disciplines.

Scientists are vividly aware that many factors constitutive of physical and biological reality are not yet within the net of scientific explanation. What is not known to the confederacy of science looms larger in the good scientist's mind than what is known. But, *qua* scientist, his aim is to extend the net in appropriate ways and to preserve *scientific* agnosticism about matters which must in principle elude the net. Theology, and theological anthropology, may win his confidence, but they will do so on grounds other than those he can call scientific. It is not within the scope of this essay to explore this possibility. The point to be made here is that if these disciplines are to commend themselves and their results to scientific workers and those impressed by scientific achievements, then those who practice or rely on them must be keenly aware of what the confederacy of science has done about its own special topic, man's knowledge of the physical universe. In very many respects the universe has become much clearer than it was. If, in other respects, it has become more bewildering, this is not a source for antiscientific propaganda or for smooth talk about the limitations of science. The new clarifications have met with resistance, frequently inspired by religious preoccupations. But what has been undermined through this resistance is the worth of the religious preoccupations and not the scientific innovations. The most embarrassing feature of the current situation is that explanations which now yield clarity have no links with religious belief, as had older explanations in terms of "purposes" or in terms of "second causes," themselves the effects of a "First Cause" to which men may make their way by "reason."[9] Man has been deprived of the "cosmos" which, on Christian-classical presuppositions, gave meaning to his life and cogency to his religion. Christian men in particular have been forced to acknowledge that the world of nature and the world of events do not keep within the framework provided by the Bible. Physical and biological reality no longer bear obvious witness to the Bible's theme of God's historical purposes with men. The physical universe

---

[8]An important pioneer work in this field is M. Polanyi, *Personal Knowledge* (Chicago: University of Chicago Press, 1958). Consult also the article "Contemporary Science and Human Life," by Erik Ingelstam, *Ecumenical Review*, 9 (1957), esp. 370 ff.

[9]The detailed analysis upon which this observation rests may be studied in the book to which this essay is heavily indebted, John Dillenberger, *Protestant Thought and Natural Science* (Garden City, N.Y.: Doubleday & Co., 1960).

has therefore become, once again, a competing authority, threatening to supersede all other alleged authorities in matters of ultimate human concern. Joseph Campbell puts the point clearly in his reference to

> that most important mythological tradition of the modern world, which can be said to have had its origin with the Greeks, to have come of age in the Renaissance, and to be flourishing today in continuous, healthy growth, in the works of those artists, poets, and philosophers of the West for whom the wonder of the world itself—as it is now being analyzed by science—is the ultimate revelation.[10]

III

Tension between scientific awareness and religious convictions imposes strains which vary from person to person. Historical study of older conflicts has eased unnecessary sources of strain and shown how much adjustment has been possible when misconceptions were cured. In the minds of people who do not think much about these matters there is a formidable legacy from earlier days of conflict, and a good deal of patient education is necessary to remove it as occasions arise. Christians equipped to lend a hand with this service, and with the more constructive tasks of relating their religious convictions to scientific culture, must take their bearings from an up-to-date diagnosis of the points of strain and from the most sensitive prescriptions for dealing with them.[11] In this essay there is room for only a quick preliminary glance at the situation as currently understood, relating it so far as possible to earlier preoccupations.

How, first of all, do we best envisage the competing authorities between which tensions arise? Is it still a matter of Darwin versus the Bible, or of a self-sustaining material and evolutionary universe versus the Bible's God? It is better to say that two personal commitments may or may not come into competition within the same human individual: commitment to the authority of God expressed in the gospel of Jesus Christ and communicated through the Bible, and commitment to the authority of the scientific enterprise and its fruits. In general these can be viewed as complementary and not as competing authorities, but difficulties can and do arise, sometimes through discordance but more seriously nowadays through lack of any co-ordination.[12] The question is whether a Christian

---

[10]Joseph Campbell, *The Masks of God*, Vol. I (New York: Viking Press, 1959), p. 7.

[11]Among the books to be recommended are two of particular merit, one by a scientist and the other by a theologian: Harold K. Schilling, *Science and Religion: An Interpretation of Two Communities* (New York: Charles Scribner's Sons, 1962) and E. L. Mascall, *Christian Theology and Natural Science* (London: Longmans, Green & Co., 1956). There is a full and helpful bibliography in Dillenberger, op. cit.—itself a book of quite outstanding merit but distinguishable from the two selected for mention by its historical rather than systematic approach.

[12]I have discussed the latter point more fully in *Order, Goodness, Glory* (London: Oxford University Press, 1960), pp. 11f.

man can commit himself to the "great spiritual adventure" of science without straying into un-Christian religion or "post-Christian" mythology. Doubts about this possibility cast a blight upon upper-class English education during the nineteenth century, for after the publication of the *Origin of Species*, science, in the eyes of clerical headmasters, became tainted with irreligion. The effects of the blight are still evident here and there in England a century later. The doubts themselves are given a further lease of life with every new disclosure of how socially dangerous science can be, though they are easily smothered by each fresh reminder that it is the key to economic and political well-being in the modern world.

To the Christian scholar and gentleman nurtured on classical literature and philosophy, commitment to science appeared to mean commitment to dogmatic "materialism" and to evolutionary "naturalism," neither of which was compatible with commitment to Christian faith. What has happened on the battlefields where these war cries once rang out so clearly? The issues at stake have become uncomfortably subtle and elusive.

The reality whose structure is disclosed by physics, chemistry, geology, and the life-sciences is not well represented by the model of a material mechanism functioning as a closed system, whose "laws" men may hope to trace, only to discover at the end that they themselves are wholly absorbed in the machine. This crude materialistic image of how man must come to terms with ultimate questions under the authority of science continues to haunt human minds, in spite of steady resistance from all points of the philosophical compass—including Marxism. Its menace lies in the suggestion that everything associated with *mind* or *spirit* is, in the last analysis, reducible to properties of "mindless nonspiritual matter." "Personal" being, whether human or divine, could then, as such, have no ultimate place in reality. This metaphysical assumption is a specter firmly disowned by scientists. The representation of so-called "mindless nonspiritual matter" has become problematic in ways which necessarily divest science of metaphysical assumptions, whether these be detrimental or favorable to humanity and to theology. The detail of this development is not easily expounded, though physicists have done their best to explain to a lay audience the source and nature of the problems. The root of their difficulty in explaining the issues is, perhaps, the essentially negative character of their story. They are faced with insurmountable obstacles if they regard the happenings which are their object of study as activities or qualities of a basic material substance, whatever character they choose to ascribe to it. The *systems* ("entities" is too loaded a word) which they study in particular *states* by means of *observables* ("qualities" again is too loaded a term) are capable of mathematical representation, but cannot, without confusions and contradictions, be represented by symbols taken from the world of everyday perception, such as *position, velocity, identity, causality*—the basic concepts with which science formally hoped to give a consistent picture of the universe in "material" terms.[13] How to formulate a *positive* concept of reality which accomodates these negative facts without strain, is still an open problem and a fascinating challenge to new exploits in "natural philosophy." To the religious person it is a relief to be told that we must all abandon the idea of an "outside" world, closed in itself, to which manhood must be subordinated. If, however, he wants to go on making the important religious declaration that God, by creation, has given to men a world in which to live, it has become very difficult to see what this declaration is *about*. The way is wide open for reducing the great issues of human living to matter-of-fact problems, soluble by man's technical know-how. Salvation, if any, can only be seriously sought from man himself, with no reference to hypothetical external factors such as God, angels, and demons, or metaphysical powers of any kind.

At this point attention shifts naturally to the impact of science on philosophy, for it is through that discipline that much of the impact is mediated to theology. The presence in this volume of a separate essay on theology and philosophy[14] must serve as some excuse for what would otherwise be an inexcusable omission from this present survey of the ground jointly occupied by scientists and theologians. There are, however, two aspects of what is happening in this field which, even so, are worth mentioning here. First, there is a new self-consciousness about the nature and use of language. The language of science is conventional language whose use, and therefore meaning, is essentially operational. The language of theology is symbolical, and over much of the field it is used analogically. Do theologians understand what they are doing with language to the extent that scientists do? Are they able to cope with problems raised about the adequacy of religious symbolism?

The second matter has to do with method. If we accept Karl Popper's "hypothetical-deductive" account of scientific method, the scientist takes a problem which may be suggested by some human need or by some scientific or prescientific belief which calls for re-examination. This redirects his attention to selected data for which he seeks an explanation. Its formal structure is "causal," but causal in a strict conventional sense. Explanations consist of statements that "x determines y" in accordance with some universal or particular law; with specified initial conditions and with an assumption of validity for the appropriate law, predictions can be made; and these must be tested experimentally, so that a selection can be made from among possible explanations, some of which will be falsified by the experimental testing. By this method, no explanation is *confirmed*

---

[13]Cf. *Ecumenical Review*, 9 (1957), for articles by H. H. Wolf ("The Old Problem: Science and the Christian Faith," 357–366) and Erik Inglestam, op. cit., alluding more fully to this topic. There is a brief bibliographical note on p. 371.

[14][John Heywood Thomas, "Theology and Philosophy," in *The Scope of Theology*, ed. Daniel T. Jenkins (Cleveland: World, 1965), pp. 133–151.]

in any absolute sense; but some survive for subsequent ordeal-by-experiment. Experimentation runs right through the fabric of this method, from the original choice of problem, through the invention of concepts for specifying initial conditions, on through the postulating of laws, to the final ordeal of practical testing. This modest epistemology has won the confidence of scientists and makes them radically suspicious of the seemingly more arrogant procedures associated with the other disciplines. They cannot, in principle, regard their own structures of explanation as either complete or unrevisable. But they cannot see how theological explanations can, with any seemliness, be added to their own achievements to produce enlarged and integrated vision. In the light of their difficulty, has the theologian thought out what it is that he has to offer, and by what method he has managed to establish it?

From these abstract, but nonetheless pressing, areas of concern, let us turn to the second of the traditional battlefields. Does commitment to scientific investigation mean that one is committed to an evolutionary view of nature which is incompatible with Christian faith? To an evolutionary thesis which is fundamental for biological theory—yes; to a position incompatible with Christian faith and theology—not necessarily! It was Augustine, chiefly, who gave to the Western Church a connected conception of nature. He presented it as the work of one true and gracious God and therefore, in the positive aspects of its existence, wholly good. The natural creation lies between God and the human soul and is a vehicle of God's communication with men. In classical thought it could scarcely be viewed as the instrument of a rational and sovereign Creator unless unchanging forms and principles were built into its structure and were manifest to the rational human mind. Augustine, his predecessors, and his medieval successors saw themselves chiefly as participants in the drama of redemption, and were liable to regard the physical universe and their participation in its processes as substratum, or even shadow, rather than as substantial constituent in their own lives. What they had to say about the physical world was limited to a few themes, obviously chosen under the influence of the struggles with other faiths which Augustine in particular had sampled. The world, they affirmed, has been created, and well created; it has been corrupted, but nevertheless preserved; it is administered with providential wisdom, both through regular government and through miraculous interventions; it is destined to be brought through judgement to renewal in glory. These themes were developed in climates of thought where it was inconceivable that evolutionary characteristics might go deep into the structure of the world. As a result, Christian tradition provided no resources for meeting and coming to terms with a scientific thesis of evolution, which offended the religious sense of propriety in many respects hardly worth reiterating here.

The evolutionary thesis has been accepted in Christian theology, and indeed has been used, somewhat loosely and romantically, to portray an "ascent toward consciousness" which fits well with theological themes about man's unique place in the universe, redemption through love, and eschatological unification. But all is not well as between Christian theology and developmental biology; and it is no accident that younger scholars of ability, from many different cultural and ecclesiastical backgrounds, are hard at work at the present time sorting out the issues at stake in this particular field.

At the same time the biologists are racing ahead with exciting new work, and the theologian cannot be at all sure that he is keeping up with them at the points which may concern him most.[15] Here is a tentative list: There is the question about continuity between living and lifeless "matter." The controversy inside biology between mechanism and vitalism is being steadily transcended by new developments in biophysics and biochemistry. There is the question about the techniques of evolution, and the epoch-making step toward an answer in the theory of genetic codes. At the other end of the biological scale there is the question about continuity and discontinuity as between human and other animal behaviour, and the new biological meanings for terms like *mind* or *spirit* as applied to men. There is a marked tendency among biologists to conduct excursions into the field of ethics, with "survival value" as a principal criterion for judgement, so that *good* is liable to mean "successful," and *evil* is deprived of its more militant and malignant connotations. There is a potent and more precise meaning for that emotive word "progress," to denote increasing all-round biological efficiency, expressed through greater independence of an environment and increased control of it. These theoretical innovations go hand in hand with developments of technical power, not only over plant and animal life, but (through biochemistry in conjunction with medicine) over the life of men in its most intimate personal depths as well as (through psychology) in its social manifestations. What has the gospel to do with all this, or this with the gospel? Of the tensions which arise from these points of strain, no end is in sight. Theology, indeed, has hardly begun to recast its anthropological thinking so as to reckon with them.

If "materialism" was a threat to the basic religious convictions enshrined in all "natural theology," Darwinism was an even graver threat for it menaced the heart of the Christian gospel—the drama of creation and redemption. At both points of erstwhile strain, much has happened to alleviate the stresses originally felt. The embarrassments for Christian theology have altered, but they have not diminished in intensity.

In the Copernican world the Christian estimate of man made good sense. But what weight can be attached to it in face of the immensities of space and time revealed by modern knowledge? What importance can be as-

---

[15]Cf. W. H. Thorpe, *Biology and the Nature of Man* (London: Oxford University Press, 1961).

signed to man if humanity itself is no more than an infinitesimal grain of sand in an immeasurable sandy waste? What answer is there to the accumulating evidence of the complete dependence of the most intimate psychological processes upon physical events? What if everything the theologian talks about is simply the effect of the reflection of conditions of the brain?[16]

To this *cri de coeur* about man's feeling of insignificance we must add the other chief source of embarrassment: that the world as known to the scientists, the world which they are teaching us all to know and live in as *one* world, is a world which does not express the reality of God in any recognizable way. The hiddenness of God in his world is an accepted theological postulate which is now being grasped more radically, but in itself it is not a sufficient remedy for the difficulties with which faith has to wrestle when commitment to the Christian gospel is taken, as it should be taken, to include commitment to the enterprise of science and its fruits.

IV

Nothing in this essay should lead the reader to assume that the writer himself is discouraged by his own theological responsibilities, or that anyone else should be discouraged by theirs. On the contrary: there is work to be done; there are resources for doing it; and there is promise of joy in the effort. In the "Notes on New Directions" toward the end of his historical survey, John Dillenberger surveys the prospects with skill and judgement, and the reader should consult his pages for advice with which I wholeheartedly concur.[17] It is difficult to forecast how future work will develop. Anything said about it must have the character of pious hopes and personal intentions and should therefore be said very briefly.

In the first place, it seems that nothing in the climate of scientific culture has a rightful claim to deflect Christian theology from fundamental fidelity to its own proper object, Jesus Christ and his Lordship. There is always more to be learnt about the practical meaning of this fidelity; and the Church's practice of theology, within this faith and as its proper discipline, has often been marred by blindness and folly. But the terms of the job have always been reasonably clear, and there is no case for a radical departure from them in order to produce some revolutionary New Theology. That the work is associated with a community of faith is no ground for disparaging it. Scientific work also, it has been pointed out, has its community aspect.[18]

The task which confronts theology, vis-a-vis the impact of physical sciences, is to help all men to see their world, and to see the work of scientists within it, "under God." What is to be done about this?

---

[16]J. H. Oldham, "Karl Heim on Faith and Science," *Theology*, 56 (1953), 243.
[17]Dillenberger, pp. 255–292.
[18]Schilling.

First, we might learn to speak more clearly about what the religious man (and the theologian) looks for, but does not expect the scientist to talk about *as part of his science*. It is something "caught in the structure of physical events"; something which, when discerned, evokes worship and trust. *Consciousness, culture, personality, values, history*, are all realities alleged to be of this non-natural kind—using the scientist's version of "natural"; but the allegation is precarious, and in any case it is not as feasible as was once hoped to build upon an awareness of these things and reach assurance about a God who evokes worship and trust. The theological affirmation should be made by pointing to the possibility—in Christian belief, the actuality—to which the word *grace* refers. Personal grace; which gives, initially, with perfect freedom; bears with corruption; rescues and regenerates in a way which brings true authority to bear upon human life and admits man as a partner with Deity by participation in the mystery of reason, healed and renewed: *this* is the actuality in which all events, all phenomena, all experiences, are embraced and by which they are permeated. The physical world is not a plain expression of such grace. And it is reasonable to hold, as Christians do, that the "order of grace" is, by God's sovereign and gracious will, dependent upon his incarnate Word and disclosed to men in Jesus and through him.

If this be clearly understood, those who believe it might find it possible to construct a "theology of nature"—*not* a "natural theology"—by looking at physical reality in the hope of recognizable hints or echoes of grace in its ambiguities, and providing an orderly report which all men could at least listen to, and perhaps find helpful, in the present stage of scientific and technological culture. At the same time, those who believe the news of grace (and their theologians) might look more closely at the communal human enterprise which is science. In developing science, *man* is expressing himself and asserting his humanity in a fashion which is creating *history*. A parallel observation holds for what he is doing in the community of Christian religion; and there it is firmly believed that history is the context in which grace appears most plainly and where its triumphs are to be looked for. Despite the tensions which occur, and will occur, between these two expressions of communal human vitality, there is a possibility of consistent mutual service, of intrinsic value to both, if each community will converse with the other about the things which bear on the *quality* of human history. It has been traditionally expected of theologians that they should have some competence in philosophy. What matters today, perhaps, is a greater competence in the fields of ethics, politics, and sociology, to be acquired, not in theological isolation, nor in a specialized school of "social studies," but precisely in conversation with partners coming from the community of science—the conversation to be assisted, of course, by helpful experts from the particular fields where scientists and theologians meet and converse. There is no assurance that mistrust will be dispelled, or that we shall come to see more clearly how faith and science interact to the glory of God and the blessing of man. But as conversation develops, in these or other fields of common human interest, there is reasonable hope that we may come to see both the achievements of the physical sciences and the resources of the Christian gospel in richer terms and deeper perspectives than any which have yet appeared.

(1965)

TOWARDS A THEOLOGY
OF NATURE[1]

I

THE PHRASE "A THEOLOGY OF NATURE" IS AN ABBREVIATION FOR "A THEO-logical account of natural happenings"—happenings which are properly investigated in the first instance by appropriate "natural sciences." A Christian theology of nature seeks to provide a systematic appreciation of the physical universe, its items and occurrences, from a Christian theological point of view. If it is to rank as a serious contribution to human wisdom, it must be a disciplined effort to understand in appropriate terms the object of interest. One version of the discipline would be to produce an extension of the natural sciences, to cover topics—God, freedom, immortality—which fall outside their scope by a "metaphysical" science which links these topics to the subject-matter of natural sciences in a theoretical account of "being as such." This would have the effect of reintroducing "Natural Theology," reshaped and revitalized, into the fabric of Christian systematic theology. This project is not being advocated in this article. It is mentioned solely in order to distinguish the present topic, a "theology of nature," from what is traditionally known as "natural theology." The purpose of this article is to explore afresh the structure of Christian intellectual response to the wonder of the world, as it is now being analysed by science, with particular attention to the "evolutionary" aspect of things, appreciation of which has radically affected modern sensibility.

"Nature," as John Stuart Mill[2] said a hundred years ago, has now become "a collective name for all facts, actual and possible: or (to speak more

---

[1]This essay contains the substance of a theological contribution made to a conference of scientists, theologians, and philosophers at Bossey, April 16–20, 1963. The conference explored the topic: *Evolution—A Fundamental Element in the Concept of Nature*. The essay has been revised in the light of discussions at the conference and in the light of comments made by Mr. John Heywood Thomas. It was originally prepared without knowledge of the chapter "Die Natur" in the *Ethik* of Wolfgang Trillhaas (Berlin, 1959) from which I have now learnt a great deal.

[2]J. S. Mill, *Three Essays on Religion* (London, 1874), p. 6.

accurately) a name for the mode, partly known to us and partly unknown, in which things take place." "Nature" means the cosmos, as a field of happenings, actual and potential. Men address themselves to its "natural reality" with confidence that the fulfilment of their own existence is a matter of successful adaptation on their part, as items therein, to the cosmos which is their environment. Scientific ways of presenting the world—and man's life in the world—have all-pervasive and revolutionary effects upon human self-awareness; and this lends new urgency to the theologian's desire to speak about those matters which the natural sciences also, and primarily, speak about. Everything, including human springs of conduct and human decisions of "faith," is subject to scientific comment; and as, in any particular field of experience, the appropriate natural sciences establish what is the case, human responses tend to be modified accordingly. "Naturalism," as a possible human attitude in these present circumstances, is much less rigid and restrictive than has sometimes been the case during the period when modern science was establishing itself. But now that "nature" has come to mean "the wonder of the world," the pertinence of theological comment has become progressively more problematic.

The term "nature" once carried a different meaning. It signified the normative structure, knowable by reason, to which appeal could be made in order to elucidate obscure physical facts and also obscure matters about human conduct and politics. The physical universe was not deemed to embody this structure to perfection, though its "portents" carried reminders of the norms in which it was rooted. Human conduct, individual and corporate, was extremely liable in practice to display "unnatural" features. Yet even so, it was feasible to look through the physical world and through human experiences, and, with the intellectual eye of reason, to see "nature" and to penetrate beyond "nature" to God. Belief in this unified vision, and the struggle to maintain it, slowly but surely collapsed as modern science developed in the centuries after Galileo. With each ensuing generation it became more difficult to detect any basic affinity between what is to be seen in the region of physical laws and technical possibilities and what men still held to be apparent in the realm of human "spirit." Information about the physical realm was processed in natural sciences. Information about man's cognitive and moral existence was processed in disciplines such as philosophy, history and the study of letters, which were accepted as complementary in some sense to natural sciences. But complementarity is collapsing into a virtual subordination of the second type of information to the first. Physical reality, far greater in size, scope and variety of component factors—and seen now as determinative for consciousness—has become the fundamental point of reference. Those who look with other visions in other directions—to human culture, to history, to divinity—may be doing a supplementary job of passing use-fulness to the human race; but it is far from clear now that questions decisive for the destiny of mankind, or for the destiny of individual men, lie at the heart of these parallel, separate, non-scientific pursuits, and are being effectively pursued there. The wonder of the world, as it is now being analysed by science, is, for many modern minds, the ultimate and solely reliable point of reference.

It is about this wonder of the world that the theologian is impelled to speak, and to speak in as concrete a fashion as possible. The natural sciences enable men to speak about it with authority and with marked effectiveness. The theologian, if he is to speak about it at all, must do so in a different way. But in what different way? From what basis? By what method?

His *basis* can only be an awareness of "God." The name "theology" is a sign that in this discourse events and phenomena of "nature" are to be related to "Deity" which transcends them. The meaning of this claim to awareness of God has to be clarified and upheld in the light of scientific (*sc.* anthropological) appraisals of man and his theological preoccupations. The theologian may not find it easy to satisfy himself that the meaning is not reducible to his being tangled up in some old-fashioned system of thought and vested interest. It will, however, suffice if he can establish an irreducible awareness of a *question* concerning God.

As to *method*, he must decide by what discipline he can best articulate the "revelation" of which he is aware—even though it be merely the "empty" revelation of a real question about God! The discipline adopted may not conform to that of any natural scientist, but it should be one which secures for his statements the marks which give cogency to scientific statements. Their cogency, briefly, is that of an "objective" assessment. They are cleansed, so far as human thinking can be cleansed, of men's private moods and arbitrary prejudices. Furthermore, they lay bare the structure of the phenomena to which they refer in ways which satisfy men's logical appetite in its current form. Theologians, self-conscious about discipline as most now tend to be, have to make a choice of method, so as to bring these, or equally cogent, marks into their own statements. A fundamental choice, which cuts across types of theological attitude evoked by the detail of some problem, is between *the way of free speculation* and *the way of fidelity to a positive tradition of historically given revelation*. The first of these ways leads towards the production, not of science-fiction as now understood and respected but of philosophy-fiction, generally of a Berg-sonian kind. Whether the second way can lead to anything but up-to-date reiteration of conventional dogmatic abstractions, which say nothing to those outside the household of faith and little enough to those within, has yet to be discovered.

II

In making his choice, the theologian should humbly bear in mind the fact that any "faith" which he helps to articulate is a "religious" phenomenon and as such susceptible to anthropological comment. Religion is a natural phenomenon and is itself to be seen in evolutionary perspectives. It is a response engendered in men to the experience of life in this natural environment. Clearer, fuller, more impelling awareness of the natural environment will have its repercussions upon religion. Recent repercussions have been mentioned already and a passage already plundered for this purpose can now be usefully quoted in full. It refers to

> that most important mythological tradition of the modern world, which can be said to have had its origin with the Greeks, to have come of age in the Renaissance, and to be flourishing today in continuous healthy growth, in the works of those artists, poets and philosophers of the West for whom the wonder of the world itself—as it is now being analysed by science—is the ultimate revelation.[3]

Mythology, a human enterprise which can be accepted as wholly natural, exhibits phenomena called "traditions." Here is one whose genesis and evolution we can trace, and whose "continuous healthy growth" commends it as a programme to be adopted. Ever since it came to maturity it has been in conflict with Christian tradition *as classically formulated*. The beginnings of conflict can be detected in Kepler, for whom knowledge of mathematical harmony in the universe was "a participation in the life of God," "an act of adoration which eclipsed the knowledge of God obtainable through the redemptive history of the biblical tradition."[4] The process thus initiated removed the God of Biblical tradition from any vital relation to the order of physical nature and robbed man of a cosmos in which he could confidently be what classical tradition assured him that he was. That "evolution" is a fundamental element in the concept of the physical order did not come home to men until a relatively late stage in the conflict. When it did so, the chief effect, was, perhaps, to lend decisive weight to the conviction that men should emancipate themselves from bondage to all traditions of lower survival-value. The balance was tipped decisively in favor of emergent non-classical naturalism, as an appropriate human attitude.

Should not the theologian follow the new fashion when he looks for a starting-point? Should he not also find it in the wonder of the physical-universe? Should he not begin with the problem of describing our humanity as it has to be expressed within this context, and analysing its needs and aspirations? Should he not proceed by some method of phil-

---

[3]Joseph Campbell, *The Masks of God*, Vol. I (New York, 1959), p. 7.
[4]John Dillenberger, *Protestant Thought and Natural Science* (New York, 1960), pp. 83f.

osophical aspiration, grounded in the data of experience but reaching out towards some ultimate explanation—not, perhaps, of a scientific-utopian kind but possibly one to be reached through an improved Hegelianism, where the dialectic of "system" and "happening" is tracked to ultimate roots in a deeper dialectic, which, when uncovered, will bring into view the authentic existence of man with God and of God with man? Theologians who reject this genuinely alluring invitation must say why they do so. It is hardly enough to say that "the wonder of the world" includes man with his "rich experience of being personal." This is a popular gambit for those who are still ready to concentrate upon the intellectual and moral features in man's life as signposts which point towards God in ways which the facts of physical nature and their overtones do not. A more sophisticated version of the gambit is to claim that "man's transcendence of nature can be guaranteed by a proper delineation of history, including the drama of redemption."[5] These lines of resistance strike the critical observer as rearguard attempts to mark off "consciousness," "culture," "history," from "physical nature," in ways that will not stand up to the thrust of scientific and technological advance. It is true that the theme of "nature as history" has begun to occupy the minds of many acute thinkers as they reflect upon the implications of man's operation within the physical world as scientist and technologist. It is evident that men's *decisions* play a determining role in the theoretical as well as the practical products of such operations. The significance of this, ignorantly overestimated in the past, no doubt, and on wrong grounds, should not be ignorantly underestimated today. Such reflections are deepened by consideration of man's peculiar experience of time-consciousness in combination with the capacity for informed and informing decision. Through man, nature actualizes itself as history, inasmuch as the world gives itself to be known by this human part of itself. This dimension of its evolutionary course may have ramifications far wider than we have so far dared to envisage. If this contingency, latent in nature for so much of its duration, has to be taken with great seriousness, there is at least room for questions about other latent factors—not least for a question about one who "hides himself so wondrously, as though there were no God."

These considerations have not, to my knowledge, led any thinker to a secure ground from which he can develop a positive theology. They may have their place in association with theistic affirmation based independently upon firmer ground and may lead to more luminous and more cogent affirmation in such a context. This firmer ground has to be sought, so it seems to me, in awareness of something which has a far stronger claim to the description "non-natural" than have "consciousness," "culture," or "history." Rudolf Otto directed attention to such a ground in his

---

[5]Dillenberger, p. 288.

discussion of men's awareness of "the Holy." I find it unsatisfactory to pin my own thinking to an awareness of "the Holy" *in general*. It is "the Holy" *with a definite character*, awareness of which drives my thought beyond everything "natural." The only term which aptly designates this definite character is the term "grace." Awareness of *grace* is the only intimation of Deity which is compelling, so far as I am concerned. It is an awareness which intimates the objective reality of one who *gives initially with perfect freedom*; one who *bears with corruption*; one who *rescues and regenerates*; who does all this in a fashion which brings *true authority* to bear upon the living of human life. Grace is not a substance, nor only a quality; rather is it an operation, to which men in their total existence may be conformed in *gratitude*; in this conformation they are admitted as *partners with Deity* and thereby granted full participation in the mystery of Reason. The physical world is not a manifest expression of such grace; and it is reasonable to hold that the fruition of grace is utterly at God's disposal and by His will is dependent upon His sovereign Word; and that this Word has been disclosed to men in and through its historical incarnation in a man. A theologian whose faith in God is thus closely bound to God's gracious self-disclosure in Jesus Christ is obliged to proceed towards a "theology of nature" along paths of obedience which may not be easy to find. Nor will such paths offer prospects of dazzling synthetic achievement comparable with those which attract an expert in free speculation. It is not my intention, nor is it within my competence, to begin on the work of construction. This is an essay in prolegomena only. It seems, however, that such a "theology of nature" might be constructed by looking at physical reality in the hope of recognizing *hints* of grace, and then of providing an orderly report on its *correlations* with grace, in the shape most helpful to men in their present phase of scientific and technical culture. The word "correlation" calls to mind the chapters on "Analogy" to be found in theological works in the eighteenth and early nineteenth centuries, where English theologians took up the theme classically developed by Joseph Butler. In a fuller exploration it would be rewarding to investigate the ways in which those writers were handicapped when they turned their steps in a direction somewhat similar to the one suggested here. Today we are bound to proceed in a more piecemeal and less abstract fashion than seemed necessary to them. Nor can we proceed with the confidence which they derived from the theological tool, "analogy," bequeathed to them by Scholasticism but whose precise character they understood very imperfectly.

III

Before saying more about the search for correlations, it will be useful to pause in order to look at technical considerations of another kind, which, rightly assessed, may help a theologian to do his work better in changed circumstances. In this section we shall ask how the Church has traditionally brought grace into view as datum for a theology of nature.

The grace of God disclosed in Jesus Christ is grace expressed dramatically and historically; it is expressed in dealings between God (characterized in anthropomorphic symbolism and then acknowledged to be present among men in a fellow-man) and the human race. The physical universe is a theatre for this drama; God's creation and mankind's realm. Its career, so to speak, is caught up into the drama. Man's dominion within his realm was so devised that his treason to God brought consequences for the realm as such. His falling into sin brought man into subordination to the cosmic powers constitutive for his realm. Yet the fulfilment of his original destiny is promised through the drama of redemption, and herein lies hope for the physical universe. Something is in store for it which corresponds to the redemption of man's body.

It is to Augustine that the Western Church chiefly owes its traditional way of developing a theology of nature. From his struggles with other faiths he brought into the Christian Church a connected conception of nature as the work of the one God, a work which exhibits goodness in all its positive aspects. It could scarcely have been viewed as wholly subject to a rational Creator, in Augustine's climate of thought, except by attaching to this judgement the conviction that unchanging forms and principles lie within its structure and can be discerned there by the rational human mind. It therefore lies, so to speak, between God and human souls as a means of communication. It is fair to regard Augustine, his predecessors and his medieval successors, as men chiefly conscious of themselves as participants in the drama of redemption and in the human history annexed to it. They were liable to regard their participation in the physical universe as mere substratum—shadow, indeed, rather than substance—of their lives. What they had to say about the physical world was limited to a few themes, the choice of themes being readily understood in the light of their cultural situation: created—and created well and good; corrupted, but preserved; administered with providential wisdom, both by way of regular government and by way of miraculous intervention; destined to be brought through judgement to renewal in glory. These themes were developed in climates of thought where it was inconceivable that evolutionary characteristics might go deep into the structure of the world. It has been argued that the theology of the Reformation (and perhaps Franciscan theology before it) provided in principle a release from metaphysical presuppositions of the static kind which were inescapable for Augustine. For this and other reasons, there was no insuperable difficulty in the way of re-articulating the chosen themes in later climates of thought. But one should perhaps ask whether these are any longer the themes to which faith is bound. Is this a sacrosanct framework for a "theology of nature"? Do these themes, in words borrowed from

Bishop Westcott, bring grace into view "under an aspect corresponding to the aspect under which the whole finite order presents itself"?[6]

This essay was written while Britain was indulging in theological controversy, sparked off by the reluctance of the Bishop of Woolwich to think any longer in "supranaturalist" terms, about God "out there," doing things to a world by remote control. The bishop was aided and abetted by Mr. Wren-Lewis, who mistrusts all talk of "powers behind the scenes," deeming such talk to be paranoiac, and who takes the view that "human togetherness" is the only theologically luminous experience. For Mr. Wren-Lewis "it's possible to see all space, time and matter as *contained within* our relations with one another." If, as I am inclined to think, this is Marcion redivivus—affinities with Augustine notwithstanding!—it may be that the traditional themes, with all their supernaturalist overtones, still have a purpose to serve in articulating Christian faith and in defence of its integrity. They should not be demythologized out of all recognition, as is likely to happen if they are interpreted only by reference to man's self-expression in faith, and not as propositions about Deity (acknowledged as existing in His own right, derived *a se*), and about a physical universe (with its own proper existence, derived *ab alio* but there independently of man). Taken in a thoroughly straightforward way, these themes contain references to "acts of God": so that theology, in expressing them, seems to be making pseudo-scientific statements about what has actually gone on, what actually goes on, and will go on, in the world. *Some* support for such statements must be found in the world to which they refer—or they are superstitions, useful perhaps for driving out other superstitions but lacking serious meaning as claims upon physical reality. Therefore we must look for correspondences of some kind between theological claims and what natural sciences have to say. Of course if Marcion after all was right, such correspondences are not worth looking for, at any rate in the directions indicated by the traditional themes, since these are misconceived, and the correspondences are simply not there to be found!

IV

There are technical considerations worth bringing into view when one looks in the other direction—towards "the physical universe" or "the whole finite order"; and again some reference to traditional practice will be of assistance. The term "nature" has always been a many-valued symbol. When used, in the past, to bring the cosmic themes of theology (creation, corruption, preservation, and government) into explicit relationship with grace, it did not directly signify the perceived universe. It was the name

---

[6]B. F. Westcott, *The Epistles of St. John* (London, 1909), p. 318 (in the second appended essay, entitled "The Gospel of Creation").

for a construct, postulated by the intellect on the supposition, to quote Mr. Wren-Lewis *via* the Bishop of Woolwich, "that the network of empirical relationships is but a veil for a world of occult realities which lie behind the outward order of things and constitute the truth about man or society or [the physical universe], however much the empirical facts may appear to dispute it."[7] Prompted by a remark made by Professor Peter Brunner at a meeting in Bossey in 1958, I have pursued this construct in the thought of Augustine, Hooker, Shakespeare, Ronsard,[8] Pascal, Goethe, Hegel—and J. S. Mill who wrote its obituary in *Three Essays on Religion*.[9] With the ardour of an explorer, lost in admiration for his Newfoundland, let me offer a report in four paragraphs of summary statement.

"Nature" was not another name either for God or for the physical universe: not another name for God in any theistic sense, for that to which it points is a combination of *norm* and *modus operandi*, and only in pagan superstition is this hypostatized (falsely and unnecessarily) into an *operator*; not another name for physical actuality, since it is normative for such actuality and only imperfectly mirrored in matters of experience. It is not the name of anything. Rather is it a mediating concept, used (but not to name an actor) in the texture of a religio-cosmic drama—the drama of grace, resisted in sinful ways, and of resistance overcome. The term does indeed refer to an *operation*, viz. the determining before any and every event of what is proper and best. This, of course, God is deemed to do. Man may participate in the Reason with which God moves in these matters—at any rate to the limited extent which suffices for men's grasp upon the limited issues involved in any finite event. Though a particular finite achievement may be perfectly conformed to natural norms, it is not therefore self-justifying nor intrinsically acceptable to God. It is open to be more deeply fulfilled by freely expressed acts of grace. And if it is faulty, it is open to be rescued by such acts of grace. To say of any thing or of any event that in such and such respects it is entitled to be called "natural"—and in other respects, perhaps, "unnatural"—is not, therefore, to say the last word about it. But whatever may be judged "natural" is, in this limited sense, *reliable*. By playing his part in the drama thus envisaged man can function *reliably* as "king" in his own situation. In this concept, it was widely held, lies the root of individual and social sanity. It is a concept which, as Hegel reaffirmed, ensures the organic coherence of all things visible and invisible.

"Nature" is the name for a theological construct, and this construct, like the religio-cosmic drama where it belongs, has a history. The early

---

[7] J. A. T. Robinson, *Honest to God* (London, 1963), p. 107. I have substituted "the physical universe" for "nature."

[8] Cf. D. B. Wilson, *Ronsard—Poet of Nature* (Manchester, 1961).

[9] I have not, so far, absorbed what can be learnt from Heidegger's effort to put new life into the concept.

stages of this history would take us back to the Patristic workshops where
the term was adapted for Christian use. The later stages have brought
the term into discredit among Protestant theologians. The crisis of the
history, as of so much else in human affairs, occurred in Europe in the
sixteenth and seventeenth centuries. The concept was mistrusted by Protestant theologians, perhaps because in actual use it suggested an idol,
standing where Christ should stand. At the same time, it became one
protagonist in a war of ideas, assailed by a new concept *with the same name*,
one newly generated to justify political realism and ruthlessness of the
kind called machiavellian.

> Crude machiavellianism says that the end justifies the means. Refined machi-
> avellianism merely says: Let what you can do indicate what you can do
> better; technique is the thing; let the ends look after themselves. It is the
> attitude underlying sixteenth-century capitalist development (in war, min-
> ing and trade) and the attitude implied in the scientific programmes which
> grew out of that development.[10]

The old concept was driven out of natural philosophy by the growing
conviction that "technique is all." It was driven out of moral philosophy
by newly conceived defences of human dignity, grounded in fresh analyses
of our distinctively moral experience which led philosophers to speak of
"the naturalistic fallacy" that imperatives may be derived from indicatives,
with "is" implying "ought." It has come to be generally dismissed as a
worthless product of anthropocentric mythologizing. The "nature" which
men have talked about during the last century and a half has not been
that about which theologians were wont to speak. The word has acquired
a modern meaning: things as they manifestly are in their freshly given
state. To expose oneself to their purity, with a vision swept clear of human
prejudice and folly, is to be invigorated and renewed. A theologian is
bound to hesitate before suggesting that it is part of his job to impose
upon clear vision some distorting lens composed of ideas. His business is
with things as they really are—with the actualities of divine grace and of
creaturely existence. But it is naïve to suppose that the world as experienced by men is a datum undisturbed by the recipient's mode of perception. It is experienced as "nature"—a construct into which ideas enter.
The question is, whether the theologian can help to articulate this experience by calling into play perhaps in a revised form, something of what
was once built into the old construct which served the European imagination so well for a thousand years, at any rate in so far as it kept men's
experience in this physical environment open towards correlative grace.
It can be safely left to the scientists to make sure that their own enterprise
is not shackled by *a priori* demands proceeding from such an interpre-
tative construct.

---

[10]J. F. Danby, *Shakespeare's Doctrine of Nature* (London, 1961), p. 91.

Of what is "natural science" the science? "Take a large view of it. What does it include? The understanding of the visible world: not only the data which the mechanistic [*sic*] sciences deal with, but all the data of order and comprehensive meaning." So the Archbishop of Canterbury exhorts an audience of teachers. I do not myself think that we can go back to the urbane vision of an eighteenth-century gentleman-amateur of science. But for purposes of new construction there is much to be appreciated in the old mediating concept. It preserved a view of the whole finite order as a *created* project—the classical rendering of this tended to be "system with ends in view," but the less rigid term "project" may suit us better. It preserved a view of this project as one with its own inherent degrees of *freedom*, complementary, therefore, to grace, and coerced by necessity only where grace is resisted and the resistance itself is opposed. It preserved a view of the finite order as something which God, in His creating of it, *authorized* and continues to authorize in so far as its eventualities are "natural." Since every man lives with resources many of which he accepts as "inherited," it is for him a vital question (deeply affecting his confidence, his competence, and his capacity to use them gratefully) whether the inheritance is authorized and from whence. A similar question is raised in every use or misuse of his freedom. The old concept suggested, too, how particular projects which are men's direct concern (as the entire mysterious project in its totality is not) should be *tested for reliability and for worth*. "Nature" could be made articulate by reason, notably in "law"—this word having a wider use than to designate coercive legislation; "law" is a combination of "authority" with "word", which serves to bring reasonable men into the project as responsible partners. It affords a criterion for assessing reliability and worth, which is more human than a simple acceptance of the thesis that "whatever is, is right," and more sensitive than those afforded by secular standards of success.

These may be reckoned among the aids to civilized living which the old "theology of nature" preserved and made vivid in men's lives. Theologians, in so developing their understanding of the world, took their bearings, not directly from the physical universe, but from a theological construct for which at present we have no substitute. In the hands of dogmatists it became a tool of tyranny which inhibited the development of empirical investigation. Though it enabled men to "know themselves" and to live with human dignity in their cosmic environment, it kept them within blinkers which had to be torn away by the combined impetus of Renaissance and Reformation. It became, in its own right, a guide to their knowledge of God, and was rightly criticized as demonic by theologians newly awakened to the authority of the Bible. Perhaps it is dead and buried for ever, even as a model for what should be newly constructed. I am myself disposed to wonder whether, nevertheless, it should not be our aim to construct something like it for our own age, under safeguards which anticipate the scope for demonic perversion. If so, material may be available for us in "correspondences" which appear to the discerning eye between scientific thinking, its methods and results, on the one hand, and on the other hand those acknowledgments of grace and glory which are the substance of Christian faith.

V

"Correspondence" (or "correlation") is a notion which demands closer investigation. It directs our attention to the possibility that methods used, or theses formulated, in the course of scientific disciplines and theological disciplines, may fit together in one of several ways—consistency being presupposed for any fitting together. The simplest form of fitting together will be "simple conjunction giving wider coverage." In Teilhard de Chardin's work, this form predominates, but it may be doubted whether his naïvety in this and other respects is the naïvety of genius. To the Hegelian, "thesis and antithesis" is the form to be expected. Between these two extremes there are milder possibilities, such as "question exposed and answer offered." The most general and non-committal way of expressing what one looks for is suggested by the imagery of "echo" or "resonance."

Superficial resonance, however, will not do. Unless the correspondence suggested by symptoms can be tracked down to the centre from which both disciplines originate and be given significance there, it is unworthy of philosophical attention. This centre is the actuality of human living, social and individual; and, as the category of "evolution" serves to remind us, this actuality is marked for us with the character of *venture* in response to challenge, with *need* as the shadow-side of this situation. From this centre both scientific and theological disciplines are developed; and in the spread of interest common to both disciplines (and in principle both cover everything) instances may arise, either of resonant theses, or of resonant uses within the divergent disciplines of logical equipment drawn from humanity's common stock. "Evolution—a fundamental element of the concept of nature" provides an example. It can be expounded, loosely and romantically, so as to bring the "venture" aspect of human living into new focus. A generalized and diluted notion of evolution may be used to bring into view "an ascent towards consciousness," with genetical evolution of living organisms and a so-called psycho-social evolution of mankind as two episodes of a continuous integral process. The thesis may then be extrapolated in correspondence with theological themes about man's unique place in the universe, redemption through love, and unification in Omega, to suggest grace sufficient for all our need.[11]

---

[11]"Evolution" provides an instance of the "thesis" type. The notion of "complementarity" is another instance which has attracted attention. Though this is not the place to discuss the matter in depth, it may be suggested that it illustrates the other possibility, i.e., of resonant uses within divergent disciplines of logical equipment.

If, as many people think, this is not the way to do serious business, it may be worth while to turn one's attention to another area of scientific enterprise where a thesis is emerging which echoes in some respects the precise evolutionary thesis within biology and is bound to have reverberations within theology. From Mr. Wren-Lewis—in his capacity as scientist and technologist, not as lay-theologian—I take the suggestion that the *concept of truth* upon which men have relied for twenty-five centuries to support them in perplexity and uncertainty, will no longer serve. This has exposed a depth of need hitherto masked, and makes venture look like a desperate hazard, to which no sure promise can conceivably attach. The quest for truth—for that which merits *trust*—was formerly regarded as the approximation of theory (and of practice in the wake of theory) to reality already rooted and held firm in some determining ground. But now, truth is the actuality which emerges in the act of testing theory against experience; often an unforeseeable actuality, which was not there "in principle" (as in a womb) waiting to be delivered by thought. It requires *for its creation* our manipulations of the world. These manipulations are guided by "concepts" and "principles"; but these are merely "tentative formulae for doing things"; their function is not to guide us to theoretical conclusions about what the world is or ought to be like, in some absolute sense— to guide us, in other words, to "truth" as a fusion of intellect and being, reliably established in some determining "ground" of truth, or of reason, or of being. Where, then, may a man turn, in his perplexity and uncertainty about the decisions which he has to make? He can turn, in the fullest awareness of which he is capable, to what actually emerges in our corporate handling of the world—to materials and to the fruits of every effective exploitation of their possibilities and energy. And if, as is the case, some point of reference is needed (other than "technique is all" or "whatever is, is best") from which these actualities may be judged trustworthy and rendered trustworthy, there is no more useful point of reference than "that the good of persons should be demonstrably served." What this means, finally, has to emerge *in practice*, and not by reference to fundamental myths.

Men cannot, I believe, live in this situation and not have their interest freshly aroused in the matters raised by religious testimony. The topics given to the theologian are "God" and "man." From these topics taken together he moves out to the topic of "the world." There he meets the physical scientist, who has "world" and "man" for his topics, and who may or may not see a real question about their relatedness to "God." But the question is there. In what "ground of truth" are the happenings of nature and the decisions of men (however these be distinguished and related) rooted, charged with importance, and, under certain conditions, made trustworthy? Can a theologian, emancipated from the chains of classical traditionalism and authoritarianism, say something at this point about the authority of grace, and say it in a way which corresponds to the question? What he finds to say will include also information about man, living in the texture of this physical universe, but entitled to respond gratefully to God in the privilege of unique partnership; his response being expressed in an activity of faith working through love, which is fully open to natural description, and whose actuality is less well described as making for "evolution" than as making for "responsible reformation." Whether, in the course of trying to say all this, he can find a newly appropriate way of talking about the physical world as such—this is the question I have chiefly been trying to raise in this discussion of a "theology of nature." I am sufficiently Augustinian to express the hope that he will be able to do so, in a fashion which justifies a remark recently made to me by my old teacher, Nathaniel Micklem: "What is nature, in the end, but the mediation of God Himself to the human heart through Jesus Christ, when once our eyes are opened?"

(1964)

NEW HEAVENS
AND A NEW EARTH

God's purpose for the physical universe is for the most part hidden from us in mystery; we do not suppose that its only function is to provide support and discipline for men's bodies and minds during their lifetime on earth. We are certain that God's purpose will be worthy of his own majesty, and that it will be consistent with the dignity and splendour apparent in the universe to minds instructed through scientific enquiry. Yet we do not know, either in Christian faith or through scientific enquiry, what God will do with his creation when he completes the open expression of his sovereignty. . . .

We look forward to acts of God which bring final transformation to human life and admit human beings to share in his own eternal joy and felicity. Creatures have been called into being to reflect the unimaginable glory of the everlasting God. Cleansed from sin we shall see God in Jesus Christ in open splendour, and he will make us like himself. We do not know in what universal framework human lives so transfigured will be set; nor how in that framework God's other purposes for his created universe will be fulfilled. We do know that God is the source, the guide and the goal of all that is, and that in his serenity he sees the end from the beginning.[1]

TAUGHT BY IMMANUEL KANT, MODERN MEN FIND IT HARD TO DECLARE confidence in God until they are satisfied that what they say accords with some "Critique of Pure Theological Reason."[2] Human speech expresses

---

[1]*A Declaration of Faith, Adopted by the Congregational Church in England and Wales* (London: Independent Press Ltd., 1967). The passages are paras. 1 and 6 from Section VI: "God Will Triumph."

[2]Modern theologians provide as best they can their own account of being and knowing. When Karl Heim produced the theology which eventually made him rank as an outstanding modern authority in the field which I am exploring, he set up the elaborate framework of "polarities" by way of preface in *God Transcendent* (Welwyn: Nisbet, 1936). Karl Rahner clears the ground in another way in *The Theology of Death* (London: Burns & Oates, 1961). My crude observations on method in sections I and V represent what I have derived, unsystematically, from two theologians whom I most respect: Edmund Schlink, *The Coming*

the awareness of human beings, physically constituted for life in a physically constituted universe. It is speech disciplined by reflection and argument, serving to clarify that with which they deal and which deals with
them, and serving also to clarify the terms on which these dealings take
place. Among much which, at first sight, merely "happens," men regard
themselves as "agents" whose "activity" provides the kind of "actuality" in
which they can have a rational interest. They ask, critically, whether this
agency-language can be applied more widely, and if so with what distinctions. It is applied, in the passages cited, to "acts of God." Human awareness has produced traditions about "God." They are traditions which
suggest that human living is open towards an unseen Lord, towards an
unseen future, and towards enigmatic fellow-creatures. Supported by these
traditions men conduct their lives by faith working through love with
hope in God. Christian men speak in their faith about "what no eye has
seen, nor ear heard, nor the heart of man conceived, which God has
prepared for those who love him"; and this, they claim, "God has revealed
to us through the Spirit" (1 Corinthians 2:6–10).

What prospect have they glimpsed? Life is theirs at present within a
physical universe of which they are part. Appearances suggest that physical fact is infested with built-in obsolescence. Physical entities wear out,
and wear one another out. Is the prospect of ever-renewed splendour,
unmarred by any taint of wearing-out, compatible with the form of being
known to us as spatio-temporal physicality? "We do not know, either in
Christian faith or through scientific inquiry, what God will do with his
Creation when he completes the open expression of his sovereignty." Yet
in worship men have seen fit to express what they hope for; and in theology "which proclaims the glory of Christ in the name of God, and
develops the proclamation in the realm of thought"[3] they have discussed
the reasonable warrant for doing so.

Our obligation is to develop a theology appropriate for men whose
own knowledge of the world and of themselves has been acquired by
experience, men who also believe that they and their world are *known by
God*. We do it within a tradition where God is revered as Creator of heaven
and earth and of all things visible and invisible. The first article of the
Creed requires us to respect a fundamental distinction between God and
all that God creates. The subordinate distinctions—heaven and earth,
things visible and things invisible—do not have clarity in use which once
they had. The varied and vague associations which these verbal signposts
have acquired may confuse and hinder the work which has to be done;
but I shall try to proceed with the main business of this essay without

---

Christ and the Coming Church (Edinburgh: Oliver & Boyd, 1966), Part I, ch. 2, "The Structure
of Dogmatic Statements As an Ecumenical Problem"; and Austin Farrer, *Faith and Speculation* (London: A. & C. Black, 1967).

[3]E. Stauffer, *New Testament Theology* (London: S.C.M. Press, 1963), note 585 on ch. 43.

stopping to put them into use afresh by careful mapwork. Let us proceed with scrupulous respect for the main distinctions: between God and all that God creates, and between the knowledge God has and the knowledge which men acquire experientially. Through God's generosity as Creator, men and their world are what God knows them to be. Men have their own awareness of created actuality and of the agencies involved. Their awareness is ill informed in many respects; it can be better informed if God gives himself to them so that they may share his knowledge. Those who believe that God does precisely this may find it appropriate to say that what men receive as the creatures of God and as his partners in knowledge comes to them by two distinguishable routes: one runs through the matrix of spatio-temporal physicality, and the other supervenes upon that matrix in the experience called "conscience."

Set thus to live, men also are aware that, with their world, they are in pilgrimage; and Christians believe that in this pilgrimage God takes his creatures from "first" and "old" things to "new" and "last" things. This faith informs their will to live. At the heart of Christian tradition lies the conviction that God in his self-giving so relates himself to men that he takes up their wills into his own. Where faith prevails in the tumult of experience, Christian men are able to express their own will in the prayer: Thy will be done on earth as it is in heaven. Through Jesus Christ, author of that prayer wherever it is truly made, faith rests upon God the Creator of heaven and earth. All things are subject to his rightful authority, and in his will is our peace.

One further comment on human habits must be made and then we can get to work. Men, apt to discern what they must deal with and what deals with them, organize their awareness in ways best fitted to serve their rational interest. This organized appreciation is aptly and frequently done by the complementary application of three sets of categorical tools: one which picks out *physical* features, one which picks out *political* features, and one which picks out *personal* features, in the actuality with which (and in which) men must engage.[4] The man of faith, whose will God has taken up into his own, claims to receive into his own knowledge something of the knowledge which God has of him and of his affairs. Paul, as we have noted, does this with particular reference to the invisible future prepared in heaven already, into which the whole creation will move at its final consummation. The three complementary category-sets are prominently in use; for this particular reference fits into a larger persuasion that God, self-expressed in Jesus Christ, is at work in creation, through a process[5]

---

[4]Readers who are inclined to press this distinction into the form of compounding reality "naturalistically," "historically," and "aesthetically and religiously" may of course do so—at some risk. Cf. W. Dantine, "Creation and Redemption," *Scottish Journal of Theology*, (1965), 129–147.

[5]The judicial associations of this term should be held in mind.

of righteousness in the course of which he overcomes nullifying opposition to his will, to achieve with his creatures a final glory. Physical actualities, affirmed as heaven and earth with mankind housed in them, are subject to political action from mankind. Within an enterprise of creation, life is being given to men; and "if anyone is in Christ he is a *new* creation; the old has passed away, behold, the new has come" (2 Corinthians 5:17).

With what expectation, reasonably entertained in hope and expressed through love, may the man of faith look forward with questions in his mind about his own physicality and about the physical universe with which he is so deeply involved in the receiving of life? With the divergent languages of apocalypse, of speculative illumination, and of philosophical apologetic, the early Christians tried to do business in this matter. They took seriously the promised access to "secret and hidden wisdom" which "God has revealed to us through the Spirit." For them, as for us, it was debatable whether the "new" and "last," fully deployed, would in any sense incorporate the facts of spatio-temporal physicality given in the "first" actuality of man in his world. An apostolic assertion that "the *form* of this world is passing away" (1 Corinthians 7:31b) is ambiguous in this respect. Its author suggests elsewhere that the whole creation will be taken up in the final consummation and share in the glory of the children of God (Romans 8:21; cf. Ephesians 1:10; Colossians 1:20); but would he have denied the predicted annihilation of the material world to which others allude (1 John 2:17a; Revelation 20:11 and 21:1b; 2 Peter 3:10f.)?

We cannot, of course, be sure that we know what is being talked about here. Every closed account of spatio-temporal physicality which men give to themselves is liable to be disreputed. But there are facts, not wholly of our making, which provoke real questions. To the man who affirms creation these are facts in which the will of God is expressed; and when God's will is finally accomplished, his purpose in so ordering things will, we hope be transparently plain. Will it be plain as the purpose of a ladder is plain to those who have climbed it and, from the height scaled, see how and why it was placed as it was, with freedom thereafter to discard it? Or will it be plain because in the end materiality for men in a physical universe will serve gloriously (in ways we do not now experience) to mediate the imperishable life which God wills to give to his creatures?[6]

---

[6]This second possibility is being explored with vigour by theologians from all the main traditions who are concerned that redemption should be affirmed in proper relation to creation. From Lutheranism we hear Wingren insisting that "belief in creation means that we cannot isolate a 'religious' part, our soul, from the rest of us, or separate body from soul on the false assumption that only the soul can have any relationship to God"; "the basic fact that we live constitutes the primary relationship to God" (G. Wingren, *Creation and Law*, [(Edinburgh: Oliver & Boyd, 1961], p. 261). E. L. Mascall has contributed substantially to the discussion in *The Christian Universe* and in *Theology and the Future* (London:

In 2 Peter 1:2–11 and 3:2–13, as in Revelation 21:1–6, the universal framework envisaged for redeemed human lives is unambiguously identified as "new heavens and a new earth." Can we find an appropriate theology which prepares men at any rate to consider what is said in those passages? If the second option about plainness is correct, it will be theology which encourages us to find here a reference to actualities which are not wholly immersed into the activity of rational human agents, as the physical universe of our present experience is not. Those who believe that man's chief and highest end is to glorify God and fully to enjoy him for ever are frequently disposed to treat as fully actual, and to envisage as finally actual, only what is incorporated into the activity of rational agents. If the raw crudities of the physical universe *repel* them, they share with other pessimists the language of gnostic illumination, whose logic is to dissociate the created world from God and to assign to some demiurge the power in physical existence. If, on the other hand, the wonder of the world *holds their admiration*, they try to share with other sensitive admirerers the language of philosophical reflection. 2 Peter 1 (notably verse 4 with its reference to becoming "partakers of the divine nature") will provide a principal theological bearing, and it will be the theological language of incarnation and transfiguration whose logic they will most readily explore.

Leaving aside gnostic dualism, let us consider the theology offered by E. L. Mascall. With a sharp eye on the misconception "that Jesus Christ is of immense significance to human beings, but of no importance whatever to the rest of the universe,"[7] Mascall draws out a theology of "Christification." This theology, as also that of Teilhard whom he cautiously invokes,[8] directs attention to the present radiation of grace, overarched by "the reality of the consummated Christ"; but it does not interpret for us the Petrine injunction to "*wait* for new heavens and a new earth in which righteousness dwells." Mascall wishes to take the cosmic symbolism of this text as more than a metaphor. The hope set before us is "that both the human race and the material universe, of which the human race is part, may be taken up into the very life of God himself and be transformed into a condition of unimaginable glory."[9] His theology, like that of Teilhard,[10] displays merit for lack of which any theology will be suspect. It maintains the proper reserve which must characterize any human effort

Darton, Longman & Todd, 1966 and 1968). Cf. papers at a colloquium in 1964—"The New Testament Doctrine of Ktisis," by G. W. H. Lampe in *Scottish Journal of Theology*, 17 (1964), 449–462; "Nature," by P. Evdokimov, ibid., 18 (1965), 1–22; "Creation and Redemption," by W. Dantine, ibid., 18 (1965), 129–147.

[7] *The Christian Universe*, p. 163.

[8] *The Christian Universe*, pp. 91ff, 142ff; *Theology and the Future*, pp. 78ff.

[9] *The Christian Universe*, p. 109.

[10] I have nothing to add, by way of direct discussion of Teilhard, to what others provide. Cf. *The Phenomenon of Man* and *Le Milieu Divin*, and also *An Introduction of Teilhard de Chardin*, by N. M. Williers.

to foretell the consummation of God's purposes. It cannot be dismissed as *idle* speculation, for it directs men's will to live into the healing channels of sacramental worship and towards a Christian handling of this world's present business. Its Omega-expectation is shaped by looking down the perspectives offered now to highly cultivated men. The hazards posed by religious language which, in pagan use, purports to divinize what is not divine, are overcome—and the perils of Nature-worship dispelled—by practical theology which points to the consecration of the world in liturgy; and experiences of transfiguration, given in the way of asceticism, come to their own. What, if anything, is missing, when the theology we seek is developed along these lines?

The divergent languages of apocalypticism, gnostic speculation, and philosophical apologetic were all employed in an effort to declare "the unseen" for which empirical languages of natural science and of history are inappropriate (however relevant to the declaration what is said in those languages may be). The particular declaration about new heavens and a new earth was originally made in the language of apocalyptic. Apocalyptic testimony declares the divine enterprise of creation, within which we, with our entire world, derive being from God. It declares that God's creation is distorted by the power which lurks in idolatrous religion and sensualist seduction. It declares that men, with their world, will be renewed and glorified as God's creation when this process of salvation is accomplished. It elicits confidence in future acts of God which will give life to men and provide a framework serving to sustain that life in imperishable glory. Where this language is used in the New Testament (and we may take 2 Peter 3:13 and Revelation 21:1 as the clearest cases), the framework, identified in both cases as "new heavens and a new earth," fills the void left by demolition of the present framework of spatio-temporal physicality. The intention, again in both cases, is that mankind should have the only kind of home in which we know human life to be possible, but should have it in a new and final form where the promise of life in unimpaired fellowship with God is gloriously fulfilled—"in which righteousness dwells" (2 Peter 3:13), into which "the new Jerusalem descends" (Revelation 21:2–4). The passion which carried this thesis into Christian eschatology is something we can share if we read Isaiah 56–65, taking it as sequel to Isaiah 40–55, with the event of Jesus Christ vivid in our experience. Isaiah 65:17, once absorbed in that discipline of faith seeking understanding, is not easily abandoned: "Behold, I create new heavens and a new earth; and the former things shall not be remembered or come into mind. Be glad and rejoice for ever in that which I create!" "Create," moreover, is a word with rich associations, and a second intention attaches itself to the thesis of new heavens and a new earth: by their establishment, the inherent goodness of all that the Creator has brought into being will at last be fully and publicly displayed.

In this apocalyptic tradition we find Papias declaring that "the kingdom of Christ will be established on this earth σωματικος." We have the allusion in Acts 3:21 to "times of ἀποκαταστάσεως πάντων (reinstatement of all things)." This theme, borrowed from paganism as Lactantius happily points out,[11] constructs the Christian hope in a fashion which speaks to longings widely entertained—though on a falsely cyclic basis—in the Graeco-Roman world. We have, too, the theologies with which Paul, Mark, and Luke mediate to us the Christ-event. If Helmut Flender is right in his recent contribution to our understanding of them, each in his own way distinguishes between the renewal of the old world to its original purpose as God's creation and the eschatological new creation, of which the restored creation, for its limited time, is parabolic.[12]

None of this, one need hardly say, stands in its own right. It rests in faith's response to Jesus Christ: a man in history whose presence bears witness to the authority of God and to his asserting of that authority through process of conflict leading to victory, in the age-long engagement with the enterprise of creation. The manhood of Jesus, from conception to burial, was wrought out in the context of "heaven and earth" which is our own present context. But in his case a unique claim is made about his manhood: that it is now re-expressed in imperishable life, bound as σῶμα πνευμάτικον in indissoluble unity with the divine origin of all life. He has passed through death into the world's future; there he is "with God"; and in post-resurrection appearances he has disclosed himself to men living where we now live—an occurrence, or set of occurrences, which throw a question-mark against every closed account of spatio-temporal physicality which men concoct.[13] He has disclosed himself as "the Lord who is to come." In the meantime, he unites our works and ways with the works and ways of God "in the Spirit." By this inaugurated

---

[11]*Inst.* VII, c. 18: "Of the fortunes of the world at the last time, and of the things foretold by soothsayers.

That these things will thus take place, all the prophets have announced from the inspiration of God, and also the soothsayers at the instigation of the demons. . . . But, withdrawn from their account, not without fraud on the part of the demons, was that the Son of God would then be sent, who, having destroyed all the wicked, would set at liberty the pious. Which, however, Hermes did not conceal. For in that book which is entitled The Complete Treatise, after an enumeration of the evils concerning which we have spoken, he added: 'But when these things come to pass, then he who is Lord, and Father, and God, and Creator of the first, and sole God, looking upon what is done, and opposing to the disorder his own will (i.e. goodness), recalling the wandering and cleansing wickedness, and partly inundating it with much water and partly burning it with most rapid fire, and sometimes pressing it with wars and pestilences, *he brought his world to its ancient state and renewed it.*' "

[12]H. Flender, "Das Verständnis der Welt bei Paulus, Markus und Lukas," in *Kerugma und Dogma* (1968), Heft 1.

[13]E. Schlink, "Zum Gespräch des Christlichen Glaubens mit der Naturwissenschaft" in *Medicus Viator* (Tübingen: J.C.B. Mohr, 1959); M. C. Perry, *The Easter Enigma* (London: Faber, 1959).

eschatology we are encouraged in faith to taste the powers of the world to come and to live in this world now as men equipped for life in the glory of God's consummated creation.

The will so to live here and now is strengthened and guided by theological explorations which are closely related to one which immediately concerns us, but are not identical with it.[14] Good work has been done on the theme of "cosmocrats" (falsely divinized authorities of culture) and their subjection to God in Christ. Work has also been done on the implications of this Christology and eschatology for the self-understanding and practice of the Church in its worldly-role and service. It must suffice here to note, without investigating, the possibility that these explorations supply signposts which suggest that cosmically the way forward is to a new heavens and a new earth, where physicality in a physical universe (a state which at present seems to be constitutive for manhood) is not abandoned but renewed—renewed by acts of God of which we have had some intimation in advance not only by the post-resurrection appearances of Christ but also by his transfiguration. But sign-posts are not maps. We have no maps. And if we take our bearings from physicality as at present we experience it, we find ourselves wrestling with difficulties which have put a brake on apocalyptic exuberance. Our task is to focus, if we can, an expectation reasonably held in faith and hope, one which bears fruit now in appropriate deeds of love; and it must be done with theological sobriety, a virtue not conspicuously present in apocalyptists, though it is worth remembering that theological exhilaration is not to be equated with theological intoxication and primly repudiated![15]

With brakes gently applied, philosophical theologians have turned into other linguistic territories where difficulties about physicality have sometimes brought them near to dissolving redemptive history into timeless myth. We need not follow those who strayed into the language of speculative illumination. The church's resistance to gnostics "who tried to dissociate the created world from God, in order to assign to the demiurge the power in physical and external existence"[16] is enshrined in the first article of the Creed. Notoriously there was not, and still is not, a comparable resistance to the temptations offered through the language of philosophical apologetic, which, in varying forms, expresses "an attitude to life which is defined by the ideal of the development of personality." These

---

[14]A. D. Galloway, *The Cosmic Christ* (Welwyn: Nisbet, 1951). In Davies and Daube, eds., *The Background of the New Testament and its Eschatology* (Cambridge: Cambridge University Press, 1954), there are highly relevant articles: "Christ, Creation and the Church," by N. A. Dahl and "Kerugma, Eschatology and Social Ethics," by A. N. Wilder.

[15]G. B. Caird, *Commentary on the Revelation of St. John the Divine* (London: A. & C. Black, 1966), provides an impressive and timely exposition of the religious and intellectual power in that piece of apocalyptic.

[16]Wingren, *Creation and Law*, p. 4.

temptations, particularly as presented in traditions stemming from Platonist "idealism," have been kept under critical scrutiny, but not always to everyone's satisfaction.[17] Good men and true have always been ready to argue that both alternatives to the language of apocalypticism evoke theological reports on God's work and ways with his world which are insufficiently *theocratic* to satisfy the Christian conscience. Be that as it may, the difficulties which men have in reconciling spatio-temporal physicality with final glory must not be evaded.

Spatio-temporal physicality, taken abstractly as a *form* of creaturely being, does not present difficulty in principle for theistic religion. It is a form appropriate to finitude; one in which creatures evidently *hold their own* and exert their God-given *power* to be. Taken materially, as matter of fact, it is riddled with suggestions of ultimate recalcitrance to the grace we look for in the works and ways of God. The suggestions fall under two broad heads, roughly corresponding to two grounds of opposition which Paul diagnosed in the resistance put up to his preaching of Christ crucified, the power of God and the wisdom of God. Men reared in Judaism put up religious opposition; Gentiles put up rational opposition; both had to be "called" out of their habitual attitudes to a fresh apprehension of grace.

Man's own physicality, and the dominant constituents in his physical environment, attract from him a confidence which easily passes into worship; and worship is rightly to be given only to God. Where men's will to live is corrupted by misplaced worship, God's enterprise of creation is distorted, not only in manhood itself but in everything with which men have dealings. Early theologians, whilst resisting the gnostics' radical mistrust of physical actuality, vehemently contested all tendencies to assume that material principles are ultimate. "The heart of the matter for Clement always lies in the doctrine of the transcendent Creator upon whose will and providence the created order is dependent and with whom this world is in no sense identical."[18] Philosophical theologians stood with apocalyptists in repudiating the power which lurks in sensualist seduction and in the refinements of idolatry to which it leads. But, asks the religious man, can actualities which serve so to seduce men be glorified in the final triumph of God's purposes?

The universe in all its physical actuality so imposes itself upon men that their effort to live is marred, to the eye of faith, by evidence of opposition to God. Where, however, is the principle of opposition properly to be

---

[17]J. Hering, "Eschatologie biblique et idealisme platonicien," in *Background*, ed. Davies and Daube. Three more recent works provide very rewarding guidance: H. Chadwick, *Early Christian Thought and the Classical Tradition* (London: Oxford University Press, 1966); R. A. Norris, *God and World in Early Christian Theology* (London: A. & C. Black, 1966); Angelo P. O'Hagan, *Material Recreation in the Apostolic Fathers* (Berlin: Akademic–Verlag).

[18]Chadwick, p. 46.

located? The gnostics had their unacceptable answer in a dualism which denied Christian belief in creation. If the principle is not to be traced to God himself, an alternative is to locate it solely in man's perverse will; but this is perhaps unduly presumptuous, and does not in any case remove theological difficulties about the goodness of the Creator's work. The evidence, moreover, is that evil is inflicted upon men from the non-human environment in ways which cannot be exhaustively covered by tracing the evil men impose on the environment. Karl Barth has tried to safeguard what is at stake in formulation of the thesis that the relationship between Creator and creature is disrupted by a nullifying element "which is compatible with neither the goodness of the Creator nor that of the creature, and which cannot be derived from either side but can only be regarded as hostility in relation to both."[19] With consistent stress on the negativity of all that comes into view, and with careful attention to appropriate distinctions, he succeeds to my mind in providing a report on God's process against evil which opens the way to a religiously tolerable hope of redemption for all that God has created, by reconciliation and renewal.

A prospect of cleansing from corruption and of liberation from distortion does not, however, necessarily suffice for minds troubled in another way about physicality. Those most troubled in this other way are men whose will to live has for its spearhead the power of intellect; men who often invite the description "rootless cosmopolitans and aristocrats of the mind." Aristocrats of the mind are unwilling to be comfortably or uncomfortably at home along with the world's minerals, vegetables, and animals. They want to *know*. Physicality being as it is, their aspiration to succeed through knowing lies under threat.[20] The difficulties posed by finitude and by death are not, perhaps insuperable; nor are those posed by the immensity and complexity of physical fact or by the dangers in physical power. The threat arises from the strong hint that what is physical is, in the last resort, opaque and therefore ultimately intractable to the rational agency of mind. One way of repelling this threat is to affirm the superiority of rational agency to physical functioning and in the end to write off whatever is not subsumed into that superior agency. The threat

---

[19]K. Barth, *Church Dogmatics* III, 3 (T. & T. Clark, (Edinburgh: 1960), ch. 50, 1—"The Creator and His Creation."

[20]A. D. Galloway (*The Cosmic Christ*) is an excellent guide to the varying ways in which men have shown awareness of this threat. Dr. Galloway's own—modern—way of putting it is that the not-self, in its physicality, seems to be an impersonal intrusion upon personal life. On pp. 150–3 he cites two passages, one from a second-century Gnostic and the other from Kant, each of which "expresses fear, awe, and a feeling of insignificance in the fact of the vast, uncontrollable, impersonal forces of nature. Each expresses this in a different way, but to both such a universe, appears to be ultimately incompatible with the fulfilment of personal life." The question raised is therefore: By what redemptive act of God is personal life in an impersonal universe fulfilled in such a way that all experience becomes an encounter with God?

is repelled but not finally dispelled. Perhaps, after all, it should not be dispelled but rather absorbed into a will to live which is transmuted into the richer way of love.

It is consistent for aristrocrats of the mind to hope that in the end men will be liberated from every trace of physicality, so that rational agents, eternally preserved, lie open to one another and to God unencumbered by the "otherness" which physicality secures for whatever displays it, including men themselves. Now all who have discovered that men live by love for what is other than themselves will find some attraction in this hope; for love is served by knowledge. An aspiration for life in which love is *transcended* by knowledge probably reflects a distortion of humanity, and a disposition towards living as a rootless cosmopolitan may be a still greater distortion; but the protest against perpetual "otherness" which lies somewhere near the root of an intellectual aversion from physicality is not to be lightly dismissed. Yet, if life can be construed in terms of love, which is served but not transcended by knowledge; and if love presupposes "otherness" which it overcomes without destroying; then it is reasonable to contemplate a consummation in which, together with God and men, creatures other than men have their part.

Traditionally this contemplation has been unfolded in thought-patterns with pyramid structure and an hierarchical system of subordination. By virtue of the Son's subjecting of all creatures to himself, and in virtue of his own subjection to the Father, God "will be everything to everything" (1 Corinthians 15:28). The pyramid is filled out by adding the thesis that non-human creatures have their place in the final glory by subjection to mankind. We do not know how to admit this thesis without arrogance; and modern man's modest estimate of his own importance in his newly seen universe provides (where it exists) a salutary echo of the warning against arrogance which Christians must listen to from another and decisive source. Men are not fit to speak about the commission given to them to "fill the earth and subdue it, and have dominion over every living thing that moves upon it," nor to act upon that commission, until the judgement of God on human pride and human hardness has been carried home. It is carried home proleptically in faith broken and remade before the cross and the empty tomb of Jesus. It will be finally carried home in death and in that to which death is the gateway. Any prospect we may hold of an "earth," given afresh to the children of men, with its "heavens," must be seen under the discipline of God's judgement on mankind. Such a prospect, and the hope which goes with it for power and joy in living, are subject to the grace in which God gives himself to free our race from its guilt. If, then, we affirm our hope, in faith which already leaps to lose its chains, we should do so with modest reserve about man's

dominion and let the emphasis rest on the glory which God will create
when nothing obstructs his will.[21]

In the present inglorious state of affairs we cannot affirm that God is
everything to everything. Idolized creatures and idolizing men offer the
plainest evidence against any such affirmation, and what nullifies it at this
centre is operative wherever we look. That the good creatures of God are
everywhere drawing their life from God must be affirmed in faith; but
the life so drawn is not being returned to him in gratitude, only to be
enjoyed afresh in the glad exchange of love. Physical actuality *as we experience it* obstructs the consummation of creation in a glory so envisaged.
God, so we may affirm, is rightly at work in judgement to demolish it,
and by dying we too shall be engulfed in that demolition. But the final
word about God's creation of mankind as physical beings in a physical
universe rests with God. It is a word already uttered in the inaugurated
eschatology from which Christians take their bearings. The possibility that
demolishing judgement is God's final word is ruled out by the presence,
in this inaugurated eschatology, of resurrection from the dead, and indeed of transfiguration as a present possibility (Mark 9:2 and parallels;
1 Corinthians 15:51). The cosmic hopes expressed in Romans 8:21, in
Ephesians 1:10, in Colossians 1:20, and spelt out in the apocalyptic passages which have claimed our special attention, must be maintained in
fidelity to God.

Throughout this paper I have deliberately used the Greek forms (derived from φύσις) of the words traditionally used to characterize spatio-
temporal actuality and have avoided the Latin derivates, "natural" and
"material." I will not argue the case for doing so here. It is, I believe,
likely that these Latin terms have acquired associations which confuse and
obscure what is under discussion. The problem is to find and to use a
language which will serve to reflect in our own awareness the knowledge
we believe God to have about us and our affairs. It must, I suggest, be
language which catches up spatio-temporal physicality into the enterprise
of "world-making" which is also "history-making": language which does
this by referring to *creation*, to a *process* of righteousness, to glorious *fulfilment* of will and purpose. Language of this kind has been made available

---

[21]Cf. E. Schlink (*The Coming Christ and the Coming Church*, pp. 62f.), where "The Basic
Forms of Human Perception" are under discussion, the pyramidal one having been introduced on p. 56. "The thought-form of a pyramid with its hierarchical system of subordination does not succeed in comprehending the relationship between God and the world,
because God meets the world in Christ as the wholly other Lord—wholly other not only
in his omnipotence, but also because He, the Most High, has come down to us in Christ
as the humblest of all."
K. Heim's discussion of the World's Perfector, in Part Three of *Jesus the World's Perfector*.
(Edinburgh: Oliver & Boyd, 1959), introduces all the insights which impose theological
reserve.

for theological use from the experience of a civic community—"founded," "defended, ruled and rectified," consolidated after episodes of critical strain with ceremonial "triumph." The peace of any such *civis* depends on the rightful authority under which it lives and on the grace and power of that authority's actual operation. When borrowed for theological use, to portray the rightful authority of God over all that is, the term *spirit* is employed to indicate by what agency God's will takes effect with grace and power. This name, alas, has been used so diversely and so loosely that we hesitate about doing further business with it. But if we abandon it the lacuna is not easily filled.

"The Spirit of God is the concept for the activity of the one and only God in history and creation. It can serve as a direct expression for God's inner being and for his present reality."[22] "Spirit" is a word which points beyond the physical to what transcends it but at the same time impinges upon it under two aspects. First, it impinges as the operation of divine authority, expressed as will, potent for salvation or destruction. Secondly, it impinges as the intrinsic power of God to give being and life from himself to another and to receive such another into his own life. It is by Spirit that God promises to be everything to everything, when what is created (as "flesh"), and corrupted by sin but judged and rectified, is finally established as the creature wholly plastic to his will; something which by his free decision he will *own* for ever as his glory.

There are discrepancies in the use of this language, associated with different branches of theological tradition, and it is difficult to track down their sources. Theologians whose habits have been formed within one branch and who try to move out into larger ecumenical freedom have not yet come together in newly confident speech. Some light has been thrown on the problems for me in an article by J. Meyendorff, from which I cite the paragraph most relevant to my own initial habits:

> The development followed by Barth in his later works and leading to a new discovery of the Word of God in the created world, to a solidarity between God and man in the natural order—this idea was always strong in the West, both in Thomism and in modern liberalism, and was also stressed by Russian sophiologists—is still quite different from the notion of a supernatural mutual participation of God and man in the Church, through the Word's historic incarnation.[23]

Is this difference generated, in part at least, by the suspect associations of "natural/supernatural" terminology; or does it go back to insufficiently criticized presuppositions about the relations in which God, mankind, and

---

[22]Kittel, *TWNT*, *"pneuma."* Cf. E. Schweitzer, et. al., *Spirit of God* (London: A. & C. Black, 1960), p. 5.

[23]J. Meyendorff, "The Significance of the Reformation in the History of Christendom," *Ecumenical Review*, 16 (1964), 177.

the world are deemed to be? From Lutheranism we have Wingren's summons to take our presuppositions more simply from the Old Testament:

> The Old Testament describes a humanity which has been created by God, and which, represented by the peculiar people of God who had been chosen for the salvation of the whole of the human race, could do no more than await the outpouring of the Spirit. The humanity which awaits the Spirit, created by God and subject to the discipline of the Law, is the same humanity into which the Spirit comes in the present time through the Gospel and the Church.[24]

Theological language is Church language. "In the Church we live under the constraint of the Holy Spirit; we know the grace of God in Jesus Christ and trust it as sufficient for the redemption of men and women in all their need; our lives are exposed to the claim of God and we learn about his will for human beings both before and after death."[25] What affirmations are we entitled to make about the physical universe?

God exerts his will to give life to creatures; through physical and historical process he rules against the principle of enmity which threatens to nullify his will; at the end he will establish what he has created in the glory of divine ownership. He has done all this already with the man upon whom the process of righteousness was concentrated. Will he not, with him, freely give us all things? Has he not already assured us that this will be so "through the Spirit"?

It is still debatable whether the "new" and "last," fully deployed, will incorporate the facts of spatio-temporal physicality given as our universe in the "first" actualizing of creation and maintained throughout the process of creation but doomed to demolition as all men are doomed to death. Is it in order to suppose that after the impending demolition—and, for the human individual, after death—these physicalities will have served their turn and can be reckoned with an "old" which has passed away? Is there any secret and hidden wisdom for us which God has revealed through the Spirit? Our modern distaste for mystery-mongering, and sceptical detachment from the Biblical presentation of God's enterprise in creation, prompt in us the reply: we do not know—and why should we care? Why, indeed, should men include within things hoped for a universe which is neither God nor their fellow men? Such a universe is theirs at present. It has features strongly suggesting that it is there in many respects for its own sake and not just for ours; nor are these features wholly ascribable to a present enslavement under sin, distorting mankind and all that mankind must deal with. It defies, and threatens to defeat, our capacity for love. Such a universe, however it be glorified, threatens to be "an impersonal intrusion upon personal life." There now, it serves in many ways to

---

[24]Wingren, *Creation and Law*, p. 16.

[25]*A Declaration of Faith* (Congregational Church in England & Wales), Preamble, p. 8.

excite and sustain men's will to live; but it is the proximate cause of defeat for that will.

All Christian hope rests in one who is not defeated by what defeats men. It looks to the God of grace who will give himself to men, dealing first with their guilt and then with the debility and corruption which weaken their creaturely power to be. The hope is that God will take men through death and final judgement and then renew them in power for a life of glory, where all experience will be participation in God's own joy. Does this presuppose a framework of which our present physical universe is parabolic? Moved by respect for God's present works and ways in the act of life-giving, I am inclined to believe that God's answer to that question will be yes! How, otherwise, will life for *men* be given to us? How, otherwise, shall we exert the power of human life?

This essay began with prolegomena evoked by the shade of Immanuel Kant. It turns back to him in a postscript where I will borrow references from Peter Baelz to Kant.[26]

> Whatever else he is, man is a child of nature and part of the natural world. He is to a large degree what he is because nature is what it is. Thus the metaphysical questions concern not simply the meanings he can give his own life, but the meaning which life can give him. (p. 32)

Reflecting on what he knows most intimately, man begins with himself, an agent acting with knowledge formed in categories of causal explanation. Man does not create all that he experiences as a subject; he is not God. His reflections are halted at frontiers of agnosticism which Kant located in his own way:

> The justification of our right to expect the external world to conform to our causal categories of explanation is accompanied by the assertion that we had no right to expect those categories to apply *beyond* the external world. They were restricted in their range to the world of space and time as it must appear to man; they could not be extended beyond the phenomenal world to whatever existed in itself apart from its appearance to man. (p. 34)

But man's worldliness "threatens to destroy his status as a rational, moral being. This threat can be held at bay only if his worldliness is in the last resort subordinated to his moral rationality" (p. 38). In Kant's analysis the postulate of God is inextricably linked with this assertion of ontological priority for man's moral rationality over whatever is phenomenally apparent.

We are now, and not for the first time, dealing within a physical universe which threatens so to impose itself as to crowd out man's coveted self-

---

[26]P. Baelz, *Christian Theology and Metaphysics* (London: Epworth Press, 1968), pp. 32ff.

esteem and to deprive his appeals to God of the weight they have been thought to carry. Theses marked by anthropocentric claims must be advanced, if at all, against critical resistance; and so, though not in consequence, must theses marked by theocentric postulates. What Eliade has called "the anxiety of man living in Time" is a fertile womb of myths, dreams, and mysteries which must not be admitted without close scrutiny into the texture of reasonable faith. The most admissible among these at present is

> that most important mythological tradition of the modern world, which can be said to have had its origin with the Greeks, to have come of age in the Renaissance, and to be flourishing today in continuous healthy growth, in the works of those artists, poets, and philosophers of the West for whom the wonder of the world itself—as it is now being analysed by science—is the ultimate revelation.[27]

If, as seems plausible, Heidegger stands to the twentieth-century European mind as Kant stood to that mind in his day, we must take seriously Heidegger's question about what it means "to be in the world," not only as mind but as concrete being. We must share too his determination to take seriously the φύσις with which beings become and remain observable: an "opening-up and inward-jutting-beyond-itself," declaring a power to be and a right to be which aristocrats of the mind must not lightly brush off. Heidegger, nevertheless, is an aristocrat of the mind who has picked up the Idealist torch and tried to carry some of its light into our own century. There is mystery in φύσις, not exhausted in our scientific dealings with physical things. "The Greeks did not learn what φύσις is through natural phenomena, but the other way round; it was through a fundamental poetic and intellectual experience of being that they discovered what they had to call φύσις."[28] Yet Heidegger can also be described as the grave-digger of German Idealism: an Idealism "rotted in the Mediator, in reconciliation in history, in the Golden Age."

> Heidegger knows no Mediator but poetry. Heidegger knows no world but the material one in which he attempts to find meaning and reconciliation. . . . Heidegger destroys the Idealist reconciliation of the spiritual and material worlds as revealing each other, through faith for Bengel or reason for Hegel.[29]

Through Heidegger's torch-bearing and grave-digging hands we inherit

> the poetical and religious visions of a universe hidden by Satan but at the same time revealing the Light (Being). Heidegger is deeply immersed in

---

[27]Joseph Campbell, *The Masks of God*, Vol. I, (New York: Viking, 1959), p. 7.

[28]M. Heidegger, *An Introduction to Metaphysics* (Garden City, N.Y.: Doubleday, Anchor edn., 1961), p. 12.

[29]M. Heidegger, *The Question of Being* (London: Vision, 1959), pp. 9–10; from the preface by W. Klubach and J. T. Wilde.

the Nothing (Satan) as the veiling of Being (Light), in the anxiety, deepened by the shocking realization of demonic possibilities, lying at the root of earthly reality. Salvation may lie in the poetically lived existence.[30]

For what poetically lived existence have men been set free in Christian faith? In their inner freedom from guilt and in their outward activities of service, in tokens of blessing which lead Cullmann to write about the proleptic deliverance of the body, and others too to write about proleptic dominion in grace over the rest of creation, Christian men have in their faith the gift of life at its best, to be enjoyed here and now in worldly circumstances and to be celebrated for the witness it bears to what is to come. Present victories over illness and promised victory even over death, enacted with and for the body; dethroning of all cosmocrats—false authorities lording it over human culture; union for men with their saviour in subjection to the Father; prospects, however enigmatic, of glorified physicality with God everything to everything—all this, we want to say, comes to us now from the future in the Spirit. It does not come as a matter of course. It comes, in a world "charged with the grandeur of God," through hints and tokens which "flame out, like shining from shook foil."[31]

Whilst we still live on this side of the judgement into which we shall be plunged by death, we do not see what God has prepared for those who love him. We play our part in world-making, in history-making, under conditions of spatio-temporal physicality which conceal the limit which embraces them and pose death as the final absurdity. The order of physical reality reflects some radiance of wisdom and love, it reflects, too, the pride and the hardness with which God is opposed. It invites demolition—and it invites restoration in free grace. Faith cannot satisfactorily state in prose what man is not yet able to see. But it is not disreputable for faith to find expression in prayer and praise—and to sing its belief in poetry as the liturgical counterpoint to the concrete obedience of poetic living. Faith finds expression in liturgical worship even among Welsh (and English) nonconformists:

Thy love is the bond of creation,
Thy love is the peace of mankind.
Make safe with thy love every nation
In concord of heart and of mind.
Thy pity alone can deliver
The earth from her sorrows, dear Lord;
Her pride and her hardness forgive her,
Thy blood for her ransom was poured.
Thy throne, O Redeemer, be founded
In radiance of wisdom and love;

[30]Ibid.
[31]Gerard Manley Hopkins, *Poems* (London: Oxford University Press, 1930), p. 26.

The name through the wide world be sounded
Till earth be as heaven above.
Though hills and high mountains should tremble,
Though all that is seen melt away,
Thy voice shall in triumph assemble
Thy loved ones at dawning of day.[32]

(1970)

---

[32]Howell Elvet Lewis, *Congregational Praise*, No. 342.

PART THREE

The Analogy of Authority

THE CHRISTIAN
IN THE UNIVERSITY

Thus saith the Lord God: Behold, I, I myself, will search for my sheep and will seek them out . . . and I will rescue them from all places where they have been scattered on a day of clouds and thick darkness. . . . I myself will be the shepherd of my sheep. . . . I will seek the lost and I will bring back the strayed; I will bind up the crippled and I will strengthen the weak, and the fat and the strong I will watch over; I will feed them in justice. Ezek. 34:11–16.

HERE IS A PICTURE OF THE UNIVERSE IN THE HANDS OF GOD AND UNDER HIS eye, and of the human race as a flock of sheep. We suspect, don't we, that there is a hidden contempt for human nature when this particular picture is used? It lends support to the paternalism of politicians, to the officiousness of administrators, to the sinister benevolence of mass-providers. Twice, in the Lake District, I have had the luck to watch, from a height, sheep being gathered in the dale-head at the foot of the crags. It is a spectacle to be admired and applauded; but all my admiration goes to the solitary man and the two dogs—three specks in a vast landscape—whose beautifully executed movements can clear three hundred sheep from the fells in an hour and take them to some convenient sheepfold. It is the shepherd, not the sheep, whom we admire and even envy.

The Bidding Prayers sometimes used at formal university services explain to those who pray that they should seek divine blessing upon the university so that "there may never be wanting a succession of persons duly qualified to serve God in Church and State"; and the service envisaged is generally understood to include leadership in society. A good deal of arrogance and lack of humour can bedevil this necessary idea of leadership within human society pictured as a flock of sheep. We shall be saved from the worst excesses and pretensions if we follow Ezekiel's metaphor accurately and refuse to think of ourselves as *shepherd*-leaders. Shepherds are beings of a higher order than the sheep they control; they tend to usurp the role of God Himself and to exploit it in their own interest. The succession of persons duly qualified by university life to serve God in Church and State *remain sheep* and not shepherds; they are men, not little gods. But they are the more gifted and enterprising sheep; well-informed sheep, who can nose out the good pasture and persuade others to feed there. Equipped to rise above the narrow horizon of petty self-interest, they are to take the measure of our human predicament in ways which are of public benefit. They tend to become the fat and the strong, mentioned by Ezekiel towards the end of his picture—a tendency mildly encouraged by the University Grants Committee and by the various Local Authorities who finance our enterprises. But if, in addition, there is a shepherd's mind and heart, moving with sure compassion behind all the appearances of nature and of history, these leading sheep above all should take heed and give thanks. Ezekiel tells us, of course, that this is the case. The scattered flock is wandering in places to which they have strayed in cloudy days and dark nights. There they are: fodder for wild beasts, herded from time to time by pseudo-shepherds who want wool and mutton but care nothing for the weak, the sick, the crippled, or the odd one who is lost. And the Lord God pledges Himself to be, in His own person, the shepherd of these sheep. He will see to pasture for them; He will seek out the lost and care for the weakling; *and* He will keep an eye on the fat and the strong.

We listen to this as persons who have been called to live for the time being in a university. These highly artificial communities are maintained, at mounting expense to the tax-payers, to be the intellectual spearheads for our country's life. We are here to *think*—to take the measure of mankind's predicament by orderly thinking; to think through a vast amount of material which clamours for attention and to push our thinking further than most people have time to do. It has been finely said (I believe by Professor Hodges of Reading) that those who live the life of the mind have a peculiar share in the Passion of Christ. "It is theirs to see and endure, not so much the broken body, the torn flesh of the world, but its twisted and distracted mind."[1] Every student has an all too sordid experience of that twisted and distracted mind as he pursues his earnest business of getting lots of lecture notes in the hope of passing examinations by reproducing them. But if you rise above that parody of academic life and really manage to *think*, you will find it is not blasphemous to link the strain upon you with that mighty and incomparable anguish in which God once and for all poured out His own compassion for the world. The twisted and distracted mind of man is wearing and wearying. Once you dig below the surface of these ideas which convention has made comfortable, you find strings of alternative considerations, unexamined possibilities, subtle errors, and utter uncertainty, all lurking behind the simplest essay subject. You will lose patience with and interest in the finer points,

---

[1] H. A. Hodges, *The Christian in the Modern University* (London: SCM, 1946), p. 24.

which in fact call for your most sensitive and painstaking alertness, precisely because they stand in the way of a plain and easy story. You will look for short cuts to a plain easy story, particularly if your taste runs only to examination fodder. But for good or ill you are here to live this life of the mind, taking the measure of human perplexity, and doing it, as I believe, with Christ.

And, of course, it is fun to be here. It is a life specially designed for the strong (and potentially fat) to enjoy. It is fun to explore the pastures on which the human race has been set to feed, and to admire the curious antics there performed. It is in the nature of our job to penetrate beneath the spiteful and sordid features of things which appear, and taste the underlying glory more fully than is possible for most men in the rough and tumble of life. And those who are persuaded that the same Christ who suffered on Calvary is now exalted and glorified and is the arbiter of creation's destiny, will commit themselves in firm delight to every hint of the glory yet to be revealed. It is therefore expected of us that we should come to live with a measure of distinction and discernment and a proper *joie de vivre*. And this is not self-indulgence—or should not be. It should be a matter of public benefit, for it can offer to depressed and bewildered fellow-mortals the most refreshing kind of leadership, and take them to the pastures where God's wisdom reaches down and prevails.

In saying this, I am of course aware that much has happened in the last two or three centuries to call into question everything that this sermon is trying to say about God. We have been shown to what extent a man's life may simply be reckoned as one slight episode in the "history of nature"; that mankind's highest achievements and experiences (not to mention the low and mediocre ones) are simply what one would expect from a natural creature adapting itself to this natural environment; that the moments of religious exaltation in which men indulge from time to time have their psychological explanation; that each of us, in fact, has been thrown up to play his little part in the "history of nature," and that the great assurance of cleaving to the personal living God at the core of all religion is plain self-deception—whistling to keep one's courage up. It is interesting that this outlook has not been fostered by cynical ignoramuses. It is the great religions, Christianity not least, which have encouraged men to look steadily and honestly at the dark, enigmatic side of life. And now men have looked, squarely and honestly, at the agony and frustration running through life's fabric, at guilt and at death. They cannot see the way of deliverance about which the great religions speak. They have spoken, with restraint but very powerfully, of the desolating possibility that man, each man, is ultimately alone; with all nature to sustain him for the time of his existence, but with no divine Shepherd to provide for him, or to rescue him when nature decrees that her purpose has been served so far as he is concerned. It is in a world thus envisaged that all of us live for much of the time. Many of your moods, your thoughts, your actions and your attitudes belong, as do many of mine, to that sort of world. And in consequence, our *joie de vivre* is already corroded and depressed.

But we have now heard again what Ezekiel has to tell us. I do not myself think that the dignity of university life, with all its strain and all its joy, can be sustained unless we are able to answer the great question about God's reality with confident faith, honest faith critically tested and reasonably adult; a faith which obeys His claims and grasps His promises which are expressed for us through the Bible in Jesus Christ. Here again, of course, there must be no short cuts to an easy answer. But some kind of answer is being expressed all the time, in every mood and every action and in the whole shape of your thought and imagination. You can try out the answers which in fact you are already giving—and perhaps come to re-fashion them—in an encounter with the Gospel and with the Church life which it creates. The Church of Jesus Christ is living in this university, in the same broken, inadequate form that you find everywhere else, but equipped nevertheless to carry its *witness* faithfully. Some people attach themselves to its life because it is like a breath of home—a merciful relief from the tension of academic life. Many do not bother at all. All these proceed, in due time, to the glory of the Bachelor's fur, which moth though not rust eventually corrupts, without having added an inch to their Christian stature. Perhaps you will see the matter in truer perspective and find yourself engaging with the Gospel and with Church life in order to discover on the properly academic level that the Lord is our Shepherd; that sheep may safely graze in this world (with or without seductive twiddles by John Sebastian Bach); and that to serve God in Church and State is the foundation of human dignity in universities and beyond them.

(1964)

AUTHORITY,
DIVINE AND HUMAN

THE CONCEPT OF "AUTHORITY" AND ITS CORRELATE "OBEDIENCE" HAD NO place in my pattern of interest during the first forty years of my life. My curiosity about them was effectively stimulated, so I suppose, by brief sojourn among the switchboards of power as Principal of a modest but exciting institution in the University of Durham beginning in 1955. This experience lent colour to dictionary definitions of authority and occasionally moved me to wonder what those who exert it suppose themselves to be doing. The dictionary connects authority with the claim proper to an author; and an author, according to Thomas Hobbes, is "he who owneth or warrenteth an action." Authority suggests "power or right to enforce obedience," "moral or legal supremacy," "the right to command or to give an ultimate decision," "personal or practical influence over the conduct or the opinion of others," "title to be believed." How was it that I had remained stubbornly insensitive for so long to the central importance of this concept in efforts to clarify the Christian tradition of theology and to probe the relationships between human politics and human science to Christian traditions about God? Some cultural exoneration from the charge of sheer stupidity may be snatched from the fact of an upbringing in the nonconformist tradition to a radical outlook in the tolerant epoch of the 1920's and early 1930's and in the liberal society of working-class life, unpretentious and thoroughly provincial, in the woollen district of the West Riding of Yorkshire. There, as I now realize, contentions established by John Locke in the reign of William and Mary, were roughly but deeply entrenched, without acknowledgement. In a recent review of Locke's correspondence from 1686 to 1690, John Dunn wrote a felicitous paragraph about the four major works fashioned in those years, works which set out to show how it is possible for men individually and collectively to live well and to know what living well consists in:

> The *Essay* shows how men can understand nature and their place within
> it. The educational texts suggest how, in practice, parents (at least among
> the gentry—there seems little hope concretely for the children of servants)
> can rear a son whose intelligence and emotions are as strictly disciplined

by this understanding as his nature permits. The *Epistle de Tolerantia* defends the claim that the role of human understanding in religious practice precludes the valid exercise of coercive authority in religious questions. ... The *Two Treatises of Government* assails the claim of secular power to authority over men on any ground other than that of palpable service to their real needs.[1]

Mr. Dunn remarks that the foundations of Locke's edifice were crumbling as he built and that it is taking us more time than is becoming to appreciate the scale of its collapse as, in the shifty vagrancy of our cognitive life, we skulk among its ruins. Instances of post-liberal "authoritarian" respect for authority abound in the current scene of politics and of religion. Consideration of authority as such (*Vollmacht*, in German speech, rather than *Obrigkeit*) from a theological point of view may serve to render any exercise of authority and any obedience to it more creative and more discriminating than these are apt to be in the pressure of events with assumptions unexamined. The difficulty, as with every important topic, is to pay due attention to what experts in fields other than theology have to say about the matter. In what follows, the selection of non-theological voices will seem odd and inadequate to a well-informed reader—and so, perhaps, will the references to theological expertise.

I

The concept of authority takes shape in human thought out of those experiences where people deal with one another in ways which require such a concept if they are to be adequately described. Dictionary definitions already cited will serve as a preliminary indication of the concept's anatomy. The theologian's concern is with the use of this concept in talk about God. Christian tradition holds that there is authority in God and from God. It maintains too, in the version offered by Sanday and Headlam of Paul's remark in Romans 13, that "the whole structure of authority in the world is God's work." Then, at the practical level, Christian tradition finds expression in Church life where people deal with one another by pleading respect for authority expressed in the Bible, the organized institution, the creeds, the ordained offices of ministry.

Ecclesiastical discussion of authority is apt to take off from this practical level—and sometimes to stay grounded on it. British writing in this century includes an essay in the volume entitled *Foundations* (1912). Its author was the Rev. Mr. A. E. J. Rawlinson, later to become Bishop of Derby,

Who cried, as joyfully he bound his Sheaves
"What I believe is what the Church believes":
Yet some might find it matter for Research

---

[1]*The Listener*, August 10, 1978, 188–89.

Whether the Church taught him, or he the Church.
Corpus had trained him Reason's Truth to doubt
And Keble added Faith, to do without. . . .
Whether our Fact be Fact, no Man can know,
But, Heav'n preserve us, we will treat it so.[2]

He returned to the charge in his Paddock Lectures for 1923, published as *Authority and Freedom*, and, assisted by Wilfred Knox, in *Essays Catholic and Critical* in 1926. T. A. Lacey wrote an ampler book, *Authority in the Church*, which I shall have occasion to draw upon later. In Scotland J. H. Leckie wrote in 1909 on *Authority in Religion* and this wider theme was treated with exemplary power by Peter Taylor Forsyth writing from English Dissent in 1913 with the title *The Principle of Authority in Relation to Certainty, Sanctity and Society*. For him:

> the principle of authority is ultimately the whole religious question; . . . an authority of any practical kind draws its meaning and its right only from the soul's relation to God; this is so not only for religion strictly so called, nor for a Church, but for public life, social life, and the whole history and career of Humanity. . . . All the authority essential in an ordered society or state has its right in proportion to its proximity to, or charter from, the last authority of all. . . . All questions run up into moral questions; and all moral questions centre in the religious, in man's attitude to the supreme ethic, which is the action of the Holy One.[3]

It is Forsyth who provides for me the parameters of any adequate discussion of authority. The most rewarding work of recent date, done with comparable scope and vision, is an Anglo-French Catholic Symposium, *Problems of Authority*, edited by John M. Todd (1962), with which one may associate also *Images of Authority* by J. M. Cameron (1966) which probes the concepts of regal and priestly power. Contributions to essentially ecclesiastical discussion have come from conservative evangelical sources, with the booklet entitled *Authority* by Martin Lloyd-Jones and published by the I.V.F. in 1958 as perhaps the most penetrating. In 1976 the Anglican/Roman Catholic Commission brought the whole topic back to ecclesiastical earth with an Agreed Statement on *Authority in the Church*.

II

Whilst Forsyth was putting together his *Principle of Authority*, Francis McDonald Cornford's book *From Religion to Philosophy* emerged from the press in 1912. It has been republished as a Harper Torch Book and a note in this new edition warns the reader that some of Cornford's more adventurous pages take off from hypotheses of the French school of so-

---

[2]Ronald Knox, "Absolute and Abitofhell," in *Essays in Satire*, pp. 86–87.
[3]P. 3.

ciologists and anthropologists and show marked affinity with the outlook of dynamic psychologists, Jung in particular. There seems to be some question as to which we learn most about from Cornford: the cultural situation in pre-Socratic Greece or the cultural situation in twentieth-century Western Europe. In either case I think there is something to learn about what may be called "the natural history of respect for authority."

Cornford studies the three great conceptions of Destiny, Law, and Nature; he defines what he calls "the primitive religious fact"; and he shows in what sense it is also the primitive *social* fact. "We find it to be a social group (*moira*), defined by its collective functions (*nomoi*); these functions constitute its nature (*physis*), considered as a vital force proper to that group. Religion begins with the first representation of this fact" (p. 87). The representations of "God" and of "soul" emerge in the process and merge together. Before the individual soul comes to define itself in distinction from the group, the individual "must first be aware of a power which both is and is not himself—a moral force which at once is superior to his own and yet is participated in by him" (p. 102). The collective consciousness, immanent in every member of the group yet lying beyond him, the primal source of religious representation, supplies what is sought. "In proportion as it comes to be felt more and more as 'not ourselves' it becomes increasingly superhuman and divine; and, on the other hand, human individuality comes to be defined, hardened and consolidated in contrast with it." The collective authority of the tribal group, at first vested in the group as a whole, finds its first individual embodiment in the repressive authority of a despotic chief, who is not, however, an independent individual. "However absolute his power may be, he is not a tyrant claiming to be the original source of all authority. He does not rule by his own right, but solely as the representative of society. . . . He is an externalised group-soul—a daemon, not yet a God." Because his authority remains distinguishable from his personality, a further and final stage is possible, in which the collective authority—now (though Cornford does not say so) operating vis-à-vis individuals with their self-awareness—rises above the human sovereign and becomes transcendent in the impersonal form of Law. It ascends from the demonic plane to the divine; and we find in Greek democracy the constitutional theory that the sovereign is that impersonal and dispassionate Reason, called *Nomos*. In a less rationalist context, which Greece also provides, the moral power insofar as it is not ourselves is projected into the universe as a supreme force, above all agents, divine or human, in which Destiny and Right are united. As for the third component of the "primitive religious fact"—*physis*—this comes to be conceived as a sort of spiritual substance carrying to souls as to gods the resources for proper discharging of their functions. "This subtle and mobile stuff, endowed with all the properties that are held to belong to soul and god . . . is what the Milesians called *physis*." We invoke it still when we claim the support of "natural authority" or "the authority of Nature."

At this point, two lines of developing human self-awareness diverge. One is marked by steady effort to cleanse itself from inherited respect for gods, heroes, daemons, kings; its feeling for Law and Nature has been transformed by philosophical criticism; and along this line we have reached the point of emancipation from "the primitive religious fact." Technology is the accepted form of practical wisdom, and technologists take the place of priest-kings in society—many of them, however, haunted by unmanageable thoughts about Destiny and Right! The other line has been marked, in a variety of ways, by efforts to assert that Destiny, Right, Law, Nature are all subordinate to the will of a personal God who has always been beyond the matrix of the primitive religious fact; and this line, for present purposes of discussion, is represented by the Christian Church.

One way of posing the duty of its theologians, in terms of this story, is that they should offer a responsible account of the reality, authentic deity, to which we must relate the structure of authority which bears down upon us—whether by way of Cornford's "primitive religious fact" or by some more reliably plotted route. Christian conviction has at its heart an acknowledgement of divine authority and much has been said and can be said to discredit this acknowledgement. The main lines of objection are: that no adequate basis can be established in principle for this acknowledgement—in the last analysis it is incurably superstitious and incoherent; and that in social practice it has served to obstruct clear thought and appropriate action. Without pretending to take the measure of the whole sprawling debate between faith and unbelief it will be useful and proper to take from it one thread which was presented quite forcefully in the symposium entitled *The Humanist Frame* which Sir Julian Huxley edited and published in the sixties. The critique of Christianity implicit in such a book has a history stemming from the eighteenth-century epoch of Enlightenment and it has created evident uneasiness in Christian thinking and Christian behaviour whenever questions of authority are raised. The thread which I select from the debate is spun by contributors who have offered a humanist account of religion as an element in human life, and of "God" or "gods" as an element in religion.

Within this account the Christian conception of divine authority is seen in a perspective where it loses much of its seriousness. I am aware, of course, that this achievement (of accounting for religion) is open to criticism as being pseudo-scientific, over-pretentious, vulnerable in detail and so forth; but nevertheless it commands respect. "Theistic religions are organizations of human thought in its interaction with the puzzling complex world with which it has to contend" and are liable (Sir Julian Huxley's word is "destined" but I am less religious than he is) liable "to disappear in competition with other, truer, and more embracing thought-organizations which are handling the same range of raw or processed experience." Now comes the lyrical passage, behind which scholars will discern, in due time, a primitive evolutionary hymn:

> Evolutionary man can no longer take refuge from his loneliness by creeping for shelter into the arms of a divinised father-figure whom he has himself created, nor escape from the responsibility of making decisions by sheltering under the umbrella of Divine Authority, nor absolve himself from the hard task of meeting his present problems and planning his future by relying on the will of an omniscient but unfortunately inscrutable Providence.[4]

Allowing for the element of hyperbole found in all lyrical writing, I am prepared to say Amen to that—without adding the face-saving clause "and of course Christians have known this all along," because they haven't.

Consider St. Augustine's way of characterizing the Christian religion:

> In following this religion our prime concern is with the prophetic history of the dispensation of divine providence in time—what God has done for the salvation of the human race, renewing and restoring it unto eternal life. When once this is believed, a way of life agreeable to the divine commandments will purge the mind and make it fit to perceive spiritual things which are neither past nor future but ever abide the same, liable to no change. There is one God: Father, Son and Holy Spirit. When this Trinity is known as far as it can be in this life, it is perceived without the slightest doubt that every creature . . . derives such existence as it has from that same creative Trinity, has its own form, and is subject to the most perfect order. . . . When this is known, it will be as clear as it can be to men that all things are subject by necessary, indefeasible and just laws to their Lord God. Then, all those things which to begin with we simply believe, following authority only [he means the assertions made in the Apostles' Creed] we come to understand. . . . They are judged to be part and parcel of the mercy of the Most High God shown towards the human race.[5]

That, in my opinion, is not a dated passage. As a statement from which to develop an up-to-date course in Systematic Theology, it is as admirable as any which I have been able to find—and more admirable than most.

Christian religion, according to what is said in that passage, provides an answer to a serious question: the question about the source from which our existence (and that of everything else) is *ordered* and *authorized*. We shall return to this question, which may, after all be a misguided one. At present I would merely draw attention to the ways in which St. Augustine's answer to it involves acknowledgement of authority: first, in the robust assertion of an "Author," from whom all is derived and to whom all is subject by necessary, indefeasible and just laws; second, in the claim that

---

[4]J. Huxley, ed., *The Humanist Frame*, pp. 18–19.
[5]*Of True Religion*, vii, 13–14.

this state of affairs may be certainly known in virtue of authoritative information. The statement contains quite remarkable correctives of the human tendency to make do with superstitious credulity and to think of obedience in terms of institutional legalism—which is why I approve so highly of it. Nevertheless, if the phenomenon of St. Augustine expressing himself thus is viewed within the perspectives afforded by the critical account of religion which coheres with modern human science, his acknowledgements of authority are robbed of any ultimate seriousness.

This does not mean, of course, that either he, or what he says, are rendered ridiculous. Here is a highly intelligent man, engaging in what is perhaps the oldest and noblest of human arts—mythology. In the light of biological psychology we are able to move towards a surer appraisal of the art itself, as a human performance, and to assess the quality of this particular performance.[6] We can view with approval the extent to which religion has served to raise

> the sights of the mass of men to some idea at least of a higher level of being. In the form of gods it has hypostasised this higher being and represented it, more or less visibly, as a possibility; and in the name of these gods it made demands on the mass of men to change their mode of existence, to be dissatisfied with a life on the physico-psychological plane, and to aspire to something higher. . . . The divine is not an object, it is a challenge.[7]

As to this particular performance—classical Christianity as represented by St. Augustine's statement—while there is much to be said about the enriching effect which his mythological exercise has had upon human life, we have in fact been carried (with its help) to a point where we should forsake it in favour of

> that most important mythological tradition of the modern world, which can be said to have had its origin with the Greeks, to have come of age in the Renaissance, and to be flourishing today in continuous healthy growth, in the works of those artists, poets, and philosophers of the West for whom the wonder of the world itself—as it is now being analysed by science—is the ultimate revelation.[8]

A theologian who is prepared to admit that there is here a serious and responsible account of how matters stand is in an embarrassing position. Divine authority is not a factor to be reckoned with, except as a notion entertained by persons disposed (as most of us still are) to rise in thought beyond the wonder of the world itself, to acknowledge what St. Augustine acknowledged—though not, perhaps, precisely in his terms—with consequential results in the thought and behaviour of such persons. Their

---

[6] Cf. Joseph Campbell, *The Masks of God*, p. 42.
[7] Kaufmann, *Critique of Religion and Philosophy*, pp. 304–05.
[8] Campbell, p. 7.

entertaining of this notion, however, is part of the wonder of the world itself; and seen like that, what they say is robbed of the ultimate seriousness it purports to have as they say it.

How, then, is a man to find his bearings in the decision he must take in the course of experience? The most enlightened answer seems to be that he should attend faithfully to whatever emerges in our corporate practice of handling the world, with particular regard for *materials* and our better exploitation of their possibilities and for *energy* and its better deployment, storage and control. If some criteria are needed for *trustworthy* conduct in all these matters, there is no more useful point of reference than that *the good of persons should be demonstrably served*. The final charge in indictment of classical and religious "authoritarianism" is that all too often the importance attached to fundamental myths leads to decision, and thus to states of affairs, where the good of persons is demonstrably not served and evidence that this would be so was underrated in the decision-making. .

Lady Wootten observes that "we no longer ask what is pleasing to God but what is good for man."[9] Our concerns, it is true, are necessarily focused on the actuality of human persons, in community, making history; and it is from this centre of attention that we must try, if we try at all, to rediscover how "there is no authority except from God" and that from Him there *is* authority. I have considered, as have others, the case for working towards a new ontology, to supply a framework of reference more adequate than the man-centred, or even personality-centred framework with which at present we tend to make do. My present view is that a purely theological task could well be undertaken first—to clarify afresh the doctrine of God with particular attention to His authority; and that any new ontology may come as a by-product of interaction between this theology and what is being said by the combined team of physicists and philosophers whose revolutionary account of "the disposition of things in truth" underlies (and is doubtless misrepresented by) what I have just been saying. Be that as it may, my reluctance to forget divine authority still stands.

There are moments in human experience which make any man-made framework of reference seem too small for the mystery in which we are caught up. This came home to me afresh as I listened to Eric Newton talking about Tintoretto and his picture *The Origin of the Milky Way*. In this picture, he said,

> Juno neither wants nor attracts our admiration; she belongs to the sun, the open air and the wind. This is Tintoretto in his blithest, his most optimistic, his most frankly pagan mood. Those who know his paintings in the Scuola San Rocco in Venice will have discovered another Tintoretto,

---

[9]*The Humanist Frame*, p. 351.

the interpreter of New Testament tragedy, full of dark overtones, full of mystery.[10]

It is beside the point that the radiant energetic mood should be expressed by pagan imagery and the mood of awe in face of tragedy by Christian imagery. The point is that both moods involve reference to a more ultimate mastery over things than that to which man may aspire—in the one case a glorious mastery freely expressed with cosmic scope, in the other a mastery, equally cosmic asserted at great cost against opposition of which man cannot take the measure.

There are many persons who cannot make Nietzsche's cry that "God is dead" their own, in spite of all the pressures to do so, of which they are fully aware. They are, however, puzzled and distressed by inability, in themselves and others, to reach, and, much more, to express, something which can confidently be called "awareness of God." Most of them, like myself, are humble individuals whose right it nevertheless is to "take God seriously" in the proper way, if it is not true to say that He is dead. Some are in high positions of influence—may be members of Governments, or of the Conference on Science and World Affairs, who would be grateful to have their minds clarified in a new way about the relevance of divine authority to their responsibilities. There are other persons who are in a state of error, not of doubt, if it is not true to say that "God is dead." Much may depend on what can be done to clarify the minds of some and change the minds of others, by stating in new terms how men may acknowledge and rely upon the authority of God.

The humanist concern with human *initiative* is common to Christians and non-Christians. Christians who have the courage of their convictions can express it by asking how human beings may, in their own exercise of authority, *represent* the authority of God. There has been an uneasy recrudescence of "authoritarianism" in our current moods and culture, that personal and political phenomenon which Lord Acton recognized in persons who

> deem that anxious preoccupation against bad government is an obstruction to good and degrades morality and mind by placing the capable at the mercy of the incapable, dethroning enlightened virtue for the benefit of the average man. They hold that great and salutary things are done for mankind by power concentrated, not by power balanced and cancelled and dispersed; and that the whig theory, sprung from decomposing sects, the theory that authority is legitimate only by virtue of its checks . . . is rebellion against the divine will manifested all down the stream of time.[11]

Persons of a more "liberal" disposition take up the theme of authority with the distaste of a man who has to track down and eradicate a nasty

---

[10]*The Listener*, June 15, 1961, 1054–55.
[11]Lord Acton, *Lectures on Modern History*, p. 26.

smell haunting the drains. Authoritarians and radical dissenters alike are apt, in my view, to fumble nowadays with an anaemic conception of the place of authority in human life and we suffer in consequence from an impoverished understanding of how authorized power should be publicly used to express and enhance human dignity. Men would do well to deal more frankly in terms of authority and power and not mask what is at stake by tranquillizing pieties of speech. If, for example, professors should have lots of extra money to pay surtax with, this is because they are *in authority*, not because they "carry responsibility." It has, of course, become a commonplace that all power is delightful and absolute power is absolutely delightful, and some malcontent will be quick to say that potentates should be paid *less* because of compensating delight. So we talk rather carefully about "responsibility" rather than about power or authority. Yet to exert authority is in itself a peculiarly burdensome task and a risky one. Those who do it put their identities—and indeed the personal substance of their selves—at risk in ways that the most intrepid insurer would hesitate to cover, not least in those ways of infectious corruption which Lord Acton mentions in the authentic version of his dictum about power. To exert authority is also, of course, a form of ministry to those who depend upon its being wisely done; but this true insight has been corrupted, more often than not in practice, by a sentimental attitude to power which produces the mode of government stigmatized by the word "paternalism." Remembering how power is publicly exerted today, through modern techniques of public relations and hidden persuasion, it is tempting to declare that government of the people, for the people, by fatherly evasiveness, should perish from the earth as soon as possible.

These, then, are the circumstances (or some of them) in which a Christian theologian may usefully set himself to trace the fabric of authority, with its analogous texture, through the world of human experience to an ultimate source, itself active with divine authority. Such consideration of authority as such, from a theological point of view, may serve to render any recognition of exercised authority and any obedience evoked by it more transparent for the light of truth and goodness, more discriminating and more creative, than is often the case in practice.

III

In the third part of this essay I invite attention to that particular place in the universe of human experience where, so Christians maintain, divine authority reaches through with unambiguous and final clarity and establishes men and women in the obedience of Christian faith. The reality to which Christian faith is a response is, in the first instance, the authority of a *Gospel* (formulated news) and the authority of the *person*, Jesus Christ, whom the news is principally and finally about. It is not clear at the outset why this authority should be recognized as "divine." Nor is it wholly clear which of several things one may properly intend to say, either about the person or about the formulated news, when one uses the word "divine" to characterize their authority. The position which I take to be most widely adopted is that the person is ultimately acknowledged to be God Himself in direct contact with humanity, and so with history; but no divine attributes inhere in the formulation of the news.

This conviction is reached, where it has been reached, by careful attention to what Jesus of Nazareth said and did and what happened in consequence. It has become clearer in recent times than it has sometimes been, how his historical humanity was shaped in every detail by what he called the proximity of the Kingdom of God; that where initiative lay with him—as in his utterances and deeds—he held this clearly in view with flawless fidelity; and that where initiative did not lie with him and events were moulded by the operation of factors not under his human control, he accepted what took place as being wholly adjusted to the actualizing of this Kingdom of God within the texture of human history. Such perfect obedience on his part did in fact make God's sovereignty actual, within the limits of one human life-history. Whether or not this has far-reaching implications, as wide as cosmic history in its entirety, depends on what limits may or may not be set to his person. Anyone who is willing to proceed with this question on the lines of Christian orthodoxy has to reckon with the difficulty that his thought may at any moment lose its anchorage in the mind of Jesus himself. Any attempt to stand with Jesus and try, as I propose to do, to look back with him and then to look forward with him, may founder on the rock of ignorance (or at any rate uncertainty) as to what he really thought and said. A double hazard is involved: of accepting from critical scholarship erroneous conclusions, and of being insensitive to the best findings of critical scholarship. With prior acknowledgement of difficulty and hazards, let us see what can be done.

We look back to the faith of Israel, as the background which provided Jesus with the terms in which to envisage what was at stake. We find, as he found, that the documents of Israel's history are eloquent of the effective presence in that community of a "Lord," whose "ways" were discerned and acknowledged, though He Himself was not to be measured or adequately described by human categories. His "ways" appear in operations which brought home to Israelite man—and which, as reported, still bring home to an attentive man—that his own finite self and all the finite things for which he cares, with all their proper glory and all their infamous shame, exist and persist at the mercy of one whose thoughts are not as men's thoughts and whose activity is not as men's activity. They are the "ways" of a *Judge*, who carries out with awesome faithfulness his adverse judgement on things in which men falsely place their trust; yet they are "ways" which reveal the Judge to be, at the same time, a *Saviour*, who reinstates what comes under His condemnation and upholds it "to the glory of his grace." Where adverse judgement implies destruction, reinstatement (if it occurs) must be by way of re-creation or resurrection. Thus his "ways" come to be acknowledged as ways only to be associated with an "Author of being," whose authority is in all respects supreme— though it may still be met with rebellion and not with obedience. Further, the "Lord," acting in these "ways," has an end in view: the effective and final subordination of all things to his authority. And so far as men are concerned, this will bring to them life at its best in communion with the "Lord." The question then becomes acute: by what means, through what special events, through the activity of what special agent (or agents), can this end be reached? Jesus saw his own ministry as the answer to the questions about means and special events, and himself as the answer to the question about special agency. We are invited to believe that his historical career came to a climax in which it was disclosed that he was right; and that testimony to this being so is still being provided in the "life of faith" which has been opened for his associates.

At this point, still standing with him so far as available testimony permits us to do, may we look forward and try to appreciate the outcome of his life-work, as he confidently looked forward to it. I must omit the technicalities, many of which have to do with his own term for self-designation, "Son of Man," and put the result in rashly over-simplified form. He evidently believed that in the actuality of his life-work taken as a whole, a link was being established between historical mankind in its entirety and the divine Judge-Saviour of whose reality Israel had become vividly aware. Once this link was completed and built into the fabric of things, the goal of divine action would be in principle secured. With his death, which he turned into the consummation of obedience, his life-work was completed—as well as terminated. The link was then there in finished form. And we are invited to believe that this whole personal historical reality, Jesus, is built into the fabric of things, not as a memory enshrined in the pages of the past, but as a *live personal* reality; this by virtue of God's power to reinstate that of which he approves by resurrection.

The next step is to recognize that the programme in terms of which Jesus lived and died is one which Jesus could not conceivably have undertaken seriously and sanely except on the basis of a capacity for personal acts of self-identification, on the one hand with Deity known to him as the holy "Father," and on the other hand with all mankind. Here we must admit that such acts of "love" exceed in scope and depth anything of which, on other evidence, we would suppose a human personality to be capable. In respect of his "Sonship," his self-identification in filial love with God his "Father," we should correct a false impression which may have been built up by telling the story in this way; the impression, namely, that here is a man rising to the stature of Deity by heroic, Titanic, feats of obedience (rather than of rebellion as is customary in myths of Titanism). That is not at all what the story looks like. The most remarkable feature of all that Jesus said and did is the complete absence from it of such aspiring egoism. That is why the identification in love between Jesus and the holy divine Father is acknowledged, in Christian theology, to rest upon a ground prior to all the detail of Christ's earthly obedience. The ground is expressed by saying that the holy Father in his eternal Godhead identifies with himself an eternal Son; and Jesus is this Son. On this ground, he was able to lift his manhood into such epoch-making union with Deity. Here, as a matter of personal conviction, I would myself insist strongly that the obedience he wrought out in historical time was achieved through human, not superhuman, resources; and I see no evidence that Jesus, during his earthly life, was conscious of metaphysical identity with God. Be that as it may, the point is that the judgement reached along this road about the manhood of Jesus having a foundation in God other than that which our manhood has, represents a new awareness of divine actuality and activity. We have been moved, in thought, beyond the fact of a man, Jesus, mythologizing in terms of God and maintaining flawless consistency, to acknowledge in this effect the agency of that which is divine.

IV

We turn now to the other act of self-identification of which the whole detail of his historical humanity is eloquent, and apart from which it does not make good sense: his self-identification with mankind—an act of love so wide in its scope as to exceed any we can envisage in terms of ordinary human experience. This identification is known as something which has happened to us, by his initiative not ours; something which we can be brought to acknowledge. It can hardly be said to be part of our experience until we acknowledge it; and we refer to the agency which makes it part of our experience by speaking of Deity acting and existing in a third mode, the Holy Spirit. Basil of Caesarea speaks of his operation as "unfolding the glory of the Son, not apart from Himself but within Himself"—so it is of the Son we are made aware, not of the Spirit as such— "and he who looks on the Son, comes to know, as from an imprint, the reality of the Father whose actuality is in him." At this point, too, we are moved to cogent awareness of divine actuality. We are moved, that is to say, beyond awareness of oneself, mythologizing in terms of God and his Christ, into awareness of being newly established in faith as a creature newly related to God, by the agency of that which is divine. And the remarkable thing is that this enactment in a man's life of faith's certainty and sanctity leaves his humanity intact in its full dignity; or, better, rescues and heals his humanity and reinvests it with the dignity proper to man.

It has taken me a long time to extract, even in this small depth, the

Christian story of how divine authority emerges in operation to establish men in Christian faith. In Christian tradition the matter is presented as operations of the world's divine "Lord." It comes to a focus in the earliest Christian confession that "*Jesus* is Lord." To be made more fully aware of what is involved, we must go on learning how to say with understanding that "*God* was in Christ"; and to say this entails an initial willingness to identify God as the Holy Trinity of whom Christian liturgy and theology speak, and a readiness to reflect upon the immensity of "Deity" in appropriate terms.

> Wise men, all ways of knowledge past,
> To the Shepherds' wonder came at last—

but for twentieth-century wise men there are formidable obstacles in the way of accepting Jesus Christ as the absolute and ultimate expression to us of divine authority.

My purpose at present, however, is not to defend or to commend, but, so far as possible, to explain. If, then, it is apparent that in this context authority of an ultimate kind can be deemed to have come into view, the important thing to observe is that it is exercised in the form of a personal relation, and a moral one, between God in Christ's person, and persons such as we are; a relation of two wills, two consciences. In this respect Forsyth is able to speak of it as:

> the ground of a religion adequate to the highest practical purposes of a world of living men and the actual situation of such a world. Something equal to the great tragedies, resolves, actions or consciences of a race of loving, acting, suffering, struggling, failing, conquering souls;

a base for religion in the last great sense of that word:

> a stay in the collapse of a cosmos, or amid the collapse of man's own self-satisfaction in guilt.

It is more than "contact with God," or "influence from God" mediated perhaps through communicated principles of being and action. It is "life from a life; conscience with conscience; soul with soul." The range and depth of this "new being" must in principle be co-extensive with all actuality, if it is true that the "life," "conscience," "soul," to which our own "life," "conscience," "soul" are joined in faith, are those of authentic deity, the *divine* Lord of whom we say: *God* was in Christ. We are empowered and required, in faith, to set about the exploration of all actuality as newly seen and newly tasted. The Christian condition of faith is known by fruits which satisfy in a way that mystifying theological utterances cannot of themselves do. From the focus of Christian religion, therefore, let us turn back again to those everyday situations when "authority" is a word appropriately used and see whether illuminating connections might appear between what is experienced in those situations and that expression of divine authority to which Christian faith is the response.

One feature of situations where authority is effectively exerted can be picked out like this. The person who responds to it recognizes in someone or something other than himself a *certainty* which he takes as final and sufficient reason for some corresponding certainty in himself. The extrinsic certainty is "exerted" to produce an effect, either of obedience (when authority is effective) or of rebellion (when it is not). An obvious instance of effective authority is where men accept opinions or directives for conduct from other *persons*. But *statements* can exert authority, when no explicit attention is paid to a personal author and no personal will is deemed to be operative upon those who accept the statements. This impersonal character is even more apparent in the case of *customs and practices* about which we feel no need to ask questions before conforming to them. Authority of this same impersonal kind is sometimes deemed also to inhere in particular *offices*—the monarch, the bishop, the father, the mother, the cultural or the industrial superior. Their certainty, in matters proper to their office, is frequently taken as a final and sufficient reason for the certainty found by obedience to them.

In his useful book called *Authority in the Church*, T. A. Lacey points out that *auctoritas* stood for something of great importance in Roman history. Politically, "it signified an influence which was rather personal than official, rather moral than legal." He offers the phrase "moral weightiness"; something which a private citizen might have in greater measure than an official, so that his word would carry more weight. "It was built up in the public conduct of the man who had it, and might be lost if he presumed upon it too far, or in other ways fell into bad mistakes." But he recognizes a derived sense, where, in all languages derived from Latin, the word means legal power; ánd in this sense it denotes the source from which "authorization" is deemed to come. Here the focus of attention is on political or economic power, or on the personal power of one individual to subordinate another to his will. Burning questions arise about who shall exercise power and what safeguards shall be established against the arbitrary use of power. *Law*, therefore, emerges as the means adopted in civilized society both for the application and for the control of power. And law operates as authority in respect of conflicts between public interest and private rights. Further, law *lends* authority to persons, practices, customs, offices, and institutions. Their authority is not generally regarded as absolute; power to enforce obedience is open to question on the ground of *right*; and the question of right can be settled in some, but not all, cases, by reference to law and constitution. "An authority of any practical kind," to use Forsyth's phrase, has to pass the test of being a *legitimate* authority or a *constituted* authority. And of all constituted authority we can ask the question: constituted as authority *through what?* To answer this question by saying that "the whole structure of authority in the world is God's work" (Sanday and Headlam's paraphrase of Romans 13:1) is to provide a dangerous short-cut to certainty; one which has led to disrespect for human freedom and to intolerance of nonconformity; and so, more blatantly, have short-cuts to creaturely substitutes for God— Bible, Church, State, Natural Law, Human Nature, the Wonder of the World, the Idea of the Good.

To attribute absolute authority to anything which is not God is blasphemous. The question comes, therefore, as to whether in fact there is a place to which we can take the question posed about any practical authority—"constituted as authority through what?"—and find an ultimate and satisfying answer in *Deity*. I have tried to make plain my own conviction that there is such a place, where man and all his enterprises have been subjected to the divine action of the holy and saving God, and may now be seen in faith to be thus subjected. At this place the case emerges for making a clear distinction between authority and power. Authority commends itself, because it serves to build into the fabric of things the virtue suggested by such words as truth, health, reliability, competence. Without going so far as to say with Nietzsche that "power always lies," one may nevertheless recognize that the resort to power, in personal and social dealings, is a remedy for situations made perilous by deficiencies in these virtues. This remedy at best masks the disease and all too often aggravates it. Authority is not to be equated with power, even with the constituted power, of a person or an institution; though our experience of it is usually inseparable from such phenomena. It is an interior enacting of certainty. It is inherently more than institutional pressure, or even rational pressure. It is personal and potentially religious, for the religious person readily pictures this interior enacting of certainty as an action of God himself bearing upon the rational soul in personal experience. In relation to freedom and to tolerance, authority creates freedom and the concern for freedom, whereas power always threatens these. It is also worth remembering that in some contexts we speak of *consulting* an authority; and this usage, which sharply distinguishes respect for authority from respect for power, may be kept in mind as an indication of the proper thing to do with any "authority of a practical kind."

Authority has for its correlatives "certainty" and "obedience." "Certainty" is a term to be understood here primarily from the context of legal theory, where it points to a state of affairs promoted by good legal operations; a less absolute, but perhaps more stable state of affairs than is suggested by this term in its psychological use, where it refers to a condition which many hardly aspire to in these days and which in any case is viewed with mistrust. "Obedience" should not be pressed very far in the direction of "subjection to a personal will," and, of course, need not and should not be construed as "servility."

Forsyth speaks of figures familiar to us all, often enough vehement antagonists of external authority, who:

> lose all influence (except with the crowd) because their type and demeanour of mind show that their ground tone is not obedience, not competency, but mere autonomy, mere recalcitrance, extending occasionally to intellectual turbulence. They do not impress us as habitually and palpably living under any authority higher than their better instincts, or their conscience at best. And their very conscience does not impress us as either a ruled or an instructed conscience. It is but a phase of their self-will, their self-assertion turned on moral or social matters.[12]

This observation serves to bring into focus the actuality of authority as it is built into human experience and serving, where it is rightly acknowledged, to build into the total fabric of things a staple of truth, health, reliability and competence. That this is a matter for concern, now as ever, is evident not only in criminal behaviour or in the attitude of the young or the dispossessed; it is evident at the other end of the scale in the habits of Top People whose practices of leadership and government takes a characteristic shape, of exerting power and persuasion with deceptive ease and aplomb, only to fall back on nerveless incompetence or vicious nastiness when their bluff is called. These public symptoms of a crisis in respect of authority are reinforced by what appears in all the private occasions where men manifestly act and react like those who have been brought to mistrust their inherited resources and their inherited situations, having no conviction about a divine Author from whom, by whose authorization, and under whose authority, these things have been bestowed.

The term "inherited" serves to express an apparently ineradicable attitude which men adopt to the powers by which they live and the situations in which they live. It is primarily a legal term, and it carries overtones of meaning acquired in the socio-legal context. There an inheritance comes from a trustworthy source, which is known, if not always to the recipient at least to the authorized persons who handle the conveyance. There is an authorized way of appropriating an inheritance. A grateful beneficiary will seek to use his bequest wisely and his confidence and competence in so doing derive, in some degree, from his being authorized to do so. It is a sad feature of our modernized world that men cannot find in this experience a parable for life as a whole. Neither in nature nor in historical tradition are they able readily to discern clear signs of authority which command respect and provide that ground of authorization in which confidence and competence can grow. In a situation where most of us are

---

[12]*Principle of Authority*, p. 306.

apt to be chronically *ungrateful* for our inherited opportunities and resources, there is a deep-seated crisis of confidence and of competence.

There is, as Forsyth remarked in the epilogue to his book (pp. 473 ff),
another counterpart of authority, more spiritual than obedience and more
apt as a guide to freedom than is certainty. It is humility:

> That we should have all but lost this sovereign feature from so much of
> our religion of the Kingdom is not surprising in the decay of authority or
> its debasement, and especially in the abeyance of that superlative form of
> authority which the mystic of the conscience calls holiness, and which
> enjoins us, if we would be perfect as our Father, to be holy as he is holy,
> and humbled to the very Cross. The holiness of God is beyond our defi-
> nition. Its appeal is to something beyond both mind and will. It carries us
> deeper into God and man. ... It is that in God which emerges upon us
> and comes home to us only in our worship. It changes that worship from
> dull abasement before God's power, or dumb amazement at the wealth of
> his nature to the deepest adoration of what He personally is, and is for
> us. Its counterpart in us and our religion is the humility that worship at
> once rears and perfects. And it is as much beyond righteousness in him
> as humility is beyond mere obedience or justice in us. Humility is not a
> chain of submissive acts, but the habitual and total and active obedience
> of the whole soul to the Holy in his act—to that which ... abashes and
> exalts the whole soul and severs it from the world by every step of its
> assumption into God. ... The true authority cannot return to order, se-
> cure, and distinguish society without a religious revolution. It cannot till
> humility pull down self-satisfaction on the one hand or lift up self-
> prostration on the other, and take the place both of self-worship or self's
> dishonour. Yet it is never the mere breaking of self that makes humility,
> as it does not make true repentance or confession; it is the sight, sense,
> and confession of that ineffable sanctity which comes home to us but in
> adoration, and makes such hours the ruling and creative hours of life. For
> in that holiness we are neither passive, soft, nor weak; we are touched by
> the one authority and reality of life; and in the amazement, the miracle,
> that he should come to us who is sublimely separated from all the sinful
> world, we have the exalted humility which teaches us to love the world in
> godly sort, and is the secret of the obedience that at once controls life and
> inspires it. ... The last authority of the soul for ever is the grace of a holy
> God, the holiness of his gracious love in Jesus Christ. And this is the last
> reality of things, the last rest of all hearts, and the last royalty of all wills.

One last quotation from Forsyth will serve to state the persuasion which
underlies all that I have written:

> The authority at the head and centre of religious experience ... is the
> final authority the soul has to reckon with, the principle of the last judge-
> ment. All other authorities for the soul stand ranged in a hierarchy as
> they are near to this God, necessary for his purpose or full of his action.[13]

---

[13]*Principle of Authority*, p. 342.

To set about the exploration of all actuality, freshly seen and freshly tasted in the certainty, the freedom, the humility, and the obedience of Christian faith, is the promised life of joy and peace in believing, so that by the power of the Holy Spirit you may abound in hope.

(1981)

INDEX OF NAMES